Japanese Business into
the 21st Century

Japanese Business into the 21st Century

OSAMU KATAYAMA
Translated by Richard Walker

ATHLONE
London & Atlantic Highlands, N.J.

First published 1996 by
THE ATHLONE PRESS
1 Park Drive, London NW11 7SG
and 165 First Avenue,
Atlantic Highlands, NJ 07716

British Library Cataloguing in Publication Data
*A catalogue record for this book is available
from the British Library*

ISBN 0 485 11462 3

Library of Congress Cataloging in Publication Data
Katayama, Osamu, 1940–
Japanese business into the 21st century: strategies for success/
Katayama Osamu; translatedby Richard Walker.
p. cm.
Includes bibliographical references and index.
ISBN 0–485–11463–3 (hb)
1. Strategic planning—Japan. 2. Industrial management—Japan.
3. Success in business—Japan. I. Title.
HD30.28.K374 1996
658.4′012′0952—dc20   95–52515
                                        CIP

Typeset by WestKey Limited, Falmouth, Cornwall

Printed and bound in Great Britain by the University Press, Cambridge

Contents

Acknowledgements

I began to write this book in 1993. The post-bubble recession was already in full bloom, but not long after I started a series of major events changed the entire Japanese landscape. During that year, the 38-year uninterrupted rule of the Liberal Democratic Party came to an end, and this was followed by two rounds of sharp gains for the yen, once in 1993 and again in 1994. These dramatic changes in the economic climate rocked the very foundations of corporate Japan. For many firms, survival was indeed at stake, and in trying to search out the conditions for resuscitation and recovery, I ended up taking far more time to complete the book than I had originally planned.

I would therefore first like to thank Mr Brian Southam, chairman of The Athlone Press, for his patience and good will in waiting for the manuscript's completion. I would also like to express my heartfelt gratitude to the many companies who graciously responded to my requests for interviews. Also, many thanks to my friends for their valuable advice and my office staff for their valuable support.

Finally, thanks to Mr Richard Walker for doing the translation and to the Suntory Foundation for their generous support.

Osamu Katayama,
Tokyo

Glossary

Kanban	A unique production management system that seeks to achieve 'just-in-time' production in which irrationality, waste and inconsistency have been eliminated.
Keiretsu	Inter-corporate linkages. May involve capital, management, production and/or sales.
Payout ratios	Technical term used in securities analysis.
Shinkansen	Bullet-train.
Zaibatsu	A giant monopolistic capitalist or corporate group, generally originating from a single family or clan. Synonymous with *konzern* or *consortia*.
billion/trillion	Reflects American usage, that is, they are equivalent to a thousand millions and a million millions respectively.

CHAPTER 1

Back to the Drawing Board

Two Goals

Is Japan washed up? Listening to Japanese managers you would think so. All they have been able to talk about since the beginning of the nineties is how they have 'lost their confidence'. Perhaps that was to be expected. After all, the world is undergoing vast changes, upheavals of historical proportions, and Japanese social and economic structures are being forced to change too.

Still one wonders if this is the same country that rose so magnificently from the ashes of military defeat to achieve an acknowledged 'economic miracle'. True, things were simpler back then. When capitalism and communism faced off in the Cold War, Japan declared for the capitalist camp and summarily turned most of the responsibility for its defence over to the US. Likewise in foreign affairs, all it had to do was follow America's lead. Having renounced war and standing armies (always a costly exercise) in Article 9 of its Constitution, the country was free to concentrate on business.

Its explicit goal after the war was to catch up with and surpass Europe and North America economically. To that end, Japan refined and improved imported technology, and its people, companies and government pulled together to turn the nation into one of the world's economic power-houses.

They were halcyon days. The Cold War had provided the political stability for the country to focus exclusively on economic growth. But then it ended, and Japan woke up to face a more complex set of challenges.

NEW WORLD ORDER

The implosion of the Soviet Union has left the US as the world's only superpower, but it is a superpower of sharply diminished economic vitality, seemingly unable to maintain the discipline of the Cold War era. As the source of 15 per cent of the world's GNP, Japan is under pressure to take on political responsibilities in the international community more befitting its economic might. These new responsibilities include committing more money to developing countries and more troops to UN peace-keeping operations. Japan's national policy can no longer be focused exclusively on the domestic economy.

Japan, however, has been unsure of how to react and seems to be interested only in its own economic development. To outsiders, it appears a selfish and self-centred country. Meanwhile, the overwhelming competitiveness of Japanese products has become a political issue, too. Countries in Europe and North America are constructing legal and political barriers to keep Japanese products from edging domestic versions out of the market. But Japanese companies are unwilling to temper the marketing strategies that make their products such a threat to local economies, the emphasis remaining on production and market share at all costs.

The resulting criticism is one of the reasons for the crisis in confidence. But more important is the fact that managers have lost their direction. There is no longer any overarching goal, any higher objective to provide the underpinning for corporate activities. This is a new experience. Since Japan opened its doors to the outside world in the late nineteenth century, it has always had a goal. The first was to overtake and surpass the West. For the Meiji-period Japanese, in fact, 'modernization' and 'Westernization' were more or less synonymous. In their quest to catch up, they rallied to slogans like 'prosperity and industry' and 'rich country, strong military', actively importing Western European political and economic systems, education, culture and technology.

The goal of modernization was temporarily crushed by defeat in World War II, but it quickly revived again in the new objective of 'rebuilding the fatherland'. If anything, the drive was even stronger the second time around. And the model for modernization was the country that emerged the clear victor from the war and the world's dominant superpower – the United States. Pre-war militaristic education taught the Japanese to think of Americans as brutes and savages, but the occupation showed them as something completely different, an America of freedom and democracy. There, before their eyes, they saw their competition, the people to catch up with, the benchmark for measuring their success.

These two goals – catching up with the US and rebuilding the country – formed the basis of postwar Japanese economic and civic life. They have been at the heart of national industrial policy, company business plans and the way the average 'salaryman' looks at his job. There has been a firm agreement among all three sectors of the country – government, business and private individuals – that since Japan is so poor in resources, the only way it will ever be able to achieve the kind of economic development enjoyed by the West is by becoming a trading nation that imports its raw materials and reprocesses them for export.

These two goals have likewise been at the core of Japanese management practices. They are the reason why managers and workers are able to pull together to overcome setbacks. People here really do work towards a 'Japanese dream' of a country powerful enough to rub shoulders with Europe and North America and a lifestyle every bit as affluent as that of the West.

Experience has taught the Japanese that a prosperous state begets prosperous companies, which in turn beget prosperous households. For most, the postwar years have been a happy time. The products of their efforts have been apparent, and they have provided the motivation needed to tackle any crisis or obstacle encountered.

YESTERDAY'S ENTREPRENEURS

The goals of rebuilding and catching up were what drove the young entrepreneurs who started their businesses right after the war and provided much of the impetus for economic development.

When Japan surrendered on August 15, 1945, it was a bleak, grim, and depressing place. Where once flourished urban night life were now black markets. The streets were crowded with unemployed workers, repatriated soldiers and colonists evicted from overseas conquests. In the railway stations and underground passageways, war orphans huddled for shelter. It was a fight just to get food, and companies had to switch production from armaments to pots and pans just to ensure enough revenue to meet their payrolls.

Hitachi, for example, was carrying 44,000 workers when the war ended, but had only one factory that was fully operational. Chikara Kurata, who was installed as president immediately after the war, recalls, 'We were living from hand to mouth. All our other factories were making pots and pans, or extracting salt from seawater. We even had one that was making crackers and candy'.[1]

War had devastated Japanese industry. At the time, Western commentators predicted that it would take at least a century before the country could even start to rebuild, and they were not necessarily upset by that timetable. But there were young entrepreneurs in Japan who saw things differently, who had faith that the economy could recover from the destruction and chaos of the war. These young entrepreneurs were strong leaders with domineering personalities and their own ideas about business. They developed a new style of management and were willing to act on it.

Take Masaru Ibuka and Akio Morita, the two young men who in 1946 invested ¥190,000 in the Tokyo Communications Industry, a venture company located on the third floor of the Shirakiya Building in the burned-out business district of Nihonbashi, Tokyo. It was from those humble and forbidding circumstances that the Sony empire was born.

The official Sony account of the event reads:

> In the afternoon of May 7, twenty men with crew cuts assembled and the incorporation ceremony began.
> Ibuka was 38 at the time; Morita 25.
> New companies were required to submit a statement of intent that clearly stated their goals. Ibuka wrote it himself and entrusted it to Tachikawa, a Sony employee. But in the hectic preparations for incorporation, the document had been forgotten. Tachikawa showed it to Ibuka, exclaiming, 'Take a look at this!'
> 'Not bad, not bad at all', Ibuka mused.
> He was so impressed by his own handiwork that his speech that day was almost a direct quote from it: 'We will not be successful doing the same things that big companies do. But there are niches in technology that we can exploit. We'll do what the big companies cannot, and use technology to help rebuild our country.'[2]

By and large, that is exactly what Sony has done. The company has been responsible for many Japanese and world firsts: Japan's first practical magnetic recording tape, Japan's first tape recorder, Japan's first transistor radio, the world's first transistor television, the world's first portable video tape recorder, the Trinitron colour television. Certainly, it took entrepreneurial spirit and creativity for Ibuka and Morita to vow that day in the bombed-out ruins of Tokyo to exploit advanced technology for the good of humanity, especially when the deck was stacked against them. And an integral part of that creativity and resolve was the overriding goal of postwar Japan to rebuild.

It was that same goal that drove Konosuke Matsushita, founder of the Matsushita Electric Industrial empire – and he faced even greater odds. MacArthur's occupation forces had declared his company a *zaibatsu*, which placed severe restrictions on what it could do. Matsushita himself was barred from public service. It was not until 1950 that the sanctions were lifted, but when they were, Matsushita announced its 'Emergency Managerial Guidelines', which were in effect a declaration of its intent to start anew. The document says, 'We, the industrialists of this generation, must rebuild our country by rebuilding our industries'.

But what of the other Japanese goal of overtaking and surpassing the West? It was not forgotten after the war. In 1951, Matsushita visited the United States and was amazed at its affluence and prosperity. The buildings of Times Square in New York made a particular impression because they kept their lights burning brightly all day long. At the time, Tokyo was so short of power that the electricity was turned off for an hour every night at 7.00. He recalls:

I asked them, and they said that the city of New York was using about 4 million kilowatts of electricity a day. That was about the same amount as being used in all of Japan! That's when I understood how they could keep the lights on all day.

As an aside, we should note the reversal today. Tokyo Electric Power, which supplies the greater Tokyo area with its electricity, now produces about 50 million kilowatts, which requires it to burn about 12 million kilolitres of oil a year, roughly enough to supply all of Italy's thermoelectric requirements. Having seen for himself the prosperity of the West, Matsushita was more resolved than ever that Japan should catch up.

I just couldn't get over the affluence of America. When I talked to people at General Electric, they said their radios were selling in the department stores for $24. Standard wages for their assembly-line workers at the time were about $1.50 an hour. Assuming an 8-hour shift, that means they would be paid $12 a day, so by working 2 days, they could afford to buy one of their company's radios. Compare that to Japan. The radios we were making at Matsushita were selling for around ¥9,000, and we were paying our workers an average of ¥6,000 a month. That meant they had to work a month and a half just to buy a radio. The differences were like night and day. I had heard about American affluence before, but when I saw it with my own eyes, Japanese realities became intolerable. I swore to myself that we had to make Japan like America, and after I returned home, I tried to rally my employees to the cause of 'creating the same thing in Japan'.[3]

Like Matsushita Electric Industrial, Toyota Motor also rebuilt out of the rubble of war to become one of Japan's leading firms. The late Taiichi Ono, former vice-president of Toyota Motor and the architect of Toyota-style manufacturing writes:

August 15, 1945 was the date of Japan's defeat, but it was also the date of a new beginning. Kiichiro Toyoda (1894–1952), then president of Toyota Motor, told us

we had to 'catch up with America in 3 years or the
Japanese automotive industry would not survive'.

Not long after the occupation landed in 1945, Mac-
Arthur informed us that Japanese productivity was
only one-eighth America's. . . . It was daunting what we
were trying to do – raise our productivity eight- or
ninefold in 3 years. It meant that ten people now had to
do the work of a 100.

But one-eighth or one-ninth represented average figures, and it wasn't that surprising that in car
manufacturing, America's most advanced industry, we
weren't even at one-eighth their levels.[4]

As Ono mulled over the situation, he had a flash of insight.
Obviously, he reasoned, American workers were not ten
times stronger than Japanese. Rather, somewhere in the way
the Japanese work there must be waste, and if he could
eliminate that waste, productivity would surely rise. That
was the beginning of Toyota-style manufacturing, a system
that would become known throughout the world. And it was
a direct product of the desire to catch up with and surpass
the United States.

A similar story is told at Canon as well. After the war,
Precision Optical Industries (the predecessor of Canon) was
obsessed with the Leica, Germany's famous 35-mm camera.
Then-president Tsuyoshi Mitarai was forever chanting slo-
gans about how his company had to 'overtake and surpass
Leica' or 'topple Leica'.[5]

Soichiro Honda, who ranks with Sony's Morita as one of
Japan's leading postwar managers, was also driven by the
desire to catch up with the West. In 1946, he founded the
Honda Technology Laboratories in his hometown of
Hamamatsu. Two years later he reorganized it into the
Honda Motor Co., capitalized at ¥1 million. The company's
motorcycles did so well that by 1956 Honda could create a
company motto that exhorted its employees to 'work from a

global perspective to manufacture high-performance, low-cost products that meet our customers' requirements'. From an early point, then, Honda was concerned with catching up and saw itself as operating 'from a global perspective'. An illustration comes from one of Honda's most famous publicity stunts. In 1954, his company still shaky, Soichiro Honda travelled to Britain's Isle of Man, and upon returning home announced that Honda would be entering the Touring Trophy Race, one of the world's most prestigious motorcycle events. Mr Honda explained the decision to his employees:

> I was brimming with confidence that we could win if we just worked at it with our usual resolve. I had to do something, I was so confident I was aching for a contest. We have just finished putting together a stunning production system. The timing is right. Honda must show the world what Japanese mechanical engineering is made of. It is our company's destiny to be a beacon for Japanese industry. And it is in expression of this resolve that I have entered us in the Touring Trophy Race. I vow on behalf of all of us to strive with all my energy and might for victory.

The 1954 trip to Europe was a scouting mission, and Honda was taken aback by the evident shortcomings in Japanese technology. But he also hated to lose. There were no racing bikes in Japan at the time, so in order to study how they were made he secretly bought racing rims, tyres and carburettors. Unfortunately, when he got to the airport in Rome, he found his luggage was over the 30-kilo limit. Having spent all of his cash on motorcycle parts, his only recourse was to stuff whatever he could under his clothes and hope for the best going through customs. It was a strange-looking man who boarded the aeroplane that day. However, as Soichiro says:

I went to those lengths because I was obsessed with the idea of winning the race. They say Rome wasn't built in a day. Well, I certainly worked up a sweat in that city. . . . But it was worth it. The parts I brought back with me were instrumental in our later business.

In 1961, Honda won the Grand Prix in the Touring Trophy Race, and then went on to win in races in Spain, France and West Germany, establishing itself as the manufacturer of the world's best motorcycles. Victory in the races represented a vindication of the Honda resolve to be the best in the world even when the odds are against success – and it too was a direct result of the Japanese drive to catch up with the rest of the world.

Young Japanese entrepreneurs were so well motivated by the dreams of rebuilding and catching up that they became active importers of advanced Western technology, which they then leveraged into the capital investments that provided a base from which their businesses could grow. In the process, they achieved an economic expansion that no one had even guessed possible.

During the decade immediately after the war, Japan achieved average growth of 8.5 per cent a year. By 1955, the standard of living was back to prewar levels, and the 'Economic White Paper' declared confidently that 'the postwar period is over'. The goal of rebuilding had been completed. It was now time to play catch up in earnest.

NAVIGATING CRISIS

Japan's postwar growth may not be as impressive as it would seem at first glance. As the saying goes, 'the deeper the valley, the higher the mountain'. When you start from a base of close to zero, it is easy to achieve high growth rates, and certainly that was part of the Japanese success story. Defeated Germany and Italy also achieved higher growth rates in the first postwar decade than did victorious

America and Britain. And for all its growth, the Japanese economy was still weak. Had they been exposed to the full brunt of free trade, frail domestic companies would have certainly been overrun and economic growth rates would have quickly dropped back to pre-war levels of 4–5 per cent. Fortunately, that did not happen. Until the first oil crisis hit in 1973, Japan achieved average annual growth in excess of 10 per cent. By 1964, it was strong enough to be admitted into the Organization for Economic Co-operation and Development (OECD), officially recognized as a member of the 'rich countries' ' club with more of a voice in international affairs.

Then in the seventies things began to unravel when the Arab oil embargoes plunged the economy into crisis. During October 1973, crude oil prices quadrupled from $3 a barrel to $11.60. Oil surged from a mere 10 per cent of Japanese imports to 36 per cent, with disastrous results. Wholesale prices rose 35 per cent, consumer prices 25 per cent. Toilet paper and soap disappeared from supermarket shelves as panicky consumers began to hoard daily necessities. In 1974, the GNP recorded a decline of 0.5 per cent, its first negative growth since the war. Inflation running rampant, workers demanded and got a rise of 33 per cent, which merely served to drive companies deeper into the red and force the government to run larger and larger deficits. Between 1974 and 1977, 55,000 Japanese companies went bankrupt, leaving behind ¥8.3 trillion in debt. Three-quarters of corporate profits were erased. If levels during the year to March 1974 are taken as 100, profits for the year to September 1975 were only 26. For manufacturers they were only 8. And by the year to March 1978 they had still only recovered to 57 and 37 respectively.

Then came round two. Oil crisis struck again in December 1978, pushing crude prices from $12.80 a barrel to $26.80, more than double. But this time round, there were no sharp price rises or panic buying. During the intervening years,

Japanese firms had reduced their dependency on oil and learned how to use energy more efficiently. Oil consumption rates had, in fact, been dropping by about 10 per cent annually. In 1975 Japan used 300 million kilolitres. By 1978, it was using only 260 million kilolitres, and by 1980 only 240 million. Companies had also been achieving productivity gains in other areas, which left them better able to absorb higher oil costs.

Toyota is a case in point. The company spared no effort in streamlining its operations. In 1973 it set up 'cost improvement committees' for each of its project teams and began examining ways in which designs, manufacturing methods, production technology, procurement, administration and accounting could be changed so as to reduce the costs for each and every model it produced. This included everything from the details of bolt shapes and surface-processing techniques to questions of whether some parts were really needed at all. But it was not satisfied merely to improve the manufacturing end of its operations. It also reformed its design departments, and indeed asked its entire staff to think up ways to shave expenses, even if it were just a yen or two.

It worked. Toyota reduced expenses by 28 per cent more than it had originally targeted. By cutting the costs for its cars and being more conservation-minded in its resource and energy use, the company saved ¥5 billion during the year to November 1973 alone.

Rigorous cost-cutting meant that Toyota could get by with only seven people to accomplish the same work that required ten before the oil crisis, which meant its cars only cost 70 per cent of what they used to. And it did this twice. During both oil crises it chopped 30 per cent off its cost structure, bringing it down to 49 per cent (0.70 × 2) of previous levels. By the end of the decade, five people were doing the work of ten, and as it trimmed the fat from its operations, Toyota sparked a revolution in manufacturing.

The oil shock in the autumn of 1973 had people around the world more interested in Toyota-style manufacturing. The crisis had a deep impact on everyone – government, companies, individuals – and the next year, the Japanese economy turned in zero growth. Industry was shaken and scared. Recession was hurting everyone and even Toyota had to cut production. But it still produced better profits than anyone else, and that drew attention to it. Toyota became known as a company that was able to withstand shocks.[4]

Toyota's profits grew in 1975, 1976 and 1978, and as it widened the gap between itself and its competitors, people began to examine its manufacturing methods. Convinced that Toyota was on to something, its competitors in the car manufacturing industry rushed to adopt similar systems. Other manufacturers eventually followed suit.

Japanese companies worked smartly to overcome the oil crises, and before they knew it, they had become strong competitors, using fewer resources and less energy and being more productive than ever before. Behind these efforts was a palpable fear that the oil embargoes would sink the country and the idea of overtaking the West would end a pipe dream. Both labour and management were agreed that being poor in resources, Japan could only survive as a trading nation if its companies were strong and growing, and therefore shared a common sense of crisis and purpose in reacting to the setbacks. The bonds developed as a result of working together through two oil embargoes gave people the power and motivation to seek even further development for the Japanese economy, something that stands in sharp contrast to the companies of Europe and North America, who required far longer to get over the shocks of the seventies.

Toshio Doko, who was appointed chairman of the

powerful *Keidanren* business organization in 1974 at the height of the oil crisis and vowed to transform it into an 'activist *Keidanren*' that would lead Japan to recovery, reflects:

It wasn't just companies that were conserving energy. Individuals pitched in too. I don't think you'll find another society anywhere in the world able to pull together so well. That ability to come together and our native industriousness are two qualities that are worthy of praise and respect. They make me proud to be a Japanese.

Incorporating responses to the oil crisis into their long-term strategies, Japanese firms were able to rid themselves of the stigma that had long equated 'made in Japan' with 'falls apart after its first use'. By the early eighties, Japanese products were able to compete in world markets as high-quality goods. The country shot to the top of the pack in cars, steel, electronics and numerically controlled machine tools, and on the strength of these industries began piling up the huge trade surplus that was the most visible manifestation of its success.

While the Japanese economy was rebounding and gaining strength, the American economy, racked by the country's costly involvement in the Vietnam War, began to weaken. Imports from Japan swelled in the early eighties, as did the US trade deficit. To reduce the deficit and stimulate the economy the US, on September 22, 1985, obtained the agreement of the Group of Five industrialized countries (the US, the UK, Japan, France and West Germany) to lead the dollar lower on the foreign exchange markets.

Known as the 'Plaza Accord', the agreement caused the yen to jump from ¥240 against the dollar to ¥160 at the end of 1986, and ¥122 by the end of 1987. The rise of the yen shook the Japanese economy every bit as much as the oil crises, but once again, companies were able to respond positively.

Firms underwent another round of thorough rationalization, and in this they were aided by their employees, who shared the perception that without rationalization the company was doomed. Toyota, for example, began cutting costs so as to still be profitable at ¥150 to the dollar. It moved more production overseas, switched its focus from export markets to domestic demand, started searching for new markets and diversified its operations. In the 'me-too' style of Japanese competition, other companies followed suit. The government also stepped in, investing heavily in public works and cutting corporate taxes. Again, it was the desire to catch up with the rest of the world that steered Japan through crisis after crisis and on to further development.

SYSTEMIC ENNUI
Goals like rebuilding and catching up are simple and easy to understand. The numbers tell you if you are on track. Today must be a bit better than yesterday, tomorrow better than today, this month better than last month, next month better than this, this year better than last, next year better than this. In 5 years, 10 years, we should be here . . . corporate profits should have grown this much, or business expanded to this point. Indeed, that is just how the numbers worked out. As the economy gained momentum, growth charted a straight line upwards. In the eighties, Japan's economic might was on par with the West's and beginning to pull ahead.

By the end of 1987, the strong yen and the cumulative current account surplus had given Japan net foreign assets of $240.7 billion, outstripping even Britain to become the world's largest creditor. The 1988 GNP of $2,850 billion translated into $23,300 per person, outdoing the United States and Sweden as the highest in the world. Aggregate trade that year was worth $437.1 billion, second only to the United States, and much to the rest of the world's consternation, the current account surplus reached $79.0 billion. The dream had been fulfilled. In the eighties, Japan caught up. Its goal of modernization had been achieved – magnificently. And then in the late eighties, everything started to fall apart again. The Cold War structures that had dominated world politics disintegrated as the Soviet Union crumbled and Eastern Europe bolted for freedom. The world was suddenly very different.

Some have remarked that Japan and West Germany were the true victors of the Cold War. While America and the Soviet Union were competing for military supremacy, the US security umbrella left Japan and West Germany free to concentrate on their economies. While military spending was sapping the vitality of the two superpowers, Japan and Germany were emerging as economic giants.

The end of the Cold War also erased capitalist vs. communist calculations from the world map. Only the capitalists were left, and they now had to compete against each other. Among the victims of these changes were the Japanese political and economic systems, which were themselves very much a product of the Cold War. Cracks began to appear and the signs of dysfunction could no longer be ignored. The political 'System of 1955' and the economic 'Japanese-style capitalism' had reached a dead-end.

For Japan, 1955 marks the beginning of postwar politics, since it was in that year that the conservative parties merged and the socialist parties united to create the current political structure. This political framework developed roughly in parallel to the economic system that would later be dubbed 'Japanese-style capitalism', and together they became the twin engines that drove the country and turned it into an economic power. Not surprisingly, they too were manifestations of the postwar resolve to rebuild and catch up.

The System of 1955 was a domestic version of US–Soviet polarization: the ruling and opposition parties staged their own conflict between capitalism and socialism. Ideological rifts were what dominated their dialogue. Under the system, the ruling Liberal Democratic Party (LDP) has consistently held about two-thirds of the seats in the Diet, with the remaining one-third divided among the Japan Socialist Party, the Japan Democratic Socialist Party and other opposition groups. The stability of this political framework gave the LDP almost 40 years of unbroken rule.

But Japanese politics have been unable to escape the dramatic upheavals that are taking place around the world. In 1993, power passed to a coalition of 'not the LDP' parties led by Morihiro Hosokawa. Still, for 38 years, the Socialists and the rest of the opposition were excluded from power. Never really wanting to govern and never evincing much aptitude for it anyway, they were content to play little brother to the LDP. In many ways, therefore, the System of 1955 is to be praised, for it provided the perfect vehicle for maintaining the status quo in the Cold War world.

But now that the Cold War is over, the System of 1955 has fulfilled its historical purpose and a new system is required. Unfortunately, neither the LDP nor its rivals has the will or the ability to deal with the dramatic changes that are occurring both domestically and abroad. Rather, they are embroiled in a seemingly endless series of scandals: the Recruit shares-for-favours swindle, the Tokyo Sagawa Kyubin payoffs, the fat bribes and evaded taxes of ex-kingmaker and former LDP vice-president Shin Kanemaru. Cosy relations between politicians, bureaucrats and businessmen have invited collusion, bid-rigging, back-room dealings and just about any other form of corruption imaginable, and in the process have rendered the country unable to adapt to the challenges of a new era.

It is clear to all that the System of 1955 has long since fulfilled whatever role it had to play. The reason why it was able to survive as long as it did was because it could appeal to such grand causes as 'protecting democracy and freedom'. Though that no longer sounds as convincing today, we have still seen no new political theory, direction or system to take its place. The country has been unable to find a new political goal, and without something to work towards, its politicians have been foundering.

The Japanese economy is in a rut too. The international community is losing patience over Japan's stubborn trade surplus and its relentless march into the markets of other countries. Japan cannot pull itself out of the slump of the nineties the way it did in the seventies and eighties by increasing productivity and quality to make its products more competitive in world markets. It does not require much thought, in fact, to see that the Japanese economy cannot continue to expand as it did in previous decades, not with the bursting of the 'bubble economy', old and new environmental problems, the labour shortage and growing trade friction. Supported as it was by the myth of never-ending growth, Japanese-style capitalism has now reached the end of the line. The question is, what to do next?

Japanese products now dominate markets throughout the world, but markets were not created exclusively for the benefit of Japanese manufacturers – the growing rancour over trade provides ample evidence of that fact. And just as clearly, unrestrained economic growth is not in the best interests of the world at large, either. The myth of growth is now a thing of the past, and so is the Japanese-style capitalism that it gave rise to.

WHAT TO DO? WHAT TO DO?

Japanese-style capitalism is already at a crossroads, as the rash of bad economic news illustrates. At the end of 1992, NEC decided to pay its bonuses in kind rather than in cash. In 1993, Pioneer dismissed selected employees over 50 years old, while Nissan Motor announced that it would be closing its Zama factory outside Tokyo. These changes would have been unthinkable a few years ago, when all were comfortable in the 'people-oriented capitalism' of Japanese firms that promised jobs for life and pay based on seniority. According to Nikko Research Centre statistics, manufacturers were carrying 1.6 million in 'hidden unemployment' (the Japanese use the more colourful term 'in-house unemployed') at the end of September 1992, far higher than the 490,000 during the first oil crisis or the 330,000 during the high-yen slump. And 'employment adjustment' is spreading from small and medium-sized businesses to Japan's flagship firms. Companies are using internal transfers and assignments to subsidiaries to encourage people to leave of their own accord. Some have even scrapped their seniority-based wage scales in favour of individually negotiated salaries.

Commentators point to three fatal flaws in Japanese-style capitalism: 1) it is too worker-oriented, as is made manifest by lifetime employment and seniority-based wages; 2) it depends on the bureaucracy to enforce 'industry order'; and 3) there is too much money tied up in cross-shareholdings between companies. In the past, none of this was very problematic, but in the past Japanese managers could look forward to growth rates of 5 per cent or more.

Japanese companies are loath to dismiss employees once they have recruited them. Pink slips (notices of dismissal) come only when the company is in crisis and has no other choice. US firms, on the other hand, quickly lay off workers at the first sign of recession. Wages would seem to be floating costs for American managers, whereas in Japan they are treated as fixed. More than anything else, it is employment for life that sets Japanese-style management apart, but at the risk of repetition, this is a luxury that can only be afforded when the economy is growing.

To take an example, let us say that a company recruited twenty new graduates this year. Ten years from now, those people will be ready to assume the position of departmental head, which means they will each need ten people to work under them. For the company, that means taking on another 200 workers. And in 10 years, those 200 workers will be ready for their own departments too, which must be staffed by 2,000 new recruits. If the company does not continue to recruit at this pace, then it has disgruntled employees on its hands who find themselves with the title of departmental head and nobody to boss around. But the situation is not impossible. As long as they are growing and their share of the market is expanding, firms can keep taking on more staff.

But when growth is low and there is no reason to think it is ever going to be high again, lifetime employment does not work. Nor does seniority pay, since it too is based on the idea that you will be with the company until retirement.

Meanwhile, the bureaucracy routinely meddles with industry in order to 'maintain order', which it defines as making sure there are no losers when the economy declines. This too is only possible when the economy can be expected to show strong growth well into the future. Likewise cross-shareholdings between firms. When the economy was booming and the bull market seemed a permanent fixture, companies were happy holding each other's shares despite the low payout ratios.

What is forcing the changes in Japanese-style capitalism are changes in the system at its core, Japanese-style management. These changes are every bit as monumental as the collapse of the System of 1955 in the political sphere, and they speak of a similar inability to adapt to new environments.

Managers are starting to get the message. In February 1992, Sony chairman Akio Morita published an article in the influential *Bungei Shunju* magazine warning that Japanese-style management was reaching the end of its usefulness. Since then, a fierce debate has raged over whether Japanese-style management is such a good thing after all.

The argument had long been coming. In 1990, the final report of the Structural Impediments Initiatives Talks contained US complaints about such common institutions of Japanese business practice as *keiretsu*. Since then, mounting criticism has forced Japanese companies to rethink their priorities.

But even without the criticism from outsiders, Japanese-style management was finding itself at a dead-end. In the past, the way to react to downturns has been to cut costs, and then to hold down capital investment while seeking improvements in productivity and quality. Companies might also try to slim down their manufacturing operations by finding ways to reduce energy and labour requirements in their factories. Only as a last resort would they trim staff. Put simply, the formula has been to expand market share by slashing expenses while producing more competitive products. Bigger shares mean higher sales volumes, which then enable merits of scale to be exploited to reduce costs even further, bringing in an even larger slice of the market. That virtuous circle in motion, results take care of themselves.

This was how Japanese got through the revaluation of the yen in 1971, the twin oil embargoes of 1973 and 1978 and the post-Plaza Accord high-yen slump of 1985. Indeed, this is the only prescription Japanese-style management theory knows for downturns. Unfortunately, it has not worked in the 'Heisei Slump' that began with the rupture of the speculative bubble early in the nineties and has continued to the present day. Managers are doing the same things as they always have done, but the world is a different place. Cold War structures have collapsed, resources are limited and environmental issues demand more attention. The old patterns no longer apply, and managers have no idea what to try next.

Many have made valiant efforts to eke out cost reductions and lower their prices, but sales volumes have failed to surge – in many cases, they have not shown any sign of growth at all. All that has happened is that profits have been squeezed. No matter how much costs are cut, the red ink continues to mount, and for many businesses that has begun to spell crisis.

At the heart of the problem is a glut of gadgets. Japan's

markets have matured. It used to be that inventory was either 'factory inventory' or 'distribution inventory', but now there is a third class of inventory that is coming into play – 'household inventory'. Japan's families already have cars and televisions and video decks – many of them more than one. Their cupboards and chests of drawers are stuffed to overflowing with clothing. They still go shopping, but find little they want to buy. They have too much already. It does not matter how enticing the price tag, how stunning the design, how slick the sales talk, they just do not want it. And it is not only domestic consumers who are sated either. Export markets are also saturated and can no longer be counted on to take up the slack from at home. Even if they could, it would just cause an already enormous trade surplus to grow larger, with all the political rancour that entails.

Jiro Ushio, chairman of Ushio Inc., a maker of lamps and optical equipment, puts it as follows:

> Exports pulled us out of the oil crises and allowed us to deal with the appreciation of the yen. But we can't turn to exports to get us out of this slump. We've got to abandon our old ideas about using export drives to achieve 5 per cent growth rates. In its 1992 'Five-Year Plan', the Miyazawa administration forecast a real growth rate of 3.5 per cent, but I think we'll have to stabilize at about 2 per cent.

'ME TOO'
An increasing individualism is also bringing changes to Japanese-style management. In the eighties, the Japanese enjoyed an unprecedented affluence. Anything they wanted was theirs for the buying; materially, they were satisfied and happy. Tokyo homes may still have been rabbit hutches, but the rabbits now had televisions, video decks, stereo systems and expensive furniture to enjoy. Their

garages held luxury cars. Their bank accounts were fat. And in the summer, they holidayed overseas. Life in Japan had become very much like life in other rich countries. We had caught up with the West. But then our values started to change. We started to abandon the ideals of the postwar generation. The people of Japan were no longer the diligent workers of the 'catch up' period who sweated and strained in the hope of achieving a Western-style standard of living. They were no longer so enamoured of growth that they treated 'bigger' as synonymous with 'better'. And they no longer worshipped numbers and statistics. Japan stopped thinking like a developing country. People no longer asked themselves what they had to do to make today better than yesterday and tomorrow better than today. Economic growth had ceased to be a given; even if they sacrificed their families and private lives for the group, the company or the country, all bets were off as to whether they would find their standard of living improved or their world any happier. No matter how much they sweated for the sake of pretty slogans, there was little chance of their being materially better off and, they realized to their chagrin, there was even less chance of their having a fulfilling personal life.

Even the obsession with economic growth, so long a mainstay of the Japanese psychology, began to wane. Their own living environments, people found, were more interesting by far. Instead of wondering how the economy would fare, the Japanese were now asking themselves how they could enjoy their lives and their families, how they could feel spiritually fulfilled. The focus of interest shifted to a more personal level. Material needs having been met, the eighties were a decade in which the common, overarching goal of the group gave way to more fragmented concerns. It was the dawning of a new period of individualism.

Writing in 1989, Bill Emmott, editor of *The Economist* of London, said that such changes will not suddenly make the Japanese more like Americans, but it will make them less like earlier Japanese. Young and youngish Japanese are becoming more flexible, more fashion conscious, more willing to borrow and to spend, more individualistic. They are more likely to live on their own, to travel, and to come up with new ideas for their companies.[6]

Emmott's scenario is already coming true. Today's young workers place more emphasis on their personal lives than on the company, are more interested in vacation time than wages and place more value on a fulfilling lifestyle than on getting ahead. They think nothing of changing jobs if they are given the chance. These are not values shared with aging 'corporate warriors' of the postwar reconstruction period and booming sixties who saw denial of the self and service to the company as the highest virtues.

The shift in values away from the group in favour of the individual is turning Japanese society on its ear. Consumers, for example, are no longer content with mass-market items. They want products that are more individualized, more varied, more distinctive. This has brought new marketing buzzwords like 'shorter product cycles' and 'aesthetic consumption' to the forefront of business thought. Consumers are now more interested in design and styling than in gadgetry. The shift in orientation has even manifested itself in common language. In the early eighties, there was much talk about the shift 'from intensity to beauty'. Where earlier generations saw quantitative expansion as a virtue, younger Japanese show more of a respect for comfort and lifestyle quality, and that orientation that the phrase tries to capture. Prosperity has awakened the Japanese to the idea of living life for themselves, and they are now looking for more personal fulfilment. There is no longer an overarching goal to bring them together. All they want is enough time and money to be able to maintain themselves at current levels of comfort.

But such changes are not coming easy. Many Japanese have been taught to seek self-fulfilment only through the group and have indeed depended on the group to provide the fulfilment they seek. Having to function as an individual, to think about one's own wants and desires, to find a role for oneself and to grope for one's own path to happiness can be a daunting task for those not used to it. At the moment goals are achieved, one always experiences a corresponding loss of purpose. When this happens to an entire society, the result is uneasiness and unrest. Not only has purpose been lost, but economic prosperity has erased such common ideals – and therefore bonds – as industriousness, community responsibility and self-improvement.

In one sense, the Japanese economy, leaping past oil embargoes and skyrocketing exchange rates to new heights of prosperity, has been too much of a success. Japan has been so successful, in fact, that neither its government, nor its companies nor its people are sure of where they are heading any more. They have lost their postwar rallying points of rebuilding and catching up. These are the causes that they have believed in and have turned to for support in their lives, and no one knows quite where to look for a replacement. This, I think, is at the heart of Japan's current doldrums.

We need to find a new purpose, and we need to rework our old systems for growth and development, the vehicles that achieved our former goals of rebuilding and catching up, into something worthy of that new aim. The old systems are now at a dead-end, having achieved what they set out to do. The evidence from national government, corporate management and personal life makes that abundantly clear. Indeed, we have already begun to grope for a new direction, for this is what is spurring the current rethink of Japanese-style management.

Professor Ken'ichi Koyama of Gakushuin University warns:

Japan will not be able to stay drunk on the wine of postwar success much longer. The reason that successful systems, policies, organizations and ways of doing things fail is precisely because they *are* successful. If you have a glorious history of success, you aren't going to change what it is that brought you that success. And when things don't adjust to changing circumstances, they fail. That is the tragedy of success.

Japan must face up to the dramatic upheavals in the international order that have occurred with the end of the Cold War and make far-reaching changes in the political and economic systems that supported its postwar prosperity. The System of 1955 suffers from a severe case of 'systemic fatigue'. It is time to put an end to it and make radical political reforms. It is also time to rethink Japanese-style capitalism. Now that a very real recession has debunked the myth of unending growth, companies must forget their obsession with market share and production volume. Lifetime employment and seniority may not disappear immediately, but they will be phased out as individualism takes root, jobs change and companies begin to expect their employees to be unique individuals rather than turned out of the same mould. Should Japan fail to change, it will miss a historical transition. And then it will really know what the tragedy of success is all about.

CHAPTER 2

Even Giants Must Change: Toyota Motor

HARD TO STARBOARD!
Economic conditions change, and companies if they want to remain viable must be involved in a process of continual and bold reform. This is especially true in times of economic upheaval, for it is during these periods that companies are called on to prove themselves. Not even the giants are excepted, as Toyota Motor, the largest car manufacturer in one of the world's largest car-producing countries, has found out.

Japanese car manufacturers have watched their profit structures deteriorate, undermined by a number of factors. First there is the drop in car sales because of prolonged domestic recession. This is coupled with the hangover (in the form of heavy depreciation charges) from the capital investment binge of the bubble period. And as if that were not bad enough, the sharp appreciation of the yen has undermined their export business as well. Toyota estimates that it loses ¥10 billion in annual profits for each ¥1 gain made against the dollar. If that is accurate, then it has seen about ¥200 billion evaporate in the last year. In July 1993 the yen zoomed up from ¥121 to the dollar to about ¥100. A year later, in July 1994, it had established itself in the high nineties. This is not the first time Toyota has been through a jump in the exchange rate. In the aftermath of the Plaza Accord of 1985, the yen gained ¥46 against the dollar in a single year, which handed Toyota a ¥290 billion loss on foreign exchange. But the situation is generally thought to be even worse this time. There are three 'cushions' that companies need in order to recover, and Toyota has very little padding left in any of them.

The first is the 'market cushion'. The domestic market has matured and the heyday of the bubble, when you could sell anything you churned out, is not going to come back. In the year to June 1994, Toyota sold 2,018,000 vehicles in Japan, which was 6 per cent less than the year before. Meanwhile, overseas it faced tough competition from the US Big Three. It used to be that Japanese cars were preferred by American drivers because they were cheaper and better than what Detroit was offering, but the Big Three have been working on their quality and the exchange rate has forced Japanese car manufacturers into repeated price rises that have sapped their competitiveness. There is now a $2,000 premium on the Toyota Camry and Honda Accord compared to similar US models such as GM's Saturn or Ford's Taurus. During the year to June 1994, Toyota exported 1,445,000 vehicles, or 16 per cent less than the year before. Gone are the (friction-causing) days when domestic downturns could be offset by flooding foreign markets.

Second, Toyota has little in the way of a 'managerial cushion'. A rigorous emphasis on efficiency made upstart Toyota the world's largest car manufacturer, but its business position quickly deteriorated about the time the bubble collapsed. Its sales and core business profits for the last 5 years tell the tale. As should be obvious from the accompanying table, sales rose steadily until 1993, but operating profits registered significant declines. The ratio of operating profits

Table 1. Toyota sales and operating profits

Year (to June)	Sales (¥)	Operating profits (¥)
1990	7,998,050 M	538,677 M
1991	8,564,040 M	338,787 M
1992	8,940,898 M	124,864 M
1993	9,030,857 M	103,629 M
1994	8,154,750 M	76,780 M

to sales went from 6.7 per cent in the year to June 1990 to 3.9 per cent in 1991, 1.39 per cent in 1992 and 1.1 per cent in 1993. Finally, in 1994, it crossed the 1 per cent line, coming in at 0.9 per cent. In other words, for every ¥1 million yen consumers pay for their cars, Toyota makes a mere ¥9,000 in profit. Though a paragon of profitability, Toyota is now in the position of making almost no money at all for its trouble.

Finally, Toyota is short on 'cost-cutting cushions'. The entire aim of the Toyota-style manufacturing system was to lower costs by eliminating all waste. Whenever Toyota finds itself in crisis, its first reaction is to slash costs. Toyota is so adamant about cutting costs that its core business principle has been described by its parts suppliers as 'wringing out a dry cloth'. This idea is the be-all and end-all for the company and the reason why it was able to become so strong. Toyota president Tatsuro Toyoda explains:

> There are basically two ways to cut costs: 'value analysis' and 'value engineering'. The purpose of value analysis is to find out where to cut costs in existing models, which parts can be made more cheaply. The purpose of value engineering is to rethink cost-performance from design stages on up.

Toyota takes three different approaches to cost-cutting: 'cost improvement', 'cost planning' and 'cost maintenance'.

Cost improvement is equivalent to value analysis. It is concerned with savings that can be had from vehicles already in mass-production. Cost planning is the equivalent of value engineering in that it occurs during model changes as the company rethinks and looks for cost savings in all processes from design to manufacturing. Once costs have been cut, cost maintenance tries to keep them at those levels. The combination of these three is what has enabled to Toyota to maximize its cost savings.

For example, during the first oil crisis, it formed a project team called the 'Cost Improvement Committee' that was charged with finding savings from the Corolla, its mass-market model. The team was given the ambitious target of slashing ¥10,000 (about ¥20,000 in today's money) from the per-vehicle cost over a period of 6 months. Later, similar teams were formed for other models – the Crown Cost Improvement Committee, the Corona Cost Improvement Committee and the like. During 1974, Toyota received about 400,000 cost improvement suggestions from its employees, up about 110,000 from a year before. During the second oil embargo in 1978, it put forward the slogan '80 per cent operation' and worked to achieve a system that would be profitable at 80 per cent of the previous capacity utilization rates. When the Plaza Accord drove the yen up in the late eighties, Toyota took aim at administrative divisions in a company-wide programme to 'cut paperwork in half'. Whenever crisis looms, Toyota's first reaction is to slim down. However, there are limits to how much moisture one can wring from a dry towel, and Toyota appears to have reached them.

Not that Toyota is the only company that is lacking a cushion. The crisis that is afflicting almost all of Japanese manufacturers is ample proof that Toyota is not alone. But Toyota is one of Japan's flagships, and it faces other problems as well. Its production division has been unable to attract enough young men to its factories; its development division is suffering from 'post-bubble hangover' after having moved too far towards the luxury end of the market; and its administration division is battling against chronic 'big company disease'. These problems too are indicative of a wider trend in Japanese manufacturing.

It is therefore worth investigating how Toyota plans to get out of this crisis and what sort of reforms it will be engaging in, for where Toyota goes other Japanese companies are sure to follow. Being Japan's largest company by virtually any measure gives it that much influence.

Japanese-style capitalism, with its emphasis on market share and priority on organizational growth, has reached a turning-point. Now that Cold War structures have been eroded, the world is unlikely to put up with a Japan that runs roughshod over its markets, winning all the prizes for itself and building up ridiculously large current account surpluses. For corporate managers, the old methods of seeking prosperity through greater international competitiveness fuelled by productivity and quality gains no longer work. One look at the long-term problems Japan faces – the labour shortage, the greying of society, environmental degradation – make it clear that Japanese companies cannot continue to grow unchecked. No wonder that rethinks of Japanese-style management have become so common.

The question before us, therefore, is which direction Toyota plans to steer in as it makes its way across this historical watershed. Will its restructuring change the way Japanese-style management is practised? Or will it reform the much-vaunted 'Toyota-style manufacturing system?' And how does it plan to regain the international competitiveness that it has lost?

No one expects the reform of such a mammoth corporation (Toyota Motor itself employs 72,000 people, and between it and its affiliates over 300,000) to be easy. Just as it takes time to turn a supertanker, it will take time for the Toyota ship to change directions even after the rudder has started to move. Only time, therefore, will tell in which direction Toyota is turning, for which horizon it will set sail.

But change it will. Toyota was one of the first to sense that upheavals were coming when the bubble was reaching its peak and it was one of the first to start shifting direction. From the time the recession brought on by the 1985 Plaza Accord (approving a higher yen) was over to the stock market crash that ruptured the bubble in January 1992, Japan was drunk on boom-time excesses, but Toyota seemed to be aware that crisis was looming. By 1989 it had already started to change the way it did business. The rudder had started to turn.

1 FACTORY REFORM
The Birth of 21st-Century Toyota-Style Manufacturing
Thirty kilometres down the motorway from the city of Hakata in Fukuoka Prefecture (Kyushu) is the Wakamiya–Miyata exit. As you leave the slip road, you enter a hilly area and are eventually confronted with a series of enormous buildings all adorned with yellow smokestacks. This is the Miyata factory of Toyota Motor Kyushu, Inc., a wholly owned subsidiary of Toyota Motor.

Completed in 1992, the factory covers 106 hectares (1,056,000 square metres) of land and was built at a cost of ¥150 billion. It manufactures two upper-mid-range models, the Mark II and the Chaser. In fact, it is here that all Mark IIs for the domestic market are produced. Though capable of putting out 800 cars a day (200,000 a year), it is only running at about half capacity, or 450 cars a day, because of slumping demand for vehicles in the wake of the bubble.

One of Toyota's strengths has always been concentration. Almost all of its production and research and development have been located in Aichi Prefecture (Nagoya area). Concentration gave it four advantages: 1) highly efficient logistics; 2) quick, effective shifts of manpower and materials between factories in response to production swings; 3) easy communication between the manufacturing and research and development departments (which makes for more efficient development of new models); and 4) absence of any need to maintain lots of employee welfare facilities scattered around the country. In short, concentration was one of the keys to Toyota's manufacturing efficiency. Unfortunately, it ran into a dead-end. Toyota has been unable to attract enough young men to its factories to make concentration viable.

The trend first became prominent in the late eighties. The company would advertise for workers, but would not get much response. Those it recruited would leave after 2 or 3 years. Soaring drop-out rates told the story of young people's disdain for manufacturing jobs. Added to that is the low birth rate (only 1.46 in 1993). The fact that fewer children are being born will obviously make it harder to recruit young men to the workforce in future years. It used to be that Toyota would go out to the provinces, hire large groups of people and bring them back to Aichi to man its factories, but that too is no longer viable. In fact, it is almost impossible to get anyone to come. On top of it all, the company is being pressurized to cut working hours. If things continued on this course, Toyota realized, it could very well find itself unable to produce cars at all in the next century. It was this labour shortage more than anything else that lured Toyota out of its 'fortress' in the Aichi city that bears its name.

Luckily, Toyota already employed a lot of Kyushu natives. About 7,000 of the 30,000 people who man its factories come from the island, which made it natural for the company to look there for a new factory site. Needless to say, the Kyushu natives were all for the idea. The Miyata factory is part of a larger industrial park set up by the prefectural government on land that used to house now-defunct coalmines. Toyota first announced its intention to build there in 1973 when the waves of motorization were just starting to hit the Japanese shore. Those plans were curtailed by the oil crisis, but by a stroke of good luck the site was still empty 17 years later when the company again decided to move out of Toyota City in 1990.

Not that Kyushu was the only site in the running. It had to compete with a number of other potential locations, but what drew the company back there was the shape of the land, which running 2 kilometres from north to south and 500 metres from east to west was ideal for vehicle production. Oblong sites allow the company to lay out its buildings in the same order as production processes occur, and indeed, production at Miyata does move from north to south. At the northern extreme is the 'plastics plant' where the front bumpers, rear bumpers and instrument panels are formed. Next in line is the 'unit plant' for producing front and rear suspension parts and fuel tanks. This is followed by the 'pressing plant', 'body plant', 'painting plant' and 'assembly plant'. When finished cars roll out of the assembly plant, they go directly to the freight yards at the southern tip, where they are sorted according to their final destinations.

'We have over 3,000 visitors touring the factory every month', beams Tsutomu Nakagawa, Chief Leader of the Public Relations Group in Toyota Motor Kyushu's Administration Department. 'We employ five guides and they're kept busy all the time'. He tells me this as we drive around the factory. The reason Miyata attracts so many visitors, he explains, is that it is an ultramodern plant that has completely changed the image of what car factories are all about. Let's look at what makes it so special.

The 'just-in-time' Toyota-style manufacturing system is the epitome of efficiency, a system that aims to eradicate waste wherever it may exist. It was the first system to earn the attribute 'lean', which was given to it by a group of researchers at the Massachusetts Institute of Technology. Certainly, Toyota-style manufacturing aims to use as little labour, inventory, development time and factory space as possible, and at its foundation is a spirit of innovation that tries to utilize limited business resources efficiently. In that respect, 'Toyotism' is an unexpectedly flexible ideology. It demands that one innovate to find the best way to get the most out of limited resources at the present time. The 'Toyotistic' response to a lack of young men coming into the workforce, therefore, is to work out ways to cover the shortfall. One way, of course, is to recruit more older workers and women. It used to be that no one past 40 was allowed to work on the assembly line. Now Toyota is finding ways to employ older workers and women usefully. That means building more 'human-oriented' production lines, which is exactly what Miyata strives to do. One extreme example of this is the division of the line into eleven parts. Nowhere else in the world will you find a car assembly line so compartmentalized.

From a different perspective, Toyota-style manufacturing has so far been a 'catch-up' system. When Japan surrendered on August 15, 1945, legend has it that the father of Toyota-style manufacturing, Taiichi Ono, told then-Toyota President Kiichiro Toyoda to 'catch up with America in 3 years'. This was supposed to have been the start of the company's 'lean production'. The first step in catching up was learning from one's rivals. At the time, Japan was estimated to have only one-eighth the productivity of America. The architects of Toyota-style manufacturing realized, sensibly, that this was not because the Japanese were only one-eighth as strong as the Americans, but because somewhere they were being egregiously wasteful. The new Toyota-style manufacturing embodied in the human-oriented assembly lincs of Miyata seeks a different goal, a production system that is suited to the twenty-first century.

As noted earlier, assembly is divided between eleven 'main' lines, with an additional six 'sub' lines making a total of seventeen. The lines are laid out more or less in process order. First are the three 'trim lines' where fittings and instruments are attached. Then come the two 'chassis lines' where the engine is mounted. After this are four 'assembly lines' for attachment of engine and boot auxiliaries and work on the interior. Then come the 'final line', where brake oil and other liquids are handled; 'assembly inspection' for general visual and workmanship inspections; 'function inspection' to test the engine, suspension and metres; a 'shower line' to look for leaks; and, at the very end, a 'dispatch line', where cars are given their final inspection. Each of these lines is about 100 metres long, and each is manned by a single work team.

Nakagawa says:

> Conventional lines are 200–300 metres long, so they have to be manned by three or four teams of fifteen or twenty each. That means you've got seventy employees working there. What we've tried to do is to divide up assembly into extremely short work units.

There are reasons for this. The first is that today's cars require more parts. Kousuke Shiramizu, a member of Toyota's board and the head of its Body Assembly Engineering Division, explains:

> Twenty years ago, the assembly section only handled about one-third the number of parts we do today, and the biggest increases have been in electronics and wire harnesses. It used to be that all you had to do was wire in the lamps, radio and engine, so the harnesses were short. Now in our top-of-the-line Celsior (Lexus) models, the harnesses are four and five kilometres long. The same goes for the interior, which used to be just plain sheet metal, and the instrument panel, which used to be a few metres embedded in painted sheet metal. One long line was all you needed to put something like that together. But today, we not only have more parts to work with, we have more operations to

perform and more complex tasks to complete. Long lines just don't work as well as they used to. Actually it should be rather obvious that lines need to change to keep pace with the numbers of parts being handled, and once we realized that, we knew that splitting the line up was the way to go.

More parts also tend to make parts supplies less efficient. On a long line, parts have to weave their way through numerous obstacles before they get to where they are needed. That involves greater distance and worse access. By contrast, highly compartmentalized lines allow supply distances to be minimized. Shiramizu says:

> The ideal is to have an octagonal space in which to divide up the line. That way, each of the smaller lines can have its parts supplies right next to it. Miyata's assembly plant comes close. It is almost a perfect square, running 280 metres east to west and 265 north to south for a total of 61,600 square metres.

Who Says Inventories Are Bad?
That still does not explain what the concrete benefits of subdivided lines are, let alone how they are any more human-friendly. Toyota says there are four basic principles behind its Miyata factory: 1) autonomous, self-contained processes; 2) continuous efforts to reduce workloads under TVAL (Toyota Verification of Assembly Line), an index developed by Toyota to provide an objective measure of workloads; 3) use of in-line mechanical automation equipment; and 4) better working environments.

The first principle tries to ensure that each line completes a certain job. Conventional assembly lines are very effective at boosting production efficiency, but they have one major demerit. Workers become cogs in the wheel and feel no satisfaction or sense of achievement from their work. They create the ironic situation of higher productivity resulting in lower morale. Toyota decided it was time to put an end to this conflict.

Workers generally say that the hardest part about being on the line is that your work is paced by machines. Up until now, car manufacturers have tried to eliminate waste from any angle they could think of: machinery layouts, tool box locations and even workers' body movements. The endless flow of car bodies down the line gives workers little time to rest; in order to keep up, they must continue in silence attaching their assigned parts. If work slows down or there is some sort of problem and the line must be stopped, all seventy people along it stop working, so stoppage is never viewed lightly. The idea that everybody loses when the line stops is embedded in workers from the beginning, and there is intense pressure on them to keep things moving. Miyata has tried to eliminate much of that stress.

Juppei Muto, a director and head of administration at Toyota Motor Kyushu, explains:

> At Toyota, it's all right for workers to stop the line if there is some sort of problem, but it's not something you can do very easily if you know that seventy people are going to have to stop working because of it. That's not the case when the line only has fifteen or twenty people. There's not as much resistance to stoppage.

From the point of view of efficiency, it would be best to line up all the processes from trim to dispatch in order, using transport hangers to bridge what would be minimal distances between them. But Toyota has decided to ignore those considerations. The distance between lines to be spanned by transport hangers is about the same as the length of the lines themselves. That provides some space for backlog to pile up. At the same time, it has decided to mix up the order. By rights, the assembly line should come next to the chassis line, but instead it is over by the opposite wall with the trim line in between them. Obviously, the extra distance means less efficiency, but it also gives workers the time to attach difficult parts without rushing. There is a buffer of about five cars between lines, so if for some reason one line has to shut down, it does not immediately affect the next line as well. Workers at Miyata say that is a great lifeboat to have. It is one product of the shift in orientation from efficiency to humanity. Old-style Toyota thinking saw inventories as a sin. Miyata says they may not always be.

This provides insights into what Toyota-style manufacturing will look like in the next century. Says Muto:

From the beginning we've had the idea that it's all right to stop the line at this factory. Shutdowns help us to spot defects, so they should lead to better quality. At most assembly plants, workers do not pay much attention to defects because they expect them to be spotted during the final quality inspections. They just let them go on down the line. We have a firm rule here, though, that if there are problems you fix them now, and you can stop the line if that's what it takes.

Hanging from the ceiling is a large electric sign that provides a graphic representation of how the line is moving. Areas moving normally are in green, those having trouble in amber and those stopped in red. On either side are four numbers, showing the day's original quota, the day's current quota, the number of cars produced so far and the achievement rate.

Looking down on the factory from the visitors' concourse on the mezzanine, Nakagawa says:

You can see from the sign that we have a quota of 211 cars for today and have produced 212, for an achievement rate of 100 per cent. The line manager is allowed to stop production at his own discretion once the quota is filled, so workers try to get it done as quickly as possible. When you work towards a goal and make it, there's a feeling of achievement. You can say to yourselves, if we get the job done 5 minutes faster today, let's clean the machinery or knock off early. At the same time, people on the line next door watch their neighbours getting ready to leave early and wish it were themselves instead. In other words, our workers are able to take responsibility for how the line runs.

While we were watching the sign, an amber light started to flash. Someone was having trouble. Workers started to move with more agitation. Apparently, they had been cleaning the engine-room when an oil leak was discovered. More workers pitched in to help them search for the cause. A similar fault was found in a second car. The sign changed from amber to red. The line had stopped.

We've got a buffer of three to five cars, so at a rate of one car a minute, the line can be stopped for 3–5 minutes without affecting the next process. If the next process stops, we've got a real shutdown, but most of the time things start moving again pretty quickly.

Nakamura glances at his watch. The line starts moving. 'See! About one minute!' The tension fades.

Subdivided lines also have the advantage of being able to do their own inspections. That is what Toyota means by 'self-contained processes'. Muto says:

The final step in each line is the quality check. We've made it so inspectors are able to provide the final quality assurances for the work done in their lines. Conventional lines just keep moving no matter what –

you do your job and let the cars continue on. Workers feel like cogs in the wheel, and so they are distanced from their work. When we subdivided the lines, we made it possible for workers to take responsibility for their own work. That has encouraged them to work harder, to take pride in what they do and to try to improve their quality.

Where the Toyota-style manufacturing system of the past tried to eliminate waste in all its forms, the Toyota-style manufacturing of the twenty-first century emphasizes the authority, responsibility and autonomy of each of its work groups. By asking them to guarantee their own quality, it provides groups and individuals with the sense of achievement that should come from building things. It gives them a feeling of satisfaction and pride.

Why Automate if You Don't Have to?

Miyata has made fundamental changes in Toyota-style manufacturing. It is where Toyota is evolving towards the next century. The changes are not only in how assembly lines are organized, but in how automation is viewed. This too is in part a correction to bubble-period excesses.

It was not just Toyota. All Japan's car manufacturers invested heavily in automation to try to keep up with global demand. The economic bubble that hit Japan in the late eighties produced a surfeit of demand that manufacturers tried to deal with by bringing in state-of-the-art robots and automation equipment. The bubble in full roar, funding that kind of capital investment was no problem. Then everything changed in the nineties as the bubble collapsed. Domestic demand dropped and a newly competitive Detroit made it hard to boost exports to the US. With sales dropping, companies found themselves carrying excess capacity that undermined their financial stability. According to Shiramizu:

The car manufacturing industry has always dealt with labour shortages by automating more of its production lines. But we had to ask ourselves if automation by itself would really take care of our problems, and the answer we got was 'not necessarily'. Obviously, things like pressing, welding and painting that can be automated ought to be automated, but in the final assembly lines it's a mistake to think that you can cavalierly switch from men to machines. I've worked on press and body lines myself and much of what I say is self-criticism. You can try to automate body and press processes, but there are parts that just are not suited for automation, and what often happens is that you end up shoving all of the dirty work off on to the assembly lines. Sure, your own section may have automated and become more simple, but now the assembly lines have more to do, and it's more complex and time-consuming too. The load just shifts in that direction. This is something I've always had misgivings about.

In the name of automation, robots and other machines were brought in to attach tyres and windows, but what nobody paid any attention to was the problems this created for processes down the line. With the windows already in place, workers found themselves bumping into the glass, or because the tyres were in the way they had to go round to the rear to get their job done. But automation was such a beautiful thing, no one wanted to look at the trouble it caused. More and more automation was introduced to try to solve the labour shortage. The competition between car manufacturers to automate was so intense, automation league tables were reported in the newspapers. Some even announced plans to 'boost automation to 50 per cent'. Shiramizu recalls:

In 1989 and 1990, we had lots of reporters coming around to ask what percentage automation Toyota had achieved. I told them I wasn't going to comment on our automation rates. I had already worked out that automation rates were worthless. It was absolutely meaningless to be sacrificing people so that we could boost our automation rates.

But Toyota became caught up in the automation race nonetheless. The Number Four Assembly Line at the Tawara Factory, completed in 1991, featured a state-of-the-art computer-controlled automation system. It had, for example, an automated engine chassis assembly unit. In rough terms, assembly of the engine chassis has three stages: mounting the engine, screwing it down and returning it to the pallet. The machine was able to tighten scores of bolts all at once and effectively turned the three processes into a single step. It also replaced two skilled workers who would otherwise have had to spend the day uncomfortably on their backs. Tyre attachment was another process that was automated. The 'fully automated tyre supply unit' set all four tyres in their proper places before robots took over to quickly tighten the nuts and bolts.

As marvellous as this may sound, the cost-performance was dismal. At Line Number Four, Toyota spent about ¥100 million for each worker it replaced – and it ended up with less flexibility than before. Big automation equipment would have been a good idea if production volumes could be counted on to expand steadily, but when volumes drop as they have today, such machines exhibit an extreme form of downwards rigidity. Companies are left with too much capacity. This is the trap of automation (not to mention its dehumanizing effects).

As we have said repeatedly, the foundations of Toyota-style manufacturing are the elimination of waste, and what has supported this are the 'just-in-time' delivery system and what Taiichi Ono calls a 'human-centred automation'. He explains:

There are lots of machines that will run with just the flick of a switch. But these new machines, they're all 'high-performance' and 'high-speed' devices, so what happens when something goes wrong – say, you get some foreign matter in the mix or scraps back up – is that the equipment or the moulds break, or maybe you damage your taps and you get tens and hundreds of defects, cars that don't have any screws where they're supposed to. In no time at all, you've got a pile of rejects.

This sort of automation is unable to prevent the mass production of defects. It can't even check itself to make sure that it is functioning properly. That's why Toyota decided to emphasize not automation itself, but a 'human-centred' automation.[1]

One example of Toyota's 'human-centred' automation is machinery with safety devices that automatically shut down when something goes wrong. Likewise, if there are problems on the production line, workers themselves can shut the line down just by pressing the stop button. Ono goes on:

Bringing humans into automation means vast changes in the way things are managed. You don't need people around as long as the machinery is functioning normally. They just have to be there if something goes wrong and the process has stopped. Because of this, a single worker can handle several different machines, which reduces the number of processes involved and provides a great jump in production efficiency.

Unfortunately, in the race for automation, companies seem to have forgotten the human part. Shiramizu looks back:

There are enormous safety problems with high-tech automation equipment. That's why they run behind cages. What's worse, the people running these high-tech machines are wearing ties! It's as if people just existed to maintain the machinery. But do you know what? It's ironic, but since we introduced the automation equipment, we've needed more people than ever. The only thing that's changed is you don't get lively, gung-ho factories with this sort of set-up.

Shiramizu had doubts about Tawara's Line Number Four before it was ever completed:

That's why we wanted to make Miyata a people-centred factory. We tried to think about how assembly lines should be 20 and 30 years from now when the grey society is in full bloom. Our idea was that automation should be a supplementary tool, but that people should be taking the lead in making cars and should be able to ensure their quality. When we built Miyata, we took care to avoid the kind of situation we had in Tawara, where some people understood the technology and others didn't. We did not want it to be a case of people not being able to work without specialized expertise.

Miyata is very much the antithesis of Tawara Number Four, or perhaps it is Toyota's repentance for Tawara and a manifestation of its change of heart.

Of interest are some estimates run by the company to compare the overall economic efficiency of Miyata against a factory that had achieved the same TVAL score through automation. The initial investment for the fully automated line was ¥18 billion, against an initial investment at Miyata of ¥11 billion. The fully automated line required 12,500 square metres of space; Miyata, for all its subdivision, only 7,500. The fully automated line employs 925 people; Miyata 825, or a saving of 100. (Miyata does not need people to maintain security or fill in when the line goes down.)

Common wisdom would have it that there is an eternal conflict in factories between productivity and humanity, but Miyata provides an answer to that. It proves that, depending on how you develop them, human-centred lines are not only the equal of fully automated lines in terms of investment, space and personnel requirements, they are superior. It goes without saying that productivity is not lost. Miyata's influence is starting to be felt elsewhere. The assembly line at the Motomachi Factory in Toyota City, where the new 'RAV4' compact recreational vehicles (launched in May 1994) are being produced, has been subdivided into four parts.

Human-oriented Working Environments
Miyata tries to make it easier to work in many other ways than just dividing up the production line. An example is its in-line mechanical automation equipment. It has replaced conventional belt conveyors with newly developed 'friction moving floors' complete with lifts. These 'moving floors' are really just large moving pathways. The drive mechanism is hidden out of sight underneath the floor, so the line looks extremely clean and simple from the outside. Workers ride on this moving floor as they go about their jobs, and their parts boxes move along with them, so they can work just as if they were standing still. The advantage of this is that it relieves the stress that comes from having to chase after the line. In addition to being psychologically relaxing it is also physically relaxing because the floor moves cars up and down depending on the worker's posture and height, eliminating the physical stress that comes from having to work stooping over.

Another innovative attempt to reduce workloads is the 'easy seat' that is used in the interior assembly process. Putting in the interior means working within the narrow confines of the car body, with all the twisting and squeezing that entails. The easy seat is a semicircular arm with a chair attached to the end of it: workers need merely to straddle it to be placed 'easily' inside the car where they can work sitting down.

Reducing the workload enables Toyota to make better use of women and older workers on its lines. Indeed, you will find women working on all the Miyata lines, slapping on front bumpers and screwing down tyres. Miyata employs a total of 2,000 people, of which 1,600 are factory workers. Fifty of them, or 3.2 per cent, are women.

The pressing plant where car bodies are formed uses presses of up to 4,000 tons. The largest machine is operated by two employees, a woman and a man, both in their twenties. Computers look at production plans to tell the workers how many of what kind of parts need to be made and when a new mould needs to be put in. All they have to do is tell a radio-controlled crane to bring the next mould over and it is set in place in about 3 minutes; a test punch is made and then the real thing follows.

'Check this out,' Nakagawa says, pointing to a car body dangling from a suspended transport hanger. 'You know what makes factories so noisy? It's the chain conveyors that transport the car bodies. When metal is constantly grinding on metal it gets on your nerves. That hanger over there doesn't use chains at all.'

Noise being the main culprit in much of the irritation and stress that comes from working in a factory, Toyota has tried to cut down on it by bringing in what it calls 'mobile electric transport hangers'. Rather than chains, the moving parts use hardened rubber, which makes them virtually noise-free. Likewise, the moving floor is also very quiet because it is powered by friction-drive rollers that 'squeeze' it out like play-dough. A normal factory is estimated to have a noise level of about 85 decibels. At Miyata, it is about 75 decibels.

The largest source of noise is the pressing plant. 'Compare the difference in noise levels on entering and leaving the building,' Nakagawa urges. I prick up my ears as we walk through the door. It is quiet. Very quiet. Standing next to a

4,000-ton press that is punching out body parts, you can feel the vibrations in the pit of your stomach, but this is far less noisy than any conventional pressing operation I have been in. All the walls have been built with soundproofed boards, the presses themselves are inside containers and the floor is supported by springs that absorb much of the sound. Nakagawa explains:

> There are homes about 100 metres away from the pressing plant. Before we came, this area was silent at night-time, so we took special care to reduce noise. The thumping of the press, those sounds in the bass range, is transmitted through the ground just like an earthquake. That's where we went all out with soundproofing.

In another concession to better working environments, Miyata is much brighter than conventional factories. Part of this is because of the skylights, but much is due to the use of bright colours on the walls. Cream is the base colour, with steel struts painted blue and the ceiling beams light green. Visually it is very soothing and pleasant. If the exterior tries to blend in with the environment, the interior strives to be relaxing, according to Nakagawa.

> Those people sitting down over there are scheduled for the late shift. It used to be that at each shift change workers would write notes to each other about what had gone on, but here we have workers come a bit early, watch how the line is flowing for themselves and talk to the early-shift workers face-to-face. Do you know what made that possible? Putting in a break corner right next to the line.

And indeed, next to the line are a couple of tables and chairs, with vending machines nearby.

Other innovations are less obvious. For example, the parts shelves and lockers next to the line are required to be no more than 1.5 metres high. Limiting their size enables workers to scan the entire building, which not only eliminates some of the feeling of isolation, it provides a sense of visual 'liberation'. Because they know what their neighbours are doing, workers can give themselves enough flexibility to pitch in and help out if need be. Being able to see what is happening is one way of sharing information.

Miyata's environmental concerns have extended to its surroundings as well. Most factories tend to be imposing buildings that are walled off from the rest of the world, but Miyata takes pains to create the impression of openness. It has done away with concrete walls and high chain-link barriers in favour of a 1.5-metre green fence. The exterior colours are also designed to be less forbidding. The base colour is off-white with three pastels – blue, green and chrome yellow – used for accents. For all their size, the Miyata buildings are not that imposing. But what really stands out are the sixteen chrome yellow smokestacks, which have become something of a landmark in the surrounding community. Nakagawa explains:

> We knew that chrome yellow would show off dirt, but we went ahead and used it anyway as a form of self-discipline. If they get dirty, then it is clear to everybody that we haven't been doing what we're supposed to.

For their contributions to production engineering and technology in the design and construction of the Miyata assembly line, Toyota Motor and Toyota Motor Kyushu were awarded the Okochi Memorial Production Prize in March 1994. The human-oriented Miyata factory is of significance far beyond the car industry. It provides a blueprint for the production lines of the future in all of Japanese manufacturing.

2 RESEARCH AND DEVELOPMENT REFORM

Brain Surgery

Japanese manufacturers are known for their production technology, but their product development systems also tend to be a couple of steps ahead of those in other countries. One of the secrets behind their strength has been their ability to shorten development lead times while improving design efficiency and quality. But this discipline was lost during the bubble as development costs spiralled, and this has been one factor in undermining companies' earnings structure. Toyota has certainly not been alone in this, but it provides a case study.

At Toyota, what happened goes under the name 'the Celsior phenomenon'. Celsior is Toyota's top-of-the-line luxury car. Since its release in 1988 it has been an overwhelming hit in Japan and in the United States, where it is marketed under the name 'Lexus' and was voted best in all around customer satisfaction 2 years running. Celsior's success, however, threw a monkey-wrench into Toyota's efficiency-oriented cost planning. The entire line, from the entry-level Corolla on up, began to move towards the high end. Again, it was not only Toyota that did this. During the bubble, car manufacturers could sell anything they churned out, so without exception they began to increase the number of models and variations available and the number of parts they used. Ostensibly, this was done to 'cope with diversifying consumer tastes'. What it did, however, was to boost their research and development costs and investment expenditures, leaving them with vastly increased fixed costs.

The Mark II provides an example. Bubble-period Mark IIs offered a choice of sixty-eight different bumpers and forty-eight side-protection molls. When a model change was made in 1992, Toyota cut them to twenty-four and thirty-six respectively. The idea behind cost planning at Toyota has always been to improve development and production costs so that profit margins could be raised without raising prices. The higher production costs go, the harder it is to make cost improvements, and that is why Toyota's earnings structure has been subject to chronic deterioration. Katsuaki Watanabe, head of the Business Planning Department and a Toyota director, tells the story:

> During the bubble, markets just kept expanding and expanding and we fell under the delusion that they were limitless. When you have a chance to expand your market, it's embarrassing to have to keep your customers waiting or not be able to meet their demands. That's why we started our 'customer satisfaction' programme – we wanted to hear what our customers wanted. Once you start doing that, though, there's no end. We decided to upgrade our cars, so immediately research and development costs rose. Then we had to make capital investments in order to get the new models on to the market, which left us with higher depreciation charges. Before we knew it, we had set ourselves up for more and more pressure on our earnings structure. During the bubble, we forgot how to say no, how to hit the brakes.

After the bubble ruptured, Japanese lifestyles changed. Consumers still wanted more variety and better quality, but they were also concerned with price now. The key to survival in such an environment is whether or not you are able to develop products that match market requirements. In September 1992, Toyota decided it was time to give itself a more efficient and attractive research and development department and embarked on major organizational reforms. It was a first for the company. Never before in its history had it found it necessary to perform 'brain surgery'. But that surgery was exactly what it needed to reform Toyota-style manufacturing at the research and development level.

At the core of Toyota's research and development system

are its chief engineers, and they are every bit as important to it as the more famous 'just-in-time' and '*kanban*' systems. Led by the chief engineers, it is the research and development system's responsibility to ensure that Toyota's cars are attractive and in line with consumer requirements. The production system, on the other hand, is responsible for manufacturing those cars as cheaply as possible with as high a quality as possible. Though developed at Toyota, this two-part system has spread to many other industries and is indeed the basis for most Japanese-style research and development and production.

The roots of the chief engineer system go back to the launch of the Toyopet Crown in 1955. The Korean War had produced a boom in the Japanese economy, and Toyota developed the Crown to take advantage of rising consumer demand. Then chairman emeritus Eiji Toyoda hand-picked the engineer responsible for developing the car and told him to do whatever he wanted. The same sort of thing happened for the Corona, Publica and Corolla, and somewhere along the way a system was born.

Each model has a single chief engineer, generally a veteran with at least 20 years' experience. Under him work the engine, body and chassis designers as a closely knit team. The company provides basic guidelines for the new model, but the chief engineer is responsible for everything else, all the way from basic design concepts to detailed designs, production planning, marketing and aftersales servicing. When it comes to the actual design of the car, he wields far more authority than even the head of the design department. At most companies, design drawings must be signed by both the designers and the head of the design department before they are considered authorized. At Toyota, it does not matter if the departmental head has already signed them, they are not authorized until the chief engineer signs too. Allowing the chief engineer to take full responsibility for the model gives him room to use his abilities to the fullest and develop cars that are more distinctive and personal. However, somewhere in the process of expanding model selection, introducing more sophisticated technology and adding more research and development personnel, distortions began to appear in the system and the personality of the chief engineer became buried.

The Damage from Overgrown Organizations

The process of developing new products can be divided into 'product engineering' (design, prototypes and tests) and 'process engineering' (design and building of the equipment and jigs required to build the product). At most Japanese firms, these phases overlap. Just as rugby players toss the ball to each other as they run down the field towards the goal, there is a point at which the pre-processes and post-processes overlap. The merit of this system is that the engineers in charge of each phase are able to share information. Additionally, they become aware of and are able to solve problems in process engineering and production earlier, which means shorter lead times. This development system, with its emphasis on horizontal ties, may look burdensome and time-consuming, but because it proceeds forward tackling each problem as it is encountered, loss-times are minimized. Rugby-style play is one of the things that sets Japanese-style development apart.

By contrast, most European and North American companies use a 'relay race' system – they wait until product engineering is completely finished before passing the baton to process engineering. While this may appear more functional than the Japanese-style overlaps, it has the disadvantage that it is impossible to discover problems in the production stage before the switch is thrown. US and European firms will often find themselves scrambling to redesign because something went wrong when production started. Some have therefore started to learn from Japan and introduce what they call 'simultaneous engineering'.

There is one pitfall in all this, however. If left unchecked, organizations can become excessively compartmentalized so that the amount of coordination and adjustment to be done reaches ridiculous levels. Eventually this demerit starts to outweigh the merits, and development efficiency suffers.

Toyota's first chief engineer had to deal with thirteen different offices and 1,600 engineers, but most of the time all he had to do was keep in touch with the three people in charge of the engine, body and chassis for the system to run smoothly and efficiently, with everyone aware of what they should be doing and able to make changes as necessary. Over the years, however, organizations became bigger and more finely divided. Eventually, the chief engineer's job was not so much leading development as coordinating between all the interested departments. A chief engineer in 1991 would have to deal with forty-eight departments and 12,000 engineers. If he wanted to do something new, he had to go around and coordinate between all the related sections. Changing the shape of some part of the body meant securing the approval of the engineering design department, notifying the people in charge of the chassis and overall design, running tests with the change and waiting for the results to be evaluated. Naturally, all this had to be done in writing, too.

Grumbling and second-guessing were not uncommon. Negativism prevailed. Meetings abounded. By rights, meetings should just be for representatives of the departments involved in a decision, but engineers from other sections began inviting themselves on the ground that they 'needed to know just in case'. More people means longer meetings means slower decision making means less scope for the ideas of the chief engineer to be given play. But for all his loss of power, the chief was far busier than ever before. When Toyota began toying with the idea of organizational reform it ran studies on the amount of time its design engineers were spending in coordination work. The results were astonishing – 30 per cent of total working hours.

Takeshi Uchiyamada, a project general manager in the Technical Administration Division, enlarges:

> We could sell anything during the bubble, so we kept bringing out new models and our chief engineers were dizzyingly busy. Usually you have about 4 years between the end of one project and the next model change, so there's time for the chief engineer to relax and recharge his batteries, but during the bubble as soon as one project was over he was expected to help out in another, so he was continually under the gun. And most of his time was spent in coordination and administration, so it's obvious why chiefs burned out.

While organizations were expanding, electronics and other technologies had become more sophisticated and specialized, making it harder for the chief engineer to be versed in all aspects of the car and able to make his decisions with confidence. As the chief lost confidence, other organizations – the engine, body, chassis and design departments – found themselves with more say over things. It was not so long ago that the chief engineer for the Crown would order a custom-made engine from the Engine Department. Today, there are so many models that it is impossible to give each its own unique engine. Instead, the Engine Department provides ready-made products and tells the chief to 'choose between our three versions in the 3,000-cc class'. True, each of these engines is a marvellous piece of workmanship employing all the latest in electronic controls, but there is no longer any scope for the chief to design an engine with some personality. If anything, he has to change the design of his car to fit the engines available. Consumers sense that something is amiss. They complain that all Toyota cars are more or less the same. No doubt much of that is because the influence of the chief engineers has waned.

Yoshiro Kimbara, former vice-president and currently advisor on technical issues, explains:

> When technology becomes more advanced, development naturally becomes more complex. There's no way around that. But Toyota is not selling engines, it's selling cars. Certainly, the engine has to be good, but a great engine is meaningless if the car isn't very impressive overall. That's why people started to say that we needed to go back to the basics of the chief engineer system.

Individual engineers also felt the detrimental effects of overgrown organizations. Many found themselves designing steering wheels or seats for over a decade. Having come to Toyota to build cars, it was a let-down to find that they might be spending their whole life doing nothing but the indicators, and morale suffered as a result.

'If You're Going to Do It, Go All the Way'

Toyota began to overhaul its product development system in the spring of 1990 when it announced its 'Future Programme 21'. At the time, the problems in the engineering departments had not yet manifested themselves in tangible form and there was much grumbling about 'why do we have to reform all of a sudden?' Management pushed it through anyway, in a testament to its insight and vision. Kimbara recalls:

> We all had this sense that crisis was looming, that if we kept on being preoccupied with matters of the moment we'd eventually deplete all the intellectual capital we had saved up. Mid-level employees eventually realized too that radical reforms were needed before something serious happened.

Not that it is easy to reform an organization of 12,000 people. If Toyota's scalpel slipped while it was performing the brain surgery, there was a chance of doing untold damage. Debilitated research and development would immediately be felt across the entire group. Changing the organization meant changing the methods that were used to develop new products, which had ramifications for allied departments such as production technology, sales and marketing. Toyota's managers had to embark on reform with the realization that they could very well start off a domino effect. Nor, given the position Toyota holds in the Japanese economy, would failure remain just Toyota's problem. Kimbara admits:

> It was all very well to talk about reforming Toyota's brains, but if we failed the damage would be immense both to Toyota and to the Japanese economy. It was always at the back of my mind that we were gambling for huge stakes.

Obviously, many employees were perfectly content with the old system and were resistant to change. The Engine Department went on record as being against reform, arguing:

> The reason we have been able to develop high-performance engines is that all the teams within the department have been able to pull together towards a single goal. We already have an ideal organization in place. Why do we need to tear it down?

Kimbara goes on to recall:

> I came out of the Engine Department myself, so I could understand what they were saying. But we had to survey the entire engineering division in making our decision, so during the Product Development Reorganization meetings I asked them, 'What's the purpose of reform?' and I told them, 'To think about how we as a company

or we as the Engineering Division can develop new products more efficiently and get them on the market. It's not as though all we have to do is build great engines. We have to build great cars. Why don't you think about that for a moment?' I convinced them, too.

While coordinating its organizational reforms internally, Toyota also brought in outside consultants for more object-ive analysis. Toyota has always been an extremely cautious, conservative company and it was in character for it to do careful studies before deciding to act. The consultants found that while the company was in generally good shape, 'there are many reasons to doubt whether or not it will be able to adapt to rapid changes in the internal environment'. As we will discuss in detail later on, Toyota tried to flatten out its administrative organization in 1989 by doing away with the post of office manager and delegating significant authority to its divisions. But where divisions in other areas of the company had an average of fifty to sixty people, in engineer-ing they still averaged 400–600. It was therefore natural that engineering be the next area up for reform. The consultants' report having been received, Toyota set to work reorganiz-ing. It had two main goals: to eliminate the damage from overgrown organizations and to remedy the efficiency losses from overly complex communication. It emphasized six points in trying to achieve them:

1 Transmitting information quickly by shortening the path of communication so that work is more efficient.
2 Minimizing coordination by giving divisions and organi-zations authority over more work so that fewer people need to attend meetings, meetings can be held less fre-quently and such meetings as are held are over with quickly.
3 Speeding up the decision-making process.
4 Enabling people to get a wider view by encouraging

movement and job rotation within divisions, offices and groups and delegating more authority.

5   Improving employees' sense of achievement by making it easier to see what their position and job is within the entire organization and making it easier for results to be recognized.

6   Eliminating waste by working more systematically and reducing the amount of coordination that needs to be done, thereby making development more efficient.

In 1991 a subcommittee, after much debate, proposed that engineering be split into 'passenger cars' and 'commercial vehicles'. The idea had merit since it would make reform easier, but it also had the disadvantage of offering very little contraction in passenger car organizations because commercial vehicle development is only about a third its size. Kimbara says:

I went to the chairman emeritus [Eiji Toyoda] to explain the idea to him. He told me, 'If you're going to do it, go all the way. I created the chief engineer system. There was opposition at the beginning, but it became established because after trying it with a few models everyone saw that it worked. Now, however, the organization has grown so large that problems are emerging. We need to get back to the essential elements that made the chief engineer system so good. Don't just stop with dividing up commercial and passenger vehicles. Go all the way!' I was pleased with how encouraging he was, but when he told me 'Let's see what you're made of' I realized the intense pressure I would be under.

Cutting 1,200 Jobs
The next step in reorganization came in 1992 when Toyota formed a top-down decision-making organization chaired by Kimbara, who was then an executive general manager, with

Akihiro Wada, then general manager and now executive general manager, as vice-chair. The committee had final approval over reorganization plans, though day-to-day operations were left to a working group formed from members of the Engineering Division. The man who led this working group was not a professional in organizational management but a veteran product development engineer, and his staff was made up of young engineers who did the line work in individual departments. This odd mix of people tossed around an odd mix of ideas for a while before finally settling on a proposal to set up 'development centres'.

It took the idea further, making imaginary appointments to the imaginary posts of centre managers and departmental heads and suggesting several discussion teams to coordinate within and between individual centres. From there it went on to set up teams for each centre that ran detailed simulations of how organizations would be distributed among them, who would be responsible for what areas, how the centres would be run and how they would coordinate with each other and with outside departments. The working group met about sixty times before finalizing its proposal to divide the Engineering Division into four development centres. The proposal was submitted in the summer of 1992.

Development Centre No. 1 is responsible for luxury-class cars like the Century and Crown (rear-drive cars). Centre No. 2 handles front-drive models like the Corolla and Corona. Centre No. 3 has everything that is not a passenger car – trucks, recreational vehicles, commercial vehicles and electric cars. Centre No. 4 develops the technologies that are common to all. The old design, body, engine, chassis and electronics departments were split into three and distributed among the first three centres.

Each design centre has full responsibility for the development of its models, all the way from conceptualization through design, prototyping and testing. No. 1 employs 1,500 people; No. 2, 1,800; No. 3, 1,400; and No. 4, 2,100, which Toyota considers more or less optimal for each area. Kimbara claims:

> Do you know how you inspire people in research and development to work? You make sure they have competition. We've got a situation now where the people in Centre No. 1 say, 'We've run comparisons from several different angles and think we should be building more luxury cars because they can be expected to sell' and No. 2 will come back with, 'No, it's small, entry-level cars we need to be emphasizing'. All of a sudden they're competing with each other. It's been great for trucks and commercial vehicles too. It used to be that they took a back seat to passenger cars and no one paid them much attention, but now they've got their own development centre, and that puts them on a par with the others, especially since we put [relatively glamorous areas like] recreational vehicles and electric cars in there too.

But did tinkering with the organization really change anything? Toyota thinks it did. The company says efficiency has improved. It is easier for different departments to communicate, so there has been a surprising leap in the speed of decision making. In the most extreme cases, all it takes is a short conversation between departmental heads. The manager of the Engine Department tells the manager of the Chassis Department that there is a problem and they decide how to solve it – no paperwork, no time-consuming coordination meetings. Instead of coordinating between forty-nine departments and teams, managers now have only twenty-seven to deal with, and the number of departmental heads has been halved from twelve to six. Problems are discussed in a weekly meeting between the centre manager and the departmental heads, and work on their solution proceeds in easy-to-manage 1-week units. Because chief engineers only have half the number of departmental heads to deal with, the time spent in coordination, which used to account for 30 per cent of their workload, has been reduced by 30 per cent. That translates into a 10 per cent efficiency gain $(0.3 \times 0.3 = 0.09)$. In workforce terms, 10 per cent of 12,000 is 1,200, which is roughly the number of jobs Toyota has eliminated. Kimbara explains:

> More efficient development means shorter lead times, but in the end, the development period is determined by how quickly the Pre-production Department is able to get things ready. What we want to do, therefore, is keep our development periods the same, and use that time to make things a little less hectic.

Toyota also reports better morale among its engineers.

> When offices are smaller, individuals are able to do more things. We don't have people spending decades designing windscreen wipers any more. Engineers know exactly where they stand in the development of the car, and that changes their attitude towards their work. And now they can talk with people from other departments too, so our people are more well-rounded.

The reorganization of Toyota has only just begun and there are of course no guarantees that any of this will lead to more attractive cars. What is certain, however, is that the Engineering Division will never be the same again.

3 SHAKING UP THE OFFICE

White-collar workers in Japan have achieved a reputation for dismal productivity by international standards. Toyota is no exception, and its low-productivity white-collar workforce was one of its earliest targets for reform. Since 1988, the company has taken three stabs at rationalizing its administration departments. All of them have tried to achieve productivity gains while tackling the problems of rigidity and lethargy that afflict all large organizations.

Flatter Organizations
The first wave of reform came when Toyota flattened its organizations in 1989. Note that this was during the heyday of the bubble, but for all the economic giddiness, Toyota's managers sensed that crisis was coming. Decision making had become horribly slow, which not only made the company late to adapt to changing economic conditions, it also sapped it of its energy. But for all the doom felt at the top, the people on the front lines, caught up in the bubble, thought everything was just perfect. Watanabe says:

> Even trivial matters had to be pushed through level after level in the pyramid before anything could be decided. I remember having to spend 6 months and sometimes a year negotiating with other departments just to get a decision on something. I knew something had to be done, so I decided to flatten things out as much as possible.

The first step was to get rid of the post of office manager and to introduce project managers in their stead, knocking out part of the pyramid and speeding up decision making in the process. Next, the company sharply boosted the weighting towards job skills in its personnel evaluations. There are some extremely difficult aspects of evaluating middle managers' performance. Not only are there no objective criteria as to what managerial ability consists of, but when employment is for life and wages based on seniority, managers feel like they are more or less guaranteed promotions as long as they do not make any major blunders. That is where project teams come in. Project teams have clear goals to achieve, which makes it very easy to evaluate their performance objectively.

When Toyota flattened its organization it took the opportunity to change its wage scale. Before, workers were paid 'base pay' plus 'productivity allowances' (to be determined by their supervisors). Today, wages for workers in administration and engineering posts are 40 per cent base pay, 40 per cent skill pay and 20 per cent age pay. For factory workers the ratio is 40 per cent base pay, 20 per cent productivity pay, 20 per cent skill pay and 20 per cent age pay. For managers, it is 40 per cent base pay and 60 per cent skill pay. Whereas skill and ability had no impact on wages in the past, they now account for at least 40 per cent of one's cheque. The seniority-based wage scales that used to characterize Japanese-style management have, at Toyota anyway, begun to crumble. Some cracks are appearing in lifetime employment too.

Iwao Isomura, executive vice-president, muses:

> Companies evaluate their employees in terms of past performance and future expectations. Our current wage scale lets past performance determine 40 per cent of wages, which moves us much closer to a Western-style yearly salary system. I think lifetime employment will eventually fall by the wayside. At Toyota, we'll probably see about 80 per cent of our staff employed for life, with the remaining 20 per cent employed on a project-by-project basis.

In point of fact, globalization, changes in young people's attitudes towards work and other shifts in the economic climate have rendered Japanese-style lifetime employment obsolete. Toyota is responding by bringing in more flexible recruiting systems. The most recent example is the 'professional contractor' system that began in 1994. Under the system, employees are given yearly employment contracts for which a yearly wage figure is determined in advance. In its first year, Toyota advertised for designers and ended up signing on an Italian and a Japanese as professional design contractors, paying them ¥10 million each for the year. Car design is a job that is very dependent on individual skills and the results of one's labours are obvious. By paying a preset wage for a year's worth of work, the company thinks it can demand more of its designers. It is especially suited to younger workers who are apt to have less loyalty to the firm, so Toyota is confident that in the long run professional contractors will boost its labour productivity.

'Now 21'
The second administrative shake-up was the 'Now 21' programme launched in 1992. As its name suggests, the programme attempts to probe the attitudes of the younger employees who will be running the company in the next century. The Business Planning Division took the lead in organizing several surveys and discussion groups for young employees where they tried to discover employees' attitudes towards the company, areas of dissatisfaction and concern and how they think improvements should be made. This, Toyota hopes, will give it the information it needs for further reforms. Watanabe says:

> We were trying to stimulate thinking at the bottom of the organization, but at the same time we wanted to let those at the top know what those at the bottom were thinking so that they would be better able to lead. At first, top managers muttered a lot about how people at the bottom were always complaining and ought to take care of their own responsibilities before they criticize their superiors. In some senses, that was the correct response, too, but we were able to move on from there to ask ourselves what we, as managers, ought to be doing to train our staff better, and whether perhaps our

own managerial skills might not be lacking in some ways.

Of particular value in this programme were the side effects. The questions stimulated employees, caused them to think and talk and helped energize them before they fell prey to 'big company disease'. Watanabe goes on:

> People talk a lot about how adaptable Toyota is. One reason for that is that we've always had a sense of crisis. There's a way you instill that in people. Instead of just saying that everything is fine and dandy, you have to get them to realize that there might be other things they should be doing.

In other words, it is the process of asking questions itself that instills the sense of crisis that serves as a springboard for new energy. To tap that energy, companies must be continually shaking up their organizations, both horizontally and vertically.

'Business Reform'

Phase three began in June 1993 with a programme called 'Business Reform' designed to change how administrative departments functioned. If 'Now 21' was change from the bottom up, 'Business Reform' came from the top down.

Over the preceding decade Toyota had watched its staff in administrative and indirect divisions grow by 45 per cent, compared to just 18 per cent in the factories. 'Business Reform' tried to trim some of that fat. Where 'Now 21' was a voluntary programme, 'Business Reform' came from on high. According to Watanabe:

> Our indirect divisions were distended and their productivity was awful. This had been an issue ever since we flattened things out, so we decided it was time

to build a system that would be able to boost productivity.

One of the goals of 'Business Reform' was to cut work by 30 per cent. Some 10 per cent of that saving was to be used to provide shorter working hours, the remaining 20 per cent to shift people into new and more creative projects. One such new endeavour was a team to look for ways to boost profits over the medium and long term. Known as the 'Maruai Project', the team included ten office managers and assistant office managers led by Watanabe himself. Describing the project, he goes on to conclude:

In the beginning, everyone tried to champion the interests of their own department. We all agreed on general principles, but when it got down to specifics people were so caught up with defending their own ground that it became a shouting match. The more we discussed things, though, the wider their perspectives became until they were finally able to think about issues and directions from a company-wide perspective. Forming project teams and discussing things is a very effective way to change attitudes and ways of thinking.

Projects took place on three levels – company-wide, divisional and departmental – depending on their content. Each division and department had its own 'Business Reform' office or group to run the projects. Toyota received about 100 topic suggestions. Ten were company-wide issues, fifty divisional and forty departmental. Examples of company-wide themes include 'better cost planning', 'creating mechanisms for profit management', 'slimming down administrative and indirect divisions', 'improving overseas cost planning' and 'more efficient vehicle and parts supplies'. Watanabe explains:

You might be tempted to see 'Business Reform' as a way to rationalize our workforce, but that wasn't the case. We knew we couldn't adapt to changing environments by going about our business in the same old way, but every time somebody wanted to do something new their first request was for more staffing. That attitude is too facile to work either. We decided that we weren't going to permit any more staff increases even if they were needed to try something new. Instead, we would stick to our present numbers and get the staff for new projects by drawing them off low-priority areas.

It is common to think of restructuring as equivalent to staff cuts and streamlining. At Toyota, however, it was more than that. 'Business Reform' aimed both to streamline organizations and to change attitudes.

BUILDING A 'COMPASS' OF BASIC PRINCIPLES
When he announced his company's results in June 1994, President Tatsuro Toyoda said the vehicle manufacturer would produce sales of ¥1 trillion and an operating profit rate of 4 per cent by fiscal 1996. That is a rather optimistic statement for a company that, thanks to falling consumer demand and a high exchange rate, is teetering on the edge of operating losses, and it displays Toyoda's confidence in Toyota Motor's ability to make it through the crisis. Results for 1994 were not necessarily encouraging. As we noted earlier in the chapter, the ratio of operating profits to sales was a mere 0.9 per cent. What is it that makes Toyoda so confident?

One reason might be strong sales for all the new 1994 models. The RAV4 compact recreational vehicle launched in May has been selling so well that production has been bumped up from initial plans of 4,500 a month to 6,600. RAV4 is the first car to come out of the new development and production systems. It uses the same 2,000-cc engine as the Corona and Camry and shares about 40 per cent of their parts. That enables Toyota to sell it for ¥1.6 million, ¥40,000 cheaper than competing compact cars.

Both of the new midsize passenger models launched on July 1, the Vista and Camry, are bringing in about 18,000 orders a month, double the initial sales target of 9,000. During their design, these two were subject to even more rigorous cost controls than the RAV4 and Toyota was able to bring the number of parts they require down from 3,900 in the old models to just 2,300, again with 40 per cent parts shared between them. For the Vista, this can shave as much as ¥61,000 off the final price.

These results can be directly attributed to Toyota's expertise at cost-cutting. Between July 1993 and June 1994 it found ways to save ¥110 billion at the design stage and ¥40 billion in factories and logistics for a grand total of ¥150 billion. During the next year it plans to save another ¥100 billion. Says executive vice-president Hiroshi Okuda:

Before, we'd decided on our 'cost plans' – we'd say, let's bring this car in at ¥1 million – but we had a hard time sticking to those goals. During the bubble, it didn't matter if you went ¥20,000 or 30,000 over on a ¥1 million car, you could still sell them profitably. But right before the bubble popped in 1991 we realized that something was very wrong and we set up a cost reduction committee to deal with it. One of the decisions we made was that we would not market cars that did not meet their cost targets. Another was that any savings we made from cost-cutting would be taken as profits [rather than passed on to consumers]. During the bubble it was all right to cut car prices by ¥100,000 if you'd shaved ¥100,000 off your costs because you had a good chance of doing more volume. However, that kept us running after market share in a game that no one could win. Now, we don't cut our selling prices even if we've cut our costs. We don't need to. Customers already say our cars are attractively priced. What we're doing, therefore, is strengthening our earnings so that we can make some money in the domestic market for a change.

In short, one of the reasons for Toyota's new-found confidence is that its reforms are providing it with a system that is able to turn profits even at low prices.

Upon reflection, one realizes that there is nothing very mysterious about Toyota's strength. What makes Toyota a great company is that once it decides on a direction, it does everything it can to get there. It is no more difficult than becoming an honor student. You do your homework and revision as you are supposed to, and voila, you are on the dean's list. Like honor students, Toyota sticks to its decisions, often with breathtaking simplicity. When it decides to cut costs, it starts examining each individual bolt to see where savings can be made. If it feels threatened because young men are shunning factory jobs, it takes measures to deal with the situation by, for example, subdividing its assembly line into eleven small groups. Once a decision is made, it does not go halfway and try to fake the rest, it does not switch horses in midstream. Toyota employees are often criticized for being 'cookie cutter' people all pressed out of the same mould and all thinking the same thoughts, but there is no denying their ability to act and get things accomplished. Okuda counters:

> Certainly, they call us 'cookie cutter' employees and maybe there's an element of truth in that, but you can't deny our ability to achieve what we set out to do. The question is whether the brains behind the organization are thinking clearly, and whether they're able to work harmoniously with the hands and feet.

Japanese car manufacturers, and Toyota especially, have found themselves trapped in a vicious circle. When the exchange rate goes up, they cut their costs to restore their competitiveness, but that just pushes the exchange rate higher again. One may question whether it is all worth it. The pains they have taken to adapt to the exchange rate will just come back to haunt them. Toyota says it is now able to compete at ¥100 to the dollar, but one might ask what for? Does not another round of yen appreciation lie in wait around the corner?

'I think we've got to put an end to this cycle somewhere, and the only way to do that is to produce more cars locally in other countries,' Okuda says. In that sense, therefore, what Toyota needs to do is return to its basic business principles.

In 1992 it developed a new set of basic guiding principles. The new principles replace *The Toyoda Legacy*, a collection of sayings and maxims from company founder Sakichi Toyoda that have been revered for the last 57 years. The new principles are a manifestation of the new Toyota that is struggling to be born.

Twice in the past the company had toyed with the idea of revising *The Toyoda Legacy*. The first time was when it won a Deming Prize in 1975, the second was when Toyota Motor and Toyota Motor Sales merged in 1982. Neither occasion bore fruit. But then in the eighties Toyota found itself in a completely different business environment. In place of quantitative performance measures like sales, market share, export volumes, profit margins and cost reductions, people were asking questions about more qualitative issues – how it viewed its responsibilities to society, how it would contribute to the local community, what its policies were towards the environment and trade friction. This marked the transition from management for quantity to management for quality. Comments Watanabe:

It's just like what happened when people started emphasizing feeling, styling and individuality in new cars rather than price and objective quality. Today, there are more issues that companies have to approach from the perspective of intuition and feelings, things like social responsibility and environmental protection. Obviously, quantifiable measurements are still an extremely important part of running a company, but we have to deal with more qualitative issues too.

Toyota's Basic Principles are based on three insights into the business environment. The first is that the international environment is changing. With friction mounting over the motor vehicle trade, it is no longer possible to flood foreign markets with products in the name of gaining share at all costs. Also, its foreign operations make Toyota an international company and as such it must have principles that can be accepted all over the world. The second insight is that the social environment is changing. For car manufacturers, this means dealing with environmental concerns above all else. Finally, the way in which business resources are utilized is changing. Today's companies are under enormous constraints. Profit structures are deteriorating, fewer young workers are coming in, workers have different attitudes towards their jobs and there is pressure to cut hours. From the perspective of efficiency, this requires more careful use of human and financial resources than ever before. The new basic principles – there are seven of them – attempt to deal with these changes.

1 Be a company of the world.
2 Serve the greater good of people everywhere by devoting careful attention to safety and to the environment.
3 Assert leadership in technology and in customer satisfaction.
4 Become a contributing member of the community in every nation.
5 Foster a corporate culture that honours individuality while promoting teamwork.

6 Pursue continuing growth through efficient, global management.

7 Build lasting relationships with business partners around the world.

This is not only the blueprint for running a company in times of upheaval, it is a compass that gives direction to the organizational and attitudinal reforms that Toyota seeks. Tatsuro Toyoda says:

> In drawing up the new Basic Principles, the Toyota Group discussed at great length the challenges the company needed to face in order to adapt to the new business environment. Should it train more internationally oriented staff? Should it change its management style? What about wage scales and employee education programmes? And how to deal with the environment and traffic congestion? After discussing these issues, we next asked ourselves what sort of a base of action Toyota employees should have, and the conclusions we reached are embodied in the new principles. This is not some abstract managerial philosophy. These are values that can and should be shared by all Toyota employees around the world.

Toyota, the giant of the Japanese fleet, has used a series of basic reforms to build for itself a new business framework. There are still many difficult and complex questions to be dealt with. Will it really be able to improve its profit structure? Will it be able to attract workers? How does it plan to deal with the hollowing out of jobs and technology that will come with shifts to offshore production? No one expects these problems to be solved overnight. But this much is certain. This mammoth ship has finished turning its rudder and is now embarking on a new voyage into the twenty-first century, its seven Basic Principles the compass that will keep it on course.

CHAPTER 3

The Dynamism of Self-Reform: The East Japan Railway Company

RESURRECTING THE NATIONAL RAILWAYS

Companies have their own ways of seeing things, their own modes of thought, their own behaviour patterns. This 'corporate paradigm' is the basis for business strategies, corporate culture and corporate atmosphere.

Japan National Railways began operations in 1872 as a government undertaking. Extending the lines was a key part of the government's modernization programme, a programme founded on such slogans as 'rich country, strong military', and 'productivity and enterprise'. The upshot of this construction was to give the national railways a monopolistic position among land transportation institutions, and to make them one of the leaders in Japanese industry. As the 'arteries' of the Japanese economy, the railways did much to develop the country's capacity in areas like mechanical and civil engineering. Past successes and a long history, however, eventually resulted in an excessive fixation on and confidence in this corporate paradigm. State-run companies are known for being irresponsible, especially when it comes to costs, and

Japan's national railways were no exception. Management was inefficient, the railways failed to adapt to changing business conditions and they finally found themselves in a decisive crisis.

It is not easy to break out of old paradigms. In fact, reforming or transforming old paradigms is much harder than creating completely new paradigms. But the national railways have indeed been reborn, and the key to this was privatization. The old Japan National Railways (JNR) was split into six passenger lines – East, Tokai, West, Hokkaido, Kyushu and Shikoku – and one freight line. And in the process, it succeeded in making the transformation to a new way of looking at the world.

PRIVATIZATION
Former British Prime Minister Margaret Thatcher became famous for her quest for smaller government, and part of this was the privatization of many of Britain's state-run giants: British Telecom, British Gas and the electric power company. The Netherlands have also been privatizing state-run businesses, most notably the postal savings system. In the United States, even prisons and courts are now moving into private hands. Economic development and technological progress have put an end to the days when public regulations were necessary to ensure that minimum services were provided. As values become more diverse, people want more individualized services and local communities demand a greater degree of adaptation to their particular circumstances. Two things must happen, however, before these services can be provided. Companies must be privatized so as to encourage competition and creativity, and regulations must be relaxed so that business can move forward. Japan owes much of its postwar reconstruction and growth to such formerly state-run companies as Japan National Railways, Nippon Telegraph and Telephone (NTT) and Japan Monopolies, but as the economy matured and people developed

more individualistic ways of thinking, whatever historical duties these companies may have once had were completed and their rigid ways of doing business began to be seen as an impediment.

Japan rose from the ashes of World War II to achieve miraculous growth and emerge as an economic superpower, and it is companies that made this economic development possible. As we have already seen, their superb adaptability enabled firms to overcome crisis after crisis and continue to expand. Neither the oil embargoes of the seventies nor the skyrocketing of the yen in the eighties could stop them. Indeed, it is that adaptability that is behind the growth of Japanese corporations. But it is precisely that ability to accommodate new trends that the state-run companies lacked. When the waves of liberalization, internationalization and technical progress began to make an impact in the seventies and eighties, private-sector firms did what they do best – adapted, restructured and went on to even greater expansion. The fossilized state-run companies, however, rejected and ran from change, and found themselves left behind. Because of their public nature, the companies enjoyed monopolies. There was no competition, and therefore no incentive to do anything about inefficiencies. Managers, in fact, could ignore inefficiency with impunity.

The railways were a prime example. JNR recorded its first operating loss in 1964 and it continued to show a deficit for 24 years, right up until it was split and privatized in 1987. Each time the red ink appeared, programmes were unveiled to 'rebuild' and 'improve' the railways. They generally consisted of three main components:

1 Self-improvement efforts: JNR-led rationalization and productivity gains.
2 User-financed improvements: fare increases.
3 Government-financed improvements: greater burdens on tax-payers.

All were failures, and the red ink continued to accumulate. At the end of fiscal 1986, right before privatization, JNR had a cumulative loss of ¥15.5 trillion and debts of ¥25 trillion. At the time, its debt burden was even larger than the entire national debt of Mexico. The company was obviously sick, and all efforts to cure it were failures. Why?

There were three reasons. First, it did not really matter if expenses outpaced revenues and the red ink ballooned because ultimate responsibility for the losses was ambiguous. Since nobody *had* to take responsibility, the company was unable to break out of the vicious circle of debt. In fact, since it was a public corporation, virtually every important aspect of JNR was under the control of the Diet or the bureaucracy, including budgets, top management posts, fares, investment plans and scope of business. Managers were unable to make independent decisions regarding debt, budgeting or fares, and workers saw themselves more as public officials than anything else. Neither, therefore, had much interest in boosting productivity or controlling costs. There was nothing that forced anybody to take responsibility for how the company was run.

Second, JNR's internal organization was crumbling, and this helped bring on the eventual crisis. Frequent strikes testify to the instability of labour – management relations, and loose work regulations sapped employee morale. Morale was so low, in fact, that there was never even a chance of rebuilding the company out in the stations and on the trains where it mattered.

Third, the excessive expectations and interference of outsiders undermined management and accelerated the breakdown. The public clearly expected the railway to do too much, demanding, for instance, that it keep loss-producing local lines open and build and electrify new lines in unprofitable areas. Business considerations were ignored and the decisions left to politicians in the national government, handing JNR even greater losses.

The entire framework of the railways seemed designed to foster unaccountable management, and because of that, the railways were unable to perceive the dramatic changes that were taking place in the business climate. By the time they woke up, they had lost their ability to adapt to the market. For the railways, one of the chief changes to be dealt with was the rapid motorization of Japanese society. During the sixties and seventies, Japan made great progress in building its motorway system, and as it did so, cars took over from trains as the main mode of transportation. JNR had effectively lost its monopoly, but it made no effort to deal with the situation and found itself behind the times, a white elephant.

On the verge of going under, the railways were finally split up and privatized in 1987. Reborn into the private sector, the railways successfully realigned their corporate paradigms and have performed far better than anyone expected. Before privatization they had planned on annual fare increases of about 5 per cent, but they have yet to raise fares even once since the break-up. Even without the increases, the seven JR companies announced an aggregate current profit of ¥307.6 billion for fiscal 1991. This is an astounding change from JNR, which in its worst year, 1985, showed a loss of ¥2,450.0 billion.

Other statistics also attest to the unmitigated success of privatization. For instance, in 1985 JNR received ¥600.1 billion in subsidies from the national government – money taken directly from tax revenues. In 1991, the seven JR companies paid ¥150.0 billion in taxes *to* the national government.

Passengers are, of course, pleased with the fact that fares have been held steady for 7 years and attribute it to the split-up and privatization. They have also been getting better services for their money. JR has brought in more modern rolling stock, increased the number of trains it runs, air-conditioned all of the stock servicing the greater

Tokyo area, developed new double-decker carriages, boosted the number of rapid-service runs it makes and renovated its stations.

But however much the paradigms may have shifted, there are still some unresolved problems, the most pressing of which is the plight of Tokyo-area commuters. Not all of this can be blamed on the railway lines. Japan's population has concentrated around Tokyo for other reasons, but in as much as JR East earns about 80 per cent of its revenues from the Greater Tokyo area, it certainly has a duty to relieve what has become known as 'commuter hell'.

Another worry is backsliding JR employees. It has now been more than 7 years since privatization, and the initial energy and enthusiasm for reform is dissipating. The novelty has worn off, and employees are becoming more lax.

Still, even taking those problems into account, the privatization has been a success. JR is unquestionably ready to stand on its own two feet as a private company. This success, however, is not merely a product of the split and privatization. The railways were only able to make the transition from state enterprise to private company because managers actively encouraged a shift in the corporate paradigm. The companies underwent dramatic organizational and conceptual reforms. That they were able to pull it off is a testament to the ability that Japanese companies have to reform themselves. That ability is, in my opinion, at the source of their energy and vitality. When a Japanese company finds itself in crisis, its employees pull together to deal with the problem. They have a dynamic adaptability that allows them to take the lead in overcoming challenges. You cannot discuss the 'conceptual reforms' or 'organizational reforms' that encourage shifts in corporate paradigms without looking at the capacity for self-reform that bubbles up from within Japanese companies like magma from a volcano.

GETTING USED TO BEING PRIVATE

Up until now, Japanese growth and development has been driven by government policies to catch up with and surpass the West. Under these 'come from behind' strategies, the national railways, which formed one of the major arteries of the economy, were generously protected and allowed to grow. In the process, JNR employees ceased to care about efficiency or effectiveness. 'It's not our money anyway' was the unspoken attitude. The railways became more bureaucratic than the bureaucracy, and the fact that this was a gigantic organization with as many as 600,000 employees only exacerbated things. It goes without saying that the larger a company becomes the harder it is to manage. It begins to suffer from 'big company disease'. JNR was no exception.

Sure that the government would always foot the bill, employees thought they were on an unsinkable ship. 'Why work hard when it is almost impossible to sack you? Just do what you're told and go through the motions,' seemed to be the refrain. There was no interest in trying anything new, and it was no easy task to change the perceptions of employees who had spent their entire lives trying only not to rock the boat. Certainly, just a change of name and managerial style was not enough. It was by and large the same workforce as before, and many were dead set against privatization. If the truth be told, before privatization nobody thought it could be done. JNR seemed to be poisoned to the marrow and ready to resist reform at all costs. Just before privatization, posters were stuck up in the trains promising to 'get better after we've been split up and privatized'. Few of the passengers believed it.

But 'get better' it did – to everyone's surprise. Previously, the railways were only interested in 'supply-side concerns' – they saw themselves as government agents who were deigning to allow passengers a place on 'our' trains. Now they have a more demand-oriented perspective – they see themselves as part of the private sector actively seeking passengers. From 'get on if you must' it is now 'please travel on JR'. While this change in service was occurring, the railways were also developing new technologies and looking for new lines of business, all of which points to the change in attitudes that employees underwent. And that is a manifestation of their capacity for self-reform.

Shoji Sumita, chairman of JR East, recalls:

> JNR was a product of the bureaucracy. It used to be known as the 'Ministry of Transport', and before that as the 'Ministry of Railways'. That's why it was prone to bureaucratic ways of thinking and centralized authority. Government agencies function according to policy, and that inevitably leads to bureaucratization and centralization. But JNR was in the railway business, which is not a bureaucratic job at all and something that can't be run effectively when all power is concentrated in the centre. When you do that, your employees lose all motivation. In a strongly centralized organization, you don't try to do anything on your own, because if you do, the chances are good that your supervisor will say no. It's better just to follow orders and do as you're told – or at least that's how you feel and because you feel that way, you stop trying to think or act on your own.

So how was the company able to change these attitudes? Usually, when a corporate paradigm is out of synch with the times or the business climate, it will be criticized for being inefficient or ineffective. Corporate activities do not proceed smoothly, and so appropriate earnings are not achieved. The company stagnates, and the only way out is to throw off the old paradigm and replace it with something new. That means changing attitudes, because what ultimately drives a company is its people – its human resources. If the people are active and energetic, then corporate activities become more dynamic, and efficiency and effectiveness improve on their own.

The attitudinal change at JR East that made it possible for fossilized organizations to be overturned and a new environment to be constructed began with an effort to break down the culture and habits that had grown up over the last century. That required far more energy than any private-sector firm would have. JR employees had to be disabused of the idea that they were 'in His Majesty's service' and therefore immune to market forces. There were five phases to this process that we will look at more closely: 'no longer servants of the state,' putting negative energy to work, stabilizing labour–management relations, capitalizing on success and developing shared values.

'NO LONGER SERVANTS OF THE STATE'

When the railways were a state-run company, employees felt as if they were doing people a favour by allowing them to ride on 'their' trains. It was clear from how they acted that they considered themselves servants of the state with special entitlements and privileges. Needless to say, that attitude made for a fat and lazy organization.

Masatake Matsuda, president of JR East, explains:

When the railways were organized back in the late nineteenth century, Japan had never seen such a modern means of transportation. It wasn't just that they were running complex engines, there was no other industry that even approached the railways in terms of either modernity or size. It was so advanced, so looked up to, that one of the sayings at the time was 'give your daughter to a railway man'. The theories developed by the railways became the theories used by all modern industries. They were one of the driving forces behind Japanese industrialization. It stayed that way well into this century: railways were an exciting growth industry that everybody wanted to be a part of. But after the war, other forms of transportation started to come along and for passengers, railways became just another option. All that remained was the pride of those on the inside.

Railways had ceased to be the leading form of transportation, but the JNR employees acted as if they were still in their heyday. There was a reality gap. The attitude of the staff no longer meshed with the way things really were. This was aggravated by the fact that, as Sumita says:

Employees were sure JNR was an unsinkable ship. They had absolute faith in that proposition. They were part of the state. They would never fail, they would never have to think about where the next meal was coming from. There was no reason to worry.

But when they were privatized and split up, the entire corporate paradigm changed, dealing a fatal blow to the myth of 'JNR the invincible'. A sense of crisis grew among the staff. If they kept loafing, they might find themselves out in the street. Those worries were not unfounded. When it was privatized, JNR employed 277,000 people. Only 200,000 of them were taken on by the new companies. Sumita explains:

They were worried that however much they might want a job with the new companies, they might not be asked to stay on. It was a great shock. It was different from what happened when NTT or Japan Tobacco were privatized. Then they just changed the legal organization, but everybody kept their jobs. When JNR was privatized, though, it was every bit as much of a shock as if we had lost a war. People were going to be employed by a *different* company. Obviously, their attitudes were going to have to be different too.

Previously, the market had played no part in JNR decisions, so it was asking too much for employees to cease to think of themselves as civil servants all of a sudden and start reacting flexibly and responsibly to market signals. They had never learned that kind of discipline. All they knew how to do was what they were told. New ideas were neither welcome nor encouraged. Privatization forced them to change those attitudes. They could no longer depend on the government for their sustenance or authority. They were on their own. It was as if a key component had been removed from their attitudes towards their jobs. Like as not, they would have to make a new start, with new ideas and new perceptions.

PUTTING NEGATIVE ENERGY TO WORK

Employees bring two types of psychological energy to their jobs. The first comes from a sense of crisis and dissatisfaction. We call it 'negative energy'. The other comes from a desire to achieve, a sense of duty, a desire for self-realization. We call it 'positive energy'. If you act only within a given system, your energy is constantly turned inwards and you eventually become unable to think or act freely. This breeds only negative energy. If, however, you are allowed to make some creative changes to the system, however small, your energy is now directed outwards and it becomes possible to move freely. You have a desire to achieve, a sense of duty, a desire for self-realization.

When JNR was privatized, there was a very strong sense among the employees that they never wanted to be in a state-run company again. During the final years, frequent strikes had earned JNR employees public wrath and resentment. They felt as if they had to walk with hunched shoulders in order to be less conspicuous on the streets. No one wanted to feel that miserable ever again. That desire sparked hidden reserves of energy. The new JNR companies had to become profitable and employees became obsessed with the idea of getting out of 'deficit hell'. They worked hard, and in the process discovered that they were indeed able to work hard. They even found that they performed better when they were enjoying themselves. It was the first concrete manifestation of an unspoken change in attitudes. President Matsuda recalls:

> You could really see the difference in our customer service. At the gates, the ticket-collectors would bow and say thank you as people got off or greet them with a cheery 'good morning!' as they left for work. Well, if you are sincere and you keep at it, eventually you'll get through to your customers. At first, it was just a few people who smiled back, but when they did, employees began to realize that how you felt determined how you worked. And then they began to think about service.

In other words, attitudes were changed by stimulating a latent awareness of problems and an energy for reform (capacity and desire for self-improvement) among the people manning the stations and trains.

This capacity for self-improvement and change inspired the employees of JR East with a longing for independence and self-determination, with a desire to build a company that they could be proud of. They worked hard to increase revenues, adopted a 'suggestion box' system and organized small quality control circles. In 1990, for example, the company had 8,800 quality control circles in which 50,400 employees participated. It received 643,000 suggestions during the year.

STABILIZING LABOUR–MANAGEMENT RELATIONS
The rifts and conflicts between JNR's management and its trade unions were so serious and rancorous that they are often pointed to as one of the prime reasons that the state

railways were a managerial failure. At the most extreme point, unions held so much control that the company could not change its organization or even make trial runs of new rolling stock without their approval.

Symbolic of the problems was the 'Job Site Discussion System'. In May 1968, after a long period of negotiation and wrangling, the railway management and the union signed an 'Agreement Concerning Job Site Discussion Meetings'. Management emphasized that the job site was 'not to be a forum for group negotiation', but the union maintained that, whatever the name, negotiations were what this was all about. The meetings were one of the chief factors undermining discipline and morale. They became forums for lynching local managers and hotbeds of back-door agreements and shoddy work practices. One of their products was 'illicit holiday time'. Thanks to the job site meetings, it became routine for workers to take the New Year holidays off in addition to their allotted leave, and to finish early on bonus days. They also demanded and got extra holiday time just for showing up to group negotiations. All this was done with impunity, and as tensions between labour and management rose, it produced a growing sense of stagnation within the organization. Sumita comments:

> If unions and management are at each other's throats like they used to be, or if negotiations are getting nowhere, or if different unions are fighting with each other, well, obviously the mood among the staff is going to be pretty black. You end up with this brooding working environment. We've been lucky in that regard. For the last 7 years, ever since privatization, labour–management relations have been very stable.

It was the 'Joint Labour–Management Declaration' of 1986 that let the first breath of fresh air into a stale relationship. Without that declaration it is doubtful whether the corporate paradigm would have shifted so smoothly. Says Akira Matsuzaki, president of the East Japan Railway Workers' Union:

> There were two patterns to the labour movement during the national railways days. It was either conflict or cooperation to overcome our differences and achieve a new start. I like to use the German word *aufheben* to explain this. You can't solve anything by dragging around baggage from the past. You have to resolve discrepancies and try to move higher.

The joint declaration provided the basis for maintaining the stable labour relations that JR East enjoys today and that guarantee stable operations for the company as a whole. Matsuda says:

> Sour labour relations left everyone desolate psychologically. It made the workplace dark and gloomy. We wanted to build a culture that would be more fruitful, that would have better 'ventilation', if you will, so labour and management have worked closely together to achieve it. When I say a 'better ventilated culture', I mean one in which we are willing to share information that can and should be shared, one in which we share a common awareness. By nature, labour and management are always going to be negotiating across a table, but both sides can still be aware that they are moving in the same direction. Obviously, that takes discussion and debate, and those discussions open the windows, let fresh air in and keep us 'well ventilated'.

In other words, both labour and management share the goal of making JR a solid, respectable company. Both understand that achieving those goals is the best way to make employees happy. Privatization gave the unions and the management a broad range of common interests. That is the same for any company that is developing normally. If both are thinking rationally and from a long-term perspective, there are very few incidences in which the interests of the unions and the management are in conflict. Stable labour relations at JR East may therefore just be a natural outcome. Still, the company is not taking them for granted. Managers meet with the East Japan Railway Workers' Union once a month to discuss business issues.

> While we were still the national railways, no one could put their abilities to full use. Even if you had something you wanted to do, there was never any room to do it because you always had union problems to think about. To some extent we were starved for work because we had all these things we wanted to do and couldn't. Since privatization, we've been able to do what we've always wanted to, and it's because attitudes have changed.

Thus Mutsutake Otsuka, a managing director for personnel development in the company's Human Resources Development Department, illustrates how stable labour relations have allowed JR East to tap its latent capacity for self-improvement.

CREATING NEW VALUES
CAPITALIZING ON SUCCESS

Before privatization, the railways had never thought seriously about what service was. They carried people much the same as they carried any other sort of freight, and having a bureaucratic mindset, they felt that people should be grateful for the privilege. Service? What use have we for that?

But once they became private companies, the railways had to ask themselves what kind of services they should be providing for the public – and no one had even a hint as to the answer. They first had to think what service really meant.

Even those who had an intellectual understanding of the concept had no idea how to put it into practice, no clue as to how privatization should manifest itself in the services provided.

One day in April 1987, not long after privatization, a certain manager from the Track and Structures Maintenance and Electric Engineering Department, the department that managed the stations, was at a Chinese restaurant drinking Shiao Xing rice wine with some colleagues. In between drinks they were discussing their new situation, when the manager said, 'They keep telling us that we need to change our attitudes now that we've gone from "public" to "private". They mutter it over and over again like some sort of mantra – "change attitudes . . . change attitudes . . .". But that alone won't get us very far.'

'Oh yeah?' came the response. 'Then what do you suggest we do?'

'Why don't we start by cleaning the toilets? Our passengers will appreciate it, and it might be just the sort of baptism of fire we need.'

Up until then, the national railways were known for having '3-D' toilets: dirty, dark and dangerous.

The group picked its target, Higashi Nakano Station on the Chuo Line in Tokyo.

'Excuse us,' they told the astonished station master, 'would it be all right if we cleaned your toilets?' He did not know quite what to think. Whatever was going on, it could not be good when a bunch of managers from the head office showed up wanting to clean your toilets. Had he perhaps committed some inadvertent error?

The eleven members of the 'Strategic Advance Forces' brushed off his worries and got to work. They had already reconnoitred the station and had put together a 'Plan of Action' complete with floor diagrams. They set to work according to plan: long-handled brushes for the floors, complete scrubbing for the toilets. Next, they removed the ventilation fans, masked everything with vinyl and applied a fresh coat of white paint. Finally, they returned to the floors, prying loose any stray drips of paint with their bare hands. The job took three and a half hours.

Six months later, they were at it again, this time completely remaking the toilets at Shinbashi, another busy Tokyo station. The new toilet, complete with a marble entrance way that rivalled anything one would find in a hotel, was dubbed '*Pausa di croma*' (Italian for 'eighth-note rest'). This 'high-value-added' production won the team the 'Good Toilet 10 Prize' for that year.

The toilet clean-up campaign of the Strategic Advance Forces demonstrated to the rest of the company the kind of new services that could be provided. By acting on their ideas, they dealt a death-blow to the old corporate culture, erasing whatever resistance and reluctance to change remained. Instead of thinking about things in the supply-side terms of 'we'll let you on our trains', JR East was now thinking of them from the demand-side perspective of how to make people want to travel by train. It had a clear, tangible model of what phrases like 'the customer comes first' and 'quality service' really meant.

Note that the drive to break through old paradigms and replace them with new values does not necessarily come from the top. In this case, the creativity and impetus came from the middle managers and the people on the front lines, those who found themselves in the thick of things, subject to all the contradictions and discrepancies inherent in any value shift.

I talked at length to Mr Shuichiro Yamanouchi, vice-chairman of the company, about what took place.

JNR was allergic to change. It didn't matter what you wanted to do, the response was always the same: 'No', 'We're opposed', 'Too hard'. At the root of the disease was this aversion to change. No one wanted to have people mad at them because they went out on a limb and tried something different. And whenever you tried to do something different you were told, 'Mind your own business. Don't you have anything better to be doing?' Say you wanted to design a new railway carriage. The inevitable response was, 'If you've got that much time on your hands, go out and pacify the unions'. That's not the way you run a business. That robs people of the motivation to do anything new. The only way around that kind of thinking once it sets in is to show people that change can be fun, that it can produce good results.

JNR was not alone in its problems. In any organization there will be pressure to maintain the paradigms that have supported the organization so far. If you try to go beyond that framework, someone will always be ready to pull you back in. One would think that the only way to head off those forces is to get them to clearly recognize the need for a change in attitudes.

No. Attitudes and recognition and all that come afterwards. The first step is just to do it. After we were privatized, we tried lots of different things. For instance, we built all sorts of new rolling stock, and it turned out that people liked the new trains. Well, if the public likes the new trains, that's gratifying both for the people who built them and for the company as a whole. And it also means more income. . . .

I thought a lot about how to change the backward-looking attitudes and aversion to change I found in our company. I decided that the quickest and most effective way was to use success stories.

Certainly, if employees are shown a success story, they can look at it and say to themselves, 'So that's what I should be doing' or 'If I do something like that, maybe I'll be a success too.' One tangible success story is worth 100 sermons.

Even so, there was still a lot of hidden resistance. When I tried to act on the success story idea, I took a lot of flak for 'wasting money' and doing things that were 'worthless' and 'unprofitable'. We had what I call a 'temporary lapse in values'. Even the clean toilet campaign met with resistance. On one level, they were right. Cleaner toilets don't affect the bottom line. There's no direct increase in income, and if you're obsessed with the idea that the purpose of a company is to make money, then you might very well question the need to clean the toilets.

Nonetheless, the middle managers in the Strategic Advanced Forces who led the clean toilet campaign became heroes in the newly privatized JR East, one of the company's first success stories.

Heroes and success stories embody the values of the organization and provide concrete expressions of the paradigms that the organization's members should be following or aspiring to. Legendary entrepreneurs and corporate saviours evince the traditional, eternal values that the organization claims as its own. Success stories from the day-to-day operation of the firm show in a more down-to-earth form its values and goals. JR East was able to capitalize on those success stories to transform itself.

DEVELOPING SHARED VALUES

Shared values provide an organization with motivation. People with the same values have a powerful psychological energy that can never be generated from work orders and rule books. Developing shared values is therefore an ideal tool for changing attitudes.

To give this depth and breadth, however, the values must

be presented in tangible, visible form. This was especially the case for JR as it tried to shift to the paradigm of a private company. Giving tangible form to commonly held standards made it easier for new ideas to take root and grow. One such manifestation was the ¥20 billion JR East spent to clean-up its toilets. The campaign spread far beyond the railway stations, sparking a clean-up of public toilets all around Japan.

The company also hit on the idea of using its stations to provide information and education rather than just to take on and discharge passengers. Station halls became the scenes of free concerts and art exhibitions. Takahata Station in Yamagata built a hot springs right on the platform. Naruko Station in Miyagi turned itself into a community centre. Others tried more trendy ideas, confident that exciting, publicity-generating products would eventually spark some response, that information once transmitted is sooner or later received. For the people who worked for the railway, it was a chance to learn that passengers do indeed appreciate good service. A virtuous circle was in motion.

One catalyst to the development of shared values was the Gala Yuzawa ski resort. Six employees stationed at the Niigata Branch Office and the Shinkansen Echigo–Yuzawa Track Maintenance Depot came up with the idea. Wouldn't it be convenient, they asked themselves, if JR East built a big ski resort out here in the mountains and put a shinkansen stop right in front of the lifts? Wouldn't it be great if we built a special skiers' platform in Echigo-Yuzawa Station so that people could go straight from the shinkansen to the gondola? Their dream came true in Gala Yuzawa, a mammoth ski resort just 80 minutes from Tokyo by shinkansen. And yes, you can go straight from the train to the lifts.

Otsuka muses:

At the end, JNR was a classic case of organizational depression. How to get people active and excited again was our biggest headache during the first couple of years. Unless people are happy and enjoying themselves, then all this talk of 'changing attitudes' is just cheerleading.

The shared values, and the success stories that supported them, became common topics of conversation among the employees: 'We should be doing something more like those guys,' or 'That's the way we ought to be thinking,' or 'We need ideas like that.' The organization began to develop broad consensus on what its models were, which contributed to the codification of the values that JR East employees were expected to share and brought on the change in attitudes that resulted in improved services.

BETTER OFF APART

As we touched upon earlier, when JNR was privatized it was split into six passenger companies and one freight company. The split was one of the things that helped reform the organization, and the JR experience stands in direct contrast to that of NTT, which was privatized a year earlier but has not necessarily achieved much that the public finds praiseworthy. Unlike the railways, when the phone company was privatized it was not split into smaller units, and that is one of the reasons why its privatization is not deemed to have been nearly as successful.

There were three main benefits from the split. First, it fostered a sense of rivalry and competition. None of the passenger lines wanted to be outdone by the others when it came to developing new services and products. Second, it turned the companies outwards. JNR used to be considered an 'entity unto itself'. It was so large that it became a walled-off world able to take care of all its needs from within. The split made the railways aware of the other industries, other companies and customer needs. Third, it meant that to the rank and file employees, the management was no longer 'faceless'. They were now closer and more visible. Where NTT employs 210,00 people, the largest of the JR companies, JR East, has only 80,000. We need not overemphasize which group of managers is closer to its staff.

The split also had several positive effects on the way the organization was managed. We will look at these in more detail in the sections that follow.

THE SPRINGBOARD OF CRISIS

There was talk of splitting up NTT too, but labour and management combined forces to quash it. JNR was unable to do so, and so the split-up brought about a kind of 'bloodletting'. It was such a shock to the corporate system that it provided a springboard to renewed vigour.

Mr Eiji Hosoya, director and general manager of the Management Administration Department in the Corporate Planning Headquarters, comments:

The people at NTT were the trail-blazers when it came to privatization, but nobody is very impressed by their results. I think the reason for that lies in three major differences between their experience and ours.

First, all 280,000 employees of Nippon Telegraph and Telephone Public Corporation kept their jobs with NTT. No doubt part of the reason it was able to keep everybody on is that even as a public company it was showing a profit. At JNR, we only kept 200,000 of our 277,000 employees. It was enough of a shock to the system to get us moving again.

Second, the principle of competition has never fully taken root in the NTT organization. True, they have competition now for long-distance services, but I still don't think they consider them as rivals. At the risk of blowing my own trumpet, when the railways were split into six passenger lines and one freight line, it gave us instant rivalries. If one of the JR companies comes up with a great new service, all the rest of us have to outdo it. In that sense, the principle of competition has greater sway here than it does at NTT.

Third, and this is a function of being in different businesses, we have more opportunity to come in contact with our customers than NTT does. At a railway, you see your customers every day; not so at a phone company. Our employees know what it means to put the customer first and that tension, that edge, helps improve our services. It even inspires the ticket-collectors to wish passengers a cheery 'good morning' as they go through. People enjoy that, and so they are more impressed with what we've achieved from privatization than with what NTT has.

During its first year as a private company, fiscal 1987, JR East announced operating revenues of ¥1,554.1 billion, exceeding the government forecast of ¥1,472.2 billion. Its current profit of ¥76.7 billion was well ahead of the government forecast of ¥14.8 billion. In its second year, fiscal 1988, it again outperformed government forecasts, recording ¥1,650.5 billion in operating revenues and ¥85.6 billion in current profits against ¥1,526.5 billion and ¥30.3 billion respectively. It has topped government forecasts every year since, as well. Hosoya comments:

The split was a shock. How we did that first year was one of the keys to recovering from it. It gave our employees a lot of confidence when we ended that first year not only in the black, but well ahead of government forecasts. They forgot the shock of the split, and their new-found confidence inspired them to provide even better service. A virtuous circle ensued, and that is one of the major reasons why we were able to undergo such a smooth transformation.

When first privatized, JR East was carrying 20 per cent more staff than it needed. It made good use of the extra numbers, seconding them to affiliates and moving them to different territories, a practice that became known as the 'study away programme'. Since Tokyo is where much of the work centres, some of the company's workers were forced to leave their home-towns and work in the city. So far, 15,000 employees, about 19 per cent of the total, have spent time working for affiliates, and another 5,000 have had to pack up and move. There has been nothing to compare with this in recent years, and the experiences have proved stimulating to those involved, themselves contributing to the change in attitudes.

It is often the case that a sense of crisis will provide a company with a springboard to change and revitalization. Crisis gives rise to new ideas, revolutionary products and systems for organizational renewal. Some top managers have been known to shake up their organizations intentionally and put them into crisis just for the salutary effects. For JR East, the split provoked a sense of alarm among the staff that translated into new motivation and energy. It revived the organization and enabled it to make a profit from its very first year. The split, therefore, was very much the trigger of organizational reform.

STREAMLINED INTERNAL ORGANIZATIONS

The downsizing at JNR did not end with the creation of a bunch of 'baby railways'. Internal organizations were also pruned and cut back. Mid-level organizations were scrapped wherever possible in an effort to shorten the chain of command. Experience had shown that the more mid-level organizations there are, the more likely goals are to be distorted, people misled and the company's centre of gravity thrown out of kilter. Just one or two additions to the chain of command reduce the likelihood that orders will be communicated faithfully, and this ends up breeding chaos and discontent. JR East's organizational reforms began with a concerted effort to streamline the main office.

'Our main office has become a lot leaner since we were privatized,' Hosoya notes. 'Back in the JNR days, we had about 3,000 people in the main office. Now JR East only has 1,200. That's a drastic cut.'

JNR used a four-tier organization: main office, mid-level liaison organizations, railway management departments and rank and file employees. JR East has only three: main office, regional offices and rank and file employees. For instance, under the JNR 'Head Office' there was a 'Greater Tokyo Head Office' that, as its name suggested, served as the mid-level liaison organization for the Tokyo area. The Tokyo office, in turn, had six local 'railway management departments': Tokyo West, Tokyo South, Tokyo North, Chiba, Takasaki and Mito. It was their job to oversee actual operations; the Greater Tokyo Head Office was not directly involved, it merely coordinated between the different departments.

JR East did away with the Greater Tokyo Head Office. In its place, it created a Tokyo Regional Headquarters, Chiba Regional Office, Takasaki Regional Office and Mito Regional Office, all of which communicate directly with the front-line employees. The organization was, in a sense, hollowed out. The middle was removed to produce a more compact body, better able to communicate, more decisive, with more efficient meetings and a greater sense of unity. Streamlining has closed the distance between top management and rank and file employees, and as a result, the ties between them are stronger.

ELIMINATION OF SECTIONALISM

JNR was an organization that had grown too large to manage effectively. In order to maintain it and clarify who had responsibility for what, it became a highly compartmentalized, vertically oriented organization. This hindered communication within the company and fostered a bureaucratic outlook among the staff. Hosoya recalls:

> On the engineering side, we also had sorts of departments – the Train Operation Department, the Rolling Stock Department, the Electrical Engineering Department, the Construction Department, the Track and Structure Department and so on and so on. As long as you were with JNR, you worked for the same department. Even after retirement, if you wanted to try a second career, the department would find something for you. That's why it was so hard to cut costs for procurement or out-sourcing. If you tried to chop your out-sourcing budget, then you were in effect reducing the amount of money you paid to the company of somebody who used to be your boss or your friend. No one wanted to do that, so they spent their time trying to find ways to justify the status quo rather than looking for savings. We talked a lot about cutting costs, but we never made any major gains.

The big *zaibatsu* trading houses use a similar system. If a new recruit is assigned to the Car Department, that will be his 'home' as long as he is with the company. At JNR, you were even known by your department. All those working for Electrical Engineering were called 'the electricians'; everyone in Train Operation, 'the drivers'. Departments' habit of finding their retired employees new jobs is similar to the *ama-kudari* (literally 'descent from heaven') practices of the bureaucracy, where, for example, people retiring from the Ministry of Finance will be placed in executive positions at large banks. No wonder JNR had a reputation for being 'more bureaucratic than the bureaucracy'!

Streamlining has brought many changes, one of the biggest being the erosion of sectionalism. Sumita comments on the changes:

When people's first loyalties are to their department – when they think of themselves as a 'maintenance man' or an 'electrician' – the company is unable to coalesce and build up the kind of energy it needs. When JR East started, one of the first things we did was streamline our organizations. We merged Electrical Engineering and Track and Structure into the 'Track and Structures Maintenance and Electrical Engineering Department', and we turned Train Operation and Rolling Stock into the 'Transport and Rolling Stock Department'. In the process, we also eliminated a lot of departmental heads. Our aim was to do away with the damage that over-compartmentalization was causing and in the process motivate the people on the front lines.

We haven't necessarily achieved all we wanted to in that regard, but there is a growing sense of unity within the company. People are becoming aware that we are all in this together and have to help each other. For example, in 1991 JR East was damaged by Typhoon No. 19. In Noshiro, a city in Akita, we had a Work Depot that had people from track maintenance, electrical engineering and construction in it. Well, the trees that we had planted along the side of the track to serve as a wind break were toppled by the typhoon and were blocking the tracks. In the past, cleaning up after something like that would have been the job of the track maintenance people and nobody would have lifted a finger to help. This time, things were different. Everybody in the Work Depot pitched in to get the lines back in operation.

In bureaucratic organizations, ideas are communicated from top to bottom, never the other way around. And in an organization that is highly compartmentalized, there is absolutely no communication between different sections. Meetings are held frequently to try to foster communication, but they are mostly empty forms. No creative decision-making takes place. Eliminating compartments can make all the difference. Once the walls are down, communication is more effective, and people realize that regardless of their department they are all working for the same goals. The firm comes together, it coalesces, becomes more motivated and more energetic.

RANK AND FILE COME FIRST

Japanese companies tend to be good at manufacturing, so they place great importance on their rank and file members, the people who actually do the work. An important point of corporate training programmes is on-the-job training, which for manufacturers means sending new recruits down to the factory to work for a while. For service industries, it means putting them in the sales offices and stores. Having experienced for themselves what it is like 'on the front lines', future managers gain a better understanding of the importance of the factory or store; they know that it is the foundation of all corporate activities. Japanese career paths tend to be different, therefore, from those in America, where new MBAs fresh out of business school are immediately placed in assistant executive positions and follow an elite course to the top. A Japanese company president, by contrast, will have spent several years running a provincial factory if he comes from an engineering background. If he comes from a sales or marketing background, he will have worked for years as a salesman (probably with legendary results). Japanese firms are agreed that experience at the front lines teaches future managers how to motivate people, how to get organizations moving and how to exert leadership. A central part of the corporate paradigm here is that the front lines, the factories and sales offices, come first.

Many state this explicitly. Honda follows what it calls the 'three realities': 'real operations, realistic thinking and real objects'. These three realities, it says, hold the keys to all managerial problems, especially the first, real operations or the front lines. After privatization, JR East also adopted this classic Japanese managerial technique. Sumita explains:

> Back in the JNR days, there was no communication between the head office and the departments, or between the departments and the front lines. And there was certainly none between the head office and the front lines! Now, however, we are trying to tie the head office and the front lines as closely together as possible, because we see that as being necessary to creating a sense of unity. When we do our semi-annual general safety checks, the president and all of the top executives go out to the trains and stations to talk to the people there. And they go alone. No one from the regional office is allowed to accompany them. It's just the executives and the rank and file, because when there are people from the regional office present, sometimes things don't get said that need to be. All of the head office mangers are involved: the president, vice-presidents, managing directors, general managers and divisional managers. We did our first general safety inspection 4 or 5 years ago and we received some very heartwarming letters afterwards. One even said that it was the first time they had had a divisional manager from the head office visit them – ever! Back in the JNR days, no one had ever gone out that far.
>
> We try to take the opinions of the rank and file into account at other times too and work hard to create opportunities for the head office and the stations to talk to each other. Obviously, the people from regional offices are visiting the stations much more frequently too.

In placing the rank and file first, the JR East Japan management has been more aware of problems and able to involve more people in their solution. This has in turn produced more active and enthusiastic organizations. A palpable result of this can be seen from how the company deals with accidents and mishaps. In the days of the national railways, it focused on 'assigning blame'. Today, it is more concerned with 'finding causes'. The changes have brought greater unity to the organization from the front lines on up.

SHARED INFORMATION
In addition to their respect for information from the front lines, Japanese companies also tend to place great importance on interdepartmental relations. This is one of the paradigms commonly at work in Japan. Often in negotiations it will be pointed out that American companies are dominated by a vertically oriented structure – things flow from top to bottom, but rarely from side to side. Japanese corporate organizations, on the other hand, tend to be relatively thin on hierarchical relations and more concerned with 'horizontal' ties. Say, for example, a factory made a revolutionary improvement in the manufacturing process. In Japan, the factory managers would have working relationships with each other, so the information would be transmitted fairly quickly. In America, such working relationships (horizontal ties) will often not exist, so a dramatic improvement at one factory is not necessarily communicated to the others and the information does not necessarily become a common asset that all can use.

Indeed, these horizontal ties that encourage people in the factories and sales offices to exchange ideas are the key to understanding how Japanese firms gather, communicate, share, analyse, evaluate and use the information they require. For instance, when drafting business plans, production plans, development plans or sales plans, managers are constantly asking the factories for information, listening to their opinions and thinking, and trying to reflect them in the final document. The reason the Japanese decision-making process is often characterized as 'bottom up' rather than 'top down' is not unrelated to this reliance on information from the shop floor.

JNR, however, more closely resembled the American paradigm. It was a classic hierarchy in which vertical divisions were everything and horizontal ties meant little. We have already seen how this affected the lines of communication, with instructions relayed from the home office through layers of regional offices, stations and track maintenance depots before finally reaching the people charged with carrying them out. After privatization, JR East decided to break out of this hierarchic mode, and one of the ways it chose to accomplish that was by appointing 'district station-masters' who would bring previously unrelated organizations into a single, regional whole, creating a new paradigm with greater emphasis on horizontal ties.

The district station-masters idea did much to establish the new paradigm among rank and file workers. It not only brought the idea of horizontal ties to the company, it served as one of the central vehicles for maintaining them and became an important forum for exchanging and sharing information.

The Tokyo Regional Headquarters, for example, oversees 33,000 employees. It divides them up into fourteen districts, but even so, the organization is still too large for a regional headquarters to try to manage entirely on its own. Instead, each of these fourteen districts has its own station-master. Previously, each phase of operations would be managed by a different regional office department. The Track and Structure Department was in charge of the track maintenance depot, the Electrical Engineering Department had charge of the electric power depot, the Sales Department controlled the stations and the Transport Department controlled the conductors' depots. The departments reported to the regional offices, the regional offices to the head office, in the pyramid-style organization that characterizes vertical compartmentalization. Thus, even though they worked in the same geographical area, people assigned to different phases of the operation had almost no opportunity to get together. Not surprisingly, horizontal ties between them were non- existent. The introduction of district station-masters added a horizontal network to the vertical chain of command and together they formed the mesh for a more tightly woven organization.

One example of the horizontal activities performed under the authority of the district station-master is the District Managers' Meeting. For Tokyo, this takes the form of two regularly scheduled meetings a month for the thirty-two local managers in the district. One of the purposes of these meetings is to enable the district station-master to communicate to local managers the information that he has gained in meetings with the regional office. Local people are thus able to learn about what is happening in the company as a whole, what policies have been adopted at the top, how the company is being run, what problems it faces. This provides for an indirectly shared base of information in the vertical plane. A second purpose of the meetings is to let local managers discuss among themselves the challenges facing the Tokyo district and the actions that should be taken. This provides for directly shared information in the horizontal plane. Jiro Yoshioka, director of JR East and station-master of Tokyo Station, enlarges:

> Besides the District Managers' Meetings, we also have District Safety Committee Meetings. The same people attend both, but the topics of the first are more general, while the topic of the second is limited to safety. For example, the district station-master uses the District Managers' Meeting to communicate information from the regional office to the local managers. He lets them know what those higher up are thinking and what problems the Tokyo District is facing. At the Safety

Meeting, though, people will study past accidents, find out what caused them and consider whether or not their areas are safe. After each meeting, I talk individually with the local managers. Often they will come to me with ideas that they'd like to try out if I can come up with some funding – say, a study group, or an event or something, but they need money to rent a hall or pay for lunch. We discuss their ideas, and that in and of itself helps foster communication.

Here is an example from a recent Tokyo District Managers' Meeting.

Shin-Nihonbashi Station-Master: We asked to have some repair work done because one of our walls was crumbling and leaking water. Whatever happened to that?

Shinbashi Track Maintenance Depot Chief: We're still studying it. Just how much repair do you think it's going to require, anyway?

Station Manager: It looks really bad, so we'd like you to do a full repair job, but we'd be happy if you'd just put up some tiles to stop the leaks. At any rate, we need something done pretty quickly.

Shinbashi Track Maintenance Depot Chief: Understood. We'll expedite it.

Tokyo District Station-Master: Any other matters to bring up?

Suidobashi Station-Master: We have a lot of events in our area and that's where many of our passengers come from, but the counters around our ticket windows are too small to hold leaflets. We asked the Building Maintenance Depot Chief to build us a bigger one last month, and we sent him the plans but we haven't had any answer.

Shinbashi Track Maintenance Depot Chief: Those plans

you sent were over the ¥2 million budget ceiling. Could you send us plans for something cheaper?

Ichigaya Station-Master: The way our platforms are set up we need a pretty powerful loudspeaker system. Would it be possible to switch it over to radio?

Shinbashi Telecommunication Operation Depot Chief: We'd need about a month to do it, but we can promise installation by the end of that time.

At first glance, this may not seem like much, but JNR never had this kind of direct communication between local managers, and they certainly never made their requests to each other directly. For example, in the JNR days, if the train operators received complaints from passengers that the trains were rocking too much, they would first have to bring the information back to their department, which would in turn send it back down to the depot (the all important track maintenance people). Communication was an arduous process of sending things up and down the ladder and very often people would lose sight of the importance of the complaint as they were shifting the paperwork around. Nuances would be changed. Things that required immediate attention would be inexplicably delayed. The District Managers' Meeting allows local people to communicate directly. Passenger complaints go straight to the track maintenance chief. Track maintenance chiefs promise to get things done quickly as long as it does not go over budget.

Once the chains of bureaucracy are unlocked, an organization concerned with how things are working on the front lines becomes able to exchange internal information on a constant and active basis. Shared information increases its ability to solve problems, sparks innovation and creativity and makes possible a more flexible response to changes in the outside world, pushing organizational reform another step forward.

BUILDING A STRONG ORGANIZATION
DELEGATION OF AUTHORITY
Hosoya recalls:

> In the JNR days, we had an incredible number of
> departmental rules and regulations. You had to spend
> an enormous amount of time complying with
> 'procedure' just to do anything. And then everything
> had to be coordinated and adjusted between depart-
> ments, so it took forever to get a decision.

Internal rules and regulations are what give authority to
a corporate paradigm, so I asked Hosoya to estimate how
many JNR had.
'It was huge, like a law library. After all, we'd been
accumulating them for over a century.'
Otsuka agrees:

> JNR was a bureaucracy. Rules were all-powerful. The
> highest virtue was doing what you were told. It was
> natural that internal regulations multiplied. Even a
> relatively minor proposal might need to be signed by
> forty or fifty people, since in order to submit it you had
> to make sure that anyone even remotely related to it
> approved. You had to carry your documents round to
> each different department and manager and get rubber
> stamps from all of them. Some people were very con-
> cerned with protocol too. Supposing they weren't there
> when you went to talk to them so you went to the next
> person on the list. They'd be all upset because 'he got
> to look at it before I did'. Depending on what it was you
> wanted to do, it might take 6 months before you gath-
> ered all the rubber stamps you needed. Even something
> small required at least a month. That meant that
> decisions were delayed on everything.

Hierarchies are very strong organizations, and

requiring that everybody sign proposals was in some sense necessary to maintain the vertical chain of command. But in another sense, it was also a way to avoid taking responsibility. If you have forty rubber stamps on your proposal, you've cut your responsibility down to one-fortieth. So you'd go around saying, 'I'd like you onboard for this . . . I'd like you onboard too. . . .' The end result was a system in which nobody was responsible for anything.

Certainly, if you need to get forty or fifty people to put a signature to every idea, it is no wonder that it takes 6 months to decide anything. But that sort of formalism and inefficiency does not work in times of dramatic change when technological progress is measured in days or hours. It can easily become an impediment to decision making and a hindrance to activity.

Delegation of authority is something that is easy to talk about and hard to accomplish. In reporting on companies, I hear constantly about how they are delegating authority, but I suspect that it is a case of the lady protesting too much. If you have to keep emphasizing delegation, it shows how hard it is to really do it. Still, delegation is one of the most effective tools there is for breathing new life into tired organizations. In fact, you can get a good idea of how active and energetic an organization really is just by finding out how free employees are to think, plan and act on their own – how much authority has been delegated to them.

I talked to Mr Sumita about how JR East is doing:

Railways are by nature conservative organizations. The only way to change them is to set up a system in which people can think and act on their own. They may be repeating the same tasks day in and day out, but unless the system is open to change then what is already a conservative business just keeps on growing more conservative. When you delegate authority to the people on the front lines, they start to think about their work on their own and adapt how they accomplish their tasks to their situation. The traditional JNR way of doing things was not to do anything at all. If we had stayed with the old centralized system where the people at the top decide everything, then we would be in the same place we were before – no one would do anything at all.

In other words, everyone would be sitting around waiting for orders, I suggested.

Exactly. As I said, railways are naturally conservative, so you have to delegate even more authority than you would in other companies. Delegation is the same thing as 'putting the front lines first'. You set it up so that the people doing the work can decide as much as possible on their own. That means giving them both authority and budget.

I asked how authority had been delegated between the main office and the regional offices.

We've delegated quite a lot. The main office cedes authority to the regional offices, and they in turn cede it to the stations and the maintenance crews. We've given them a lot of authority over their budgets, for instance. There are still some regional offices where the general manager is holding on to authority, but when we go out to talk to local people about budget concerns, most tell us that they've been given the budget they need to do what they want.

As Sumita points out, delegation of authority only starts to be meaningful when it is backed up by budget. In JR East's case, the head office gives the regional office targets for its revenues and expenses. The regional office is then free to draw up its own targets, the only constraint being that it has to stay within the bounds and budget established by the head office. The general managers of regional offices are free to spend money at their own discretion, just as long as they do not go over budget. Some may place priority on safety investments, others may think their funds are better used buying everybody new desks and chairs and sprucing up the office. There are virtually no limits on how the offices can use normal, everyday sums of money. JNR gave the operating divisions some discretion over their budgets, but in principle everything was controlled at the headquarters. One can see, therefore, just how far JR East has come in delegating even budgetary authority, and one of the results of this is a new awareness among employees of the need to balance expenses against income.

The district station-master system is symbolic of the thoroughness with which JR East has delegated authority, budgetary and otherwise. Much of the authority that used to belong to the regional office (the Railway Operating Division at JNR) is now in the hands of the district station-masters. They are able to call meetings and conferences in the district as they see fit, and they also have responsibility for managing their own revenues and expenses, which means the district station-master can now use budget on his own authority that used to require approval from the regional office. The Tokyo Regional Office lets its district station-masters approve construction projects up to ¥2 million.

Mr Jiro Yoshioka, talked to me about how the new system works.

The district station-master system has two meanings. First, it enables communication and coordination between the thirty-two stations, conductors' depots, electric train depots and maintenance depots that are under my supervision. These are all vertically defined organizations. Stations, for example, used to report to the Management Department, and Motive Power Crew (conductors' depot) to the Train and Operation Department, and there were rarely any ties between them. The new system provides us with a horizontal network in which to issue work instructions, communicate and hold meetings. The desire to strengthen these horizontal connections was the reason why we district station-masters were given the authority to call District Managers' Meetings, and it's one of the most significant products of delegation. People now interact horizontally.

I suggested that there were now ties between departments that used to be unrelated.

I guess you'd call it a horizontal network. The reason why it worked is because we district station-masters were given responsibility over income and expenditures. They delegated budgetary authority to us. Wages are still basically up to the head office, but the districts have responsibility for most other things, like repairs, meetings and study groups, quality circles and recreation and welfare facilities. They say that managerial resources are either 'human', 'material', or 'financial'. Well, we've been given authority over the material and financial parts. Let's say that there's a spot in one of our stations that looks dirty to passengers or that has grown old and rickety and dangerous. With our new horizontal integration we can go straight to the construction people and ask them to fix it and they say, 'Sure, we'll get right on to it, and we'll take care of the budget too'. So now we can get our repairs done promptly and we don't need to bother with drafting proposals and going through a lot of rigmarole. We don't need to sound out the people on high first.

I asked whether it had previously been necessary to get approval for everything from above.

Yes. Before, everything had to go up the ladder and then back down. Now we don't need to write proposals, we just have the people at the bottom negotiate among themselves.

I asked what would have been the equivalent of the district station-master in the JNR system. I wondered if there was even a post that compared to it.

No, there really wasn't. Maybe the transport chief came close. But even the transport chief just managed the business and transport divisions. He didn't have any budgetary authority and his work was almost exclusively concerned with just those two divisions. He had nothing at all to do with the track and structures depots, for example. You see, there were so many stations that we needed somebody in the middle to manage the stations, the conductors' depots and the train drivers' depots. That was the transport chief's job. But he only provided leadership, whereas the district station-masters provide both leadership and business management. Because of that, we district station-masters – and the local managers too – have become very interested in the bottom line. We've gained an awareness of costs, and it's not big, unimaginable numbers in the trillions of yen. We're working in units of ¥100 million[1] or so, which are easier to understand. Our district's revenue goal this year is ¥200 billion.

I suggested that nevertheless, ¥200 billion is quite a sum. It's the equivalent of a year's sales for some fairly big listed companies.

> Yes, I know. When you've got a target, you spend a lot of time thinking about how you're going to meet it. There are only two ways – you either increase your intake or you cut your expenses. Our track maintenance depots can't increase intake, so their job is to hold down outflow and ensure safety. The motive power crew depots, on the other hand, are responsible for providing better service and boosting intake. But the thing is, all it takes is one accident and you lose passengers, and therefore income. So we have to make sure that people understand that safety comes before sales. Then there's service. You provide good services and people travel on your trains. That boosts your intake. So I keep reminding my people that nobody's going to get on unless we maintain safety and provide quality service. Those are things that both the maintenance and the operations people have to be thinking about. For the maintenance crews, safety means good tracks, tracks that aren't rickety. People in both areas have to think about what they do.

Delegation means more freedom. It gives employees the ambition to do things on their own. And that results in a more powerful organization. JR East has tried to get the most out of delegation, and in doing so it has found new reserves of energy for self-reform.

NEW INCENTIVES

People generally do more than they are expected to if their jobs enable them to fulfill their desire for self-realization or provide some sort of support for goal achievement. In short, they need incentives. JR East has successfully introduced an incentive system into its revenue and expense management.

If we meet our targets, they pay us a certain percentage of what we take in. There are four kinds of revenue: regular revenue, normal revenue, travel revenue and business revenue. The incentives are highest for travel revenue because that's the hardest to produce. Business revenue covers things like commuter passes and soft drink sales. You don't have to do anything for that. Customers come looking for you. But when it comes to travel revenue, you've got to go out and find people. You have to sell them the idea of taking a trip. Naturally, the incentives are higher. We have to attract people who wouldn't travel if we didn't ask them to.

I asked whether the incentives went to the section or to the individual.

They go to the district. Let's say the district has something it really wants to do. We set a goal, and when we achieve it, we get the payback. We've got the money to fix something that had been bothering everybody for a long time, or we can improve our services, or put up a flashy new lighted acrylic message board. Employees can see the results of their work with their own eyes, and that makes them happy. Customers are happy too because we've finally fixed something that's been bothering them. The results take concrete form.

On the other hand, if revenues aren't in excess of expenses, then you've got no right to expect incentives. If revenues aren't growing, you've got to cut your outlays and learn how to economize. For example, we used to change the slate roofing on our platforms once every 3–5 years, but we found that if we used impregnated coatings we could get by changing them only once every

10 years. Yes, the coatings do cost money, but we don't spend as much on slate, so the net result is a saving of about ¥100 million. We learn things like this, and there's a payback if we boost our income and cut our costs. Everybody gets what they want, and the work environment improves. We have money to fix things up. People don't have to eat in dirty dining halls any more, and they can have new desks or curtains. That motivates them. Being the Tokyo district station-master is sort of like being president of Tokyo District, Inc.

I said that I understood that the awards system provided another incentive and that under the district station-master system good use had been made of it.

We talk a lot about 'punishment and reward'. JNR was hot on punishment, but didn't do much when it came to rewards. Now we've set up a system of five different levels of award for meritorious service: the President's Award, Regional Office Manager's Award, Departmental Manager's Award, District Station-Master's Award and Local Manager's Award. You don't need to do much to get a Local Manager's Award. If somebody does something good, we want to give them positive feedback immediately. If somebody did something praiseworthy yesterday, then tomorrow you call everybody together and give them a gift worth about ¥1,000. 'I understand you did such-and-such yesterday. That was a great idea. Keep up the good work,' you tell them.

I asked whether, when it came to the District Station-Master's Awards, he had the employee come to his office in Tokyo Station.

Yes, I do, as a matter of fact. People are delighted just to be invited to come to the station-master's office.

We've even had some who have been with the railway for 30 years and it was the first time they had ever entered the station-master's office at Tokyo Station.

I said that I could see how it would be very moving for somebody out working the trains to be asked to come to what is probably the most prestigious station-master's office in the country.

I used to have one of my assistants present the awards because we had so many of them to give out, but I've changed that. Everybody likes to be praised. I certainly do. It makes people happy. And it makes them even more happy if they are praised in the station-master's office by the station-master himself. So the man goes home at night and he tells his wife, 'The station-master praised me today'. She's proud of him because he's doing a good job, and that makes him even prouder. You can bet he's going to enjoy his dinner that night, and the next day he's going to be motivated to do even better.

In 1990, there were 1,200 Local Managers' Awards given in the Tokyo District. Some people received more than one.

Awards have another purpose besides motivation – communication. They increase the communication between workers and their managers. For example, the awards give the local manager a chance to talk to each of the employees under him and give the employees a chance to see what kind of a person their manager is. When they receive their award, they may take the opportunity to see what he thinks about something else, too. Awards help clear the air. Concluded Yoshioka at the end of our conversation:

Praise breeds an important form of communication. Obviously, there are stages in how you communicate with someone, but if you praise them, it leads to deeper, more meaningful communication. Local Managers' Awards have played a great role in fostering closer communication.

Delegation has allowed JR East to put its rank and file workers first and that has necessarily improved the atmosphere in the company. In the process of going from a stiff organization to one that is more flexible, JR East has found new vigour and energy.

Thinking about it, all these issues were things that the company would have had to deal with sooner or later, whether it be changing attitudes (convincing employees that they were no longer servants of the state, stabilizing labour relations and developing share values) or reforming organizations (streamlining, putting the rank and file first, delegating authority). JR East, however, attacked them with an almost embarrassing forthrightness, and perhaps it was that naiveté that enabled it to bring off the change in corporate paradigms so successfully. Japanese companies are famous for pulling together and working towards a goal once they have decided on it. This often draws criticism from overseas, where it sometimes appears that we are too group-oriented. But if you look at it from a different perspective, it is just a manifestation of good teamwork. Maybe this is obvious, but JR's success was only possible because its employees rallied to the cause of rebuilding the railways, adopted the same course, and worked together to improve things.

In 1992 *Fortune*, the US business magazine, ranked the East Japan Railway Company, with sales of approximately $18.8 billion, as the top transportation company in the world.

CHAPTER 4

On the Frontiers of Distribution: Seven-Eleven Japan

WHEN A SELLERS' MARKET BECOMES A BUYERS' MARKET
Japanese companies are extremely adaptable, and none more
so, perhaps, than distribution powerhouse Seven-Eleven
Japan, which franchises a chain of convenience stores often
considered to be more like 'mini-supermarkets'. Chairman
Toshifumi Suzuki talks about his industry:

> All the recognized, established companies have a full
> array of resources at their disposal, be it talent, goods
> or money. But they've all fallen on hard times since the
> bubble popped. Look at the department stores, who are
> usually considered the kings of the distribution sector.
> Their results have plunged and many are on the verge
> of crisis. Do you know what the reason is? It's because
> they haven't been able to keep up with a rapidly chang-
> ing world. The world is changing in vast ways, and we
> have to change with it.

'Adapting to change' has, in fact, become one of Suzuki's favourite phrases; you will find him constantly preaching about how retailing must adapt to the changes that are taking place.

An example of Suzuki's ability to grasp the essential nature of change comes from the summer of 1989 when he declared the 'bubble economy' to be over 6 months before the stock market crashed. It was a bold statement. The bubble was reaching its peak. All the talk in the business community was about whether or not this boom would set a new longevity record; few managers were willing to acknowledge the danger that the economy might be on the way down. Certainly, managers of major retailing companies were not. Convinced that consumer demand would continue to surge, they had embarked on major store upgrades and expansions, with new openings wherever they could be had.

But Suzuki perceived the danger. The tip-off came from a slight slowdown in per-store sales. Prior to that time, Seven-Eleven's per-store sales had been growing at a rate of about 15 per cent a year, but in 1989 growth slowed to 13 per cent. Suzuki was particularly worried by the fact that the drop was the greatest for daily food items – boxed meals and *onigiri* (rice balls). A drop-off might be understandable for luxury items, but what does it mean, Suzuki asked himself, when daily necessities aren't selling? They only cost a few hundred yen, there is no reason why people should not be able to afford them. Suzuki saw it as a sign of a mood-swing among consumers. They had started to economize. He immediately announced to his company that the bubble economy was over and urged his managers to start tightening their belts.

According to Suzuki, Japan went from a sellers' market to a buyers' market in the nineties. The bubble was a sellers' market. All you had to do was put products on the shelves and they would be snatched up; there were few if any losses from remainders. But once the bubble popped, merchandise could not be turned over that easily any more. Stores might even end up with remainders on the loss-leaders they had been hoping to attract customers with. When the bubble was in full swing, consumers would suck up everything manufacturers could churn out like a sandpit absorbing water, but today there is such a glut of products on the markets that they only feel inclined to buy what they really want.

> Products produced on a whim merely flood the markets with losses. They're a waste of global resources, if you will. What managers have to figure out, I think, is how manufacturers, wholesalers, retailers and consumers can work together to eliminate waste. Adapting to change means boosting your efficiency and cutting down on your waste

says Suzuki describing his managerial philosophy. The key, he says, is how early you are able to read the signs of change and how sensitively you are able to react to the information that comes your way.

The adaptability of Japanese companies has been proved in the oil embargoes of the seventies and the rise of the yen in the eighties. But however dramatic, these were changes in the external environment and the adaptations that Japanese companies made were for the most part passive. Seven-Eleven Japan, by contrast, has been more active. Thanks to the strong will and leadership of Toshifumi Suzuki, it has been able to anticipate change and establish internal systems to deal with it. This makes it something of a rarity among Japanese companies. It is this fine-tuned ability to adapt *actively* to change that has turned the company into Japan's leading retailer.

CONVENIENCE JAPANESE-STYLE
Suzuki had long been intrigued by the low worker productivity in the retail distribution sector. After graduating in

economics from Chuo University in 1956, he joined book-seller Tokyo Shuppan Hanbai Corporation, Ltd (now known as 'Tohan'), where he spent some time as a union official before leaving in 1963 for a post in the personnel department of Ito-Yokado, the supermarket chain that is Seven-Eleven Japan's parent company. It was his experience in personnel that drew his interest to worker productivity.

A simple comparison between the Japanese retail and manufacturing sectors will show how low the former's worker productivity is, a gap that has only widened since the late sixties, when manufacturing embarked on a course of rapid modernization. Satisfied with low productivity, retailers had little choice but to become family operations since there was no money left over to take on outside employees. Suzuki, however, recognized the problems that were inherent in this. Unless retailing was able to boost its worker productivity, it would never be able to attract talented people, since they would go to more lucrative jobs in manufacturing, which meant that retailing would be doomed to stagnation.

The official company history, *Seven-Eleven Japan: Endless Innovation 1973–1991*, contains this description of the retail sector at the time:

> If you want to increase your sales, you must have accurate information about what consumers want. The way to do that is to develop a wide selection of merchandise and see what consumers are willing to buy. Unfortunately, it is almost impossible for owner-operated stores to gather and analyse this information, let alone use it to adapt to changing consumer preferences, no matter how well informed their owners are or how hard they try. And because of this, the subsistence-scale retailers that made up the majority of neighbourhood stores had serious anxieties about their future.

In spite of the fact that productivity was the most pressing problem facing retailing, stores operated on such a small scale that their value-added and labour productivity rates merely deteriorated. In manufacturing, there is not necessarily a clear match between the scale of operations and the degree of productivity, but in retailing there is indeed a direct correlation. The reason for the decline, according to the company history, was that

the managerial abilities of the retail sector had been sapped by a unilateral, manufacturer-led upstream–downstream flow of products and information. There was talk of 'marketing' and 'consumer orientation', but these were words and strategies that came out of the manufacturing side. For the retailers, who should have been closest to consumers, marketing was, unfortunately, non-existent. Manufacturing-sector marketing strategies turned into manufacturer-led distribution strategies in which 'authorized surplus wholesalers' saw retailers merely as sales agents. Meanwhile, for all the talk of 'consumer orientation', nothing of substance happened on this front at all; it was just talk. Consumer awareness and behaviour were changing, but manufacturers were stuck in the ideas and habits of the high-growth period when they could sell anything they produced.

Suzuki saw something of social significance – and an incredible business opportunity – if he could break through the structural limitations of the retail sector, improve its productivity and find a way to trade alongside existing stores.

At the time, he was in charge of the Business Development Department at Ito-Yokado. His job was to find new business for the company and in that capacity he often visited the United States. Every time he went, there was one store that kept arousing his interest. He was not quite sure if it was a grocery store or a dry goods shop, but whenever he turned the corner in American residential areas he saw that same sign: '7-Eleven'. After some hunting revealed that the chain already had 4,000 franchisees, he knew there was something important going on. There had to be some sort of system at work, and he decided to find out what it was. His research showed that the basic concept behind the store was 'consumer convenience', and because of that there were three things that set 7-Elevens apart from conventional stores. First, they were open every day all year round and for long hours. Second, they were located in residential areas. And third, they carried a full line of basic necessities, especially items that were likely to be needed in an emergency. The franchiser was an American company called Southland that was known for being one of the world's most efficient retailers. If he could bring the chain to Japan, Suzuki realized, he might have a way to wean retailing from its inefficiency.

He approached Southland, but the going was rocky at first and the match seemed uneven. Where Southland was an up-and-coming powerhouse in the US, Ito-Yokado, at number eleven in the retail industry in terms of sales, was still a relatively minor player in the Japanese market. Finally, after more than 8 months of frustrating negotiations, the two companies were able to sign 'area service' and 'licensing' contracts in November 1973. The preceding August, Ito-Yokado had established a subsidiary called 'York Seven', the predecessor of Seven-Eleven Japan, to run the chain. It was, incidently, 2 months before the first oil embargo.

Under the terms of the licence contract, Japan's first convenience store opened in Koto-ku, Tokyo on May 15, 1974.

We were scheduled to open at 7.00 in the morning, but some of the products that were supposed to be delivered the night before were late. We had the store open a bit before we were scheduled to start business because we were waiting for the delivery lorry. At about 6.30, a middle-aged gentleman poked his head through the door and asked if it would be all right to come in. That was all the excuse we needed. Seven-Eleven Japan was open for business. The man bought a pair of sunglasses that were positioned near the cash register. It was our first sale.[1]

Convenience stores had arrived. During 1974, fifteen Seven-Elevens opened. The next year the chain was up to sixty-nine. Then in 1976 it topped 100. The company celebrated by renting out a hotel function room and holding a 'Seven-Eleven Convenience Store 100th Opening Commemoration', for which John Thompson, chairman of Southland, travelled to Japan. In his speech, he told the audience, 'It took Southland 25 years to reach 100 stores. Seven-Eleven Japan has accomplished the same thing in just 2.' Suzuki was next on the podium, but he was so choked up that the master of ceremonies had to come to his rescue. Only 4 years later, in 1980, he would dwarf that accomplishment by signing on his 1,000th store, but he says in the company history that for number 1,000 he 'didn't cry.... It was getting those first 100 that was such an emotional thing'.

Seven-Eleven held strictly to a strategy of 'domination' when it chose new locations. During its first year it focused on the Fukagawa area of Koto ward. Suzuki ordered the people in charge of finding new locations 'not to take so much as a single step out of Fukagawa'. As the embodiment of efficient management, Suzuki was obsessed with the domination strategy. By concentrating new openings on a particular district, he felt that he would be better able to increase Seven-Eleven's recognition and appeal among the local population, which would allow him to use his advertising budget more effectively and save on his distribution costs too. Added to this was the fact that his stores would be able to carry a certain breadth of merchandise that would enable him to verify in great detail what customers wanted.

When viewed from the perspective of merchandise trade, there is a synergy between the sales of individual franchises and the number of franchises in a given area, and this translates into buying power. This difference in buying power between us and other chains is what we give back to franchisees in the form of services. It is perhaps the most extreme manifestation of the domination effect. If you compare the dominance of different chains in different areas, you have a good measure of their respective strengths. Obviously, in distribution it is more effective to have a certain density of stores rather than scatter them far and wide.[1]

Seven-Eleven Japan still follows the domination strategy today. It operated 5,475 stores in twenty-one prefectures as of February 1994, two-thirds of which were located in the Kanto (Greater Tokyo) area. This is in stark contrast to the number two convenience store chain, Lawson, which had 4,836 stores in thirty-nine prefectures, spreading itself out over virtually the entire country. The Seven-Eleven corporate culture is one in which a strategy, once decided on, is carried out regardless of the difficulties that may be encountered along the way. It is a philosophy the company learned from the iron will of its chairman, Toshifumi Suzuki.

Seven-Eleven began by importing advanced business know-how from Southland, but it later began to adapt the convenience store system to Japanese conditions. To be frank, it created something entirely new. Only three of the original Southland elements are still with the company today: the Seven-Eleven trademark, the basic concept of convenience stores and the franchise accounting system (gross profit division – the store owner and the chain share gross profits on a 55–45 basis). As we will see later in this chapter, Seven-Eleven Japan went on to create an entirely Japanese-style convenience store that today has surpassed even what Southland was able to achieve.

This is a recurring pattern in Japanese business history. Manufacturers began by learning manufacturing systems from Europe and North America, making incremental improvements until they had produced something more suited to Japan, which in many cases went on to surpass its Western models. Toyota's 'just-in-time' system is the most famous example of this.

Seven-Eleven did much the same thing as it pioneered convenience stores in Japan. By demanding of itself an efficiency on a par with manufacturers, it perfected a Japanese style of convenience store management that outstripped the original American version. In March 1991, Seven-Eleven Japan bought out what had become a deeply troubled Southland, paying $430 million for a 70 per cent stake in its former mentor. Ito-Yokado took 51 per cent of the 287 million shares acquired, Seven-Eleven Japan 49 per cent.

Charged with rescuing Southland, Suzuki exported Japanese-style convenience store management back to America. At the first rebuilding meeting with the Southland management, he began his remarks by taking them to task for looking to price-cuts for their salvation: 'Why are convenience stores discounting? Convenience stores sell convenience, they don't sell discounts.' The first step was to make them more Japanese, and he set about reworking their merchandise mix, pricing, display techniques and signs. The result was an astounding success. American Seven-Elevens were turning single-year profits only 2 years after the takeover. There have been few other examples in history of a foreign company rebuilding a ¥1 trillion firm in just 2 years. It is a testament both to the business skills of Toshifumi Suzuki and to the global viability of the Japanese-style convenience store system.

Having taken the US Southland under its wing, Ito-

Yokado is using it as a base from which to expand the Seven-Eleven chain into twenty-one countries, including Canada, Hong Kong and Taiwan. Between Ito-Yokado's ¥3 trillion in annual sales and Southland's ¥1 trillion, they are a ¥4 trillion company, which puts them in the same league as US retail giant K-Mart. Indeed, Seven-Eleven has by its own efforts joined the top rung of world retailers.

During the year to February 1993, Seven-Eleven Japan announced operating profits of ¥181.9 billion on sales of ¥1,194.9 billion, a gain of 11.8 per cent over the year before. Current profits jumped 9.7 per cent to ¥85.1 billion. During the same time period, Ito-Yokado posted current profits of ¥85.0 billion. In the space of just two decades, Seven-Eleven Japan has surpassed even its parent.

Limited Choices
Seven-Eleven is often described as having turned retailing into a factory operation. This is a back-handed compliment. Everyone recognizes the company's success in bringing factory-like efficiency to the backward Japanese retailing sector, but they also know the unimaginable lengths it went to in doing so.

The fatal weakness of retailing is that, unlike manufacturing, it deals with people instead of things. The only way you know what will sell is to ask people what they would like to buy. You cannot sell merchandise the way factories plan production. In fact, when Seven-Eleven Japan was established, the dominant opinion (at least in the retail sector) was that retailing and manufacturing were so different they could not even be talked about in the same breath. Suzuki rejected that idea and brought to retailing an efficiency never before seen anywhere in the world.

His strategy was to apply the Toyota '*Kanban*' system of zero inventories and 'just-in-time' deliveries. This was not as far-fetched an idea as it may appear. Toyota got its hint from American supermarkets, but Seven-Eleven went at it with a vigour that surpassed even Toyota's. It was this absolute commitment to reducing labour requirements and eliminating waste that made the company such a success.

You can see that obsession from the number of items the company's stores carry, and it is in sharp contrast to the car-manufacturing industry. During the bubble, the car manufacturers produced more and more models with more and more functions in an attempt to move up-market. When the bubble popped, they found themselves over-extended and forced to go on a 'crash diet' of discontinuing super-fluous products and using more common parts. Seven-Eleven took the opposite tack, cutting back the number of items it carried to a bare minimum. When you walk into a Seven-Eleven store, one of the first things you are struck with is how neatly everything is arranged. This is not just fastidi-ousness; you get the impression that everything has been precisely calculated. And it has.

Usually, the number of items carried by retail stores will vary widely according to the season and it tends to increase year-to-year. The idea at most stores is to carry anything that looks as though it might sell. What happens, however, is that sales floors gradually become more crowded and displays more cluttered. In the end, stores have a hard time knowing exactly what is and is not selling. Seven-Eleven, by contrast, limits itself to about 3,000 items. The concept behind conven-ience stores, it says, is to provide 'convenient' products – things that are consumed within about 30 minutes of pur-chase or things that must be had immediately. That covers about 3,000 different items, according to its research.

Indeed, if you were to count everything a person required from the time he got up in the morning until the time he went to bed at night, you would probably come up with a number in that range. In Seven-Eleven's case, many years of sales data show 3,000 to be the most efficient merchandise level. Anything more than that produces waste; anything less, and you fail to meet the needs of your customers. Common wisdom says that since consumption is growing more individualized, sellers should carry more merchandise, thereby giving their customers a wider range of choices. Certainly the car-manufacturing industry followed this philosophy, riding the waves of 'diversification' during the bubble to turn out a plethora of new options. Seven-Eleven Japan, however, has stuck to its original focus of 3,000.

Suzuki explains, 'The essence of diversification is concentration. "Diversification" is just a clever way of saying it.' In the first place, Seven-Eleven stores have a set floor space of 100 square metres, so it is impossible for them to carry lots of merchandise even if they wanted to. But this excuse is a bit disingenuous. According to company calculations, 100 square metres just happens to be the optimum space for efficiently displaying 3,000 items.

The problem is not so much with the number 3,000, but with the mix – how to make sure that only strong sellers are included. Most retailers choose their merchandise mix on the basis of a combination of the manager's intuition and the wholesaler's advice. Intuition, however, is by definition based on which products sold best in the past. The loss of opportunity potentially arising from this time lag can be substantial, and when presented with new products intuition provides a very poor guide for decision makers. That is why retailing is of necessity an inefficient business.

Instead of relying on intuition to choose its merchandise mix, Seven-Eleven Japan relies on computer-gathered data. One of the things that sets it apart from the competition is the thoroughness with which it has systematized the process of gathering data, analysing it and applying it to marketing decisions. The company has been so systematic in laying out its managerial know-how that it has even earned Suzuki the nickname Mr System!

Obviously, the purpose of all this is efficiency. The company has replaced vague experiential values with numerical data, thereby underpinning intuition with algorithm. It has tried to boost predictability even farther by utilizing two different types of information: macrodata on market trends and microdata on local characteristics. Products in the intersection between the two are what make it on to the shelves. The macrodata are handled by experts in the chain headquarters; the microdata by individual store owners, who are obviously the most knowledgeable about their own locales. Headquarters uses its macrodata to select about 5,000 items a year from among the millions of possibilities. These items it recommends to its franchisees, who then choose 3,000 of them that best suit local conditions. Products that do not sell – 'dead merchandise' – are removed from the list at a rate of about eighty a week, or 5,000 a year. This rigorous selection and discontinuation system is one of the keys to efficient operation; in the end, only strong sellers remain.

Let us look at soft drinks to see how it works. The Japanese market for soft drinks is divided into carbonated beverages, teas, canned coffees, colas and sports drinks. There are currently about 3,000 different varieties available, with each of the big manufacturers launching some 700–800 new drinks a year. Seven-Eleven recommends only 130 of these to its franchises, and they are expected to choose from among that number the drinks they will carry, usually between ninety and 100. Some 70 per cent of these will have been replaced within a year; particularly poor sellers in as little as a few weeks. Contrary to appearances, therefore, the ubiquitous soft drinks in convenience stores are anything but ordinary. They are part of a select group of 100 screened from a pool of over 3,000.

ITEMIZED CONTROL
The business of retailing is to meet the needs of consumers. Upstream in manufacturing you can develop new products and create new markets, but downstream at the very bottom in retail distribution your job is to develop an accurate understanding of what it is consumers want and find a way

to sell it to them. The key, therefore, is how sensitively you are able to respond to the needs you observe.

Some 85 per cent of Seven-Eleven's customers come in at least once a week; 20 per cent of these are dailies. The average customer visits the store between three and four times a week. Sales areas are not determined by distance, but by time and lines of movement. About 80 per cent of regular customers walk to the store, usually no more than 5 minutes. Those who drive are also usually no more than about 5 minutes from the store. In terms of lines of movement, walkers form a rough circle around the store, but drivers are located along a straight line. In the most extreme cases there will be a completely different clientele depending on which side of a busy thoroughfare the store is located on. Their extremely small territories and dependence on high-frequency regulars are among the things that set convenience stores apart from other retailers. For them to succeed, they must be tuned exactly to their clientele's needs, as if they had gone out and done the shopping on the customers' behalf.

They must also develop a merchandise mix that fits their location. Most of the merchandise carried by convenience stores consists of daily necessities; almost 40 per cent is in the deli section – boxed meals and sandwiches. The demand for these products changes on a daily basis. If a nearby school is holding a sports festival or having a field trip, lunch sales will shoot up. At the beginning of the school year, paper and pencils are likely to do well. Nor can weather be ignored. If it is raining on Sunday morning, people are not going to leave home, so lunch sales will drop. But if the rain does not start until afternoon, people are already out, so sales will hold steady. Needs, it can be seen, are in a constant state of flux. It is not just the obvious things like fashion, economic conditions and market trends that influence them, but the day of the week, the time of day and whether there are clouds in the sky. How well it is able to follow these trends can be a question of life or death for a retailer. Seen from this angle,

Suzuki's constant reminder that 'retailing means adapting to change' begins to make sense.

Fine-tuned adaptation to these kinds of change consists in the ability to read conditions on an hourly basis (or less) and change the merchandise mix accordingly. Obviously, this requires store managers who are in touch with their communities. Each outlet must adapt to local conditions.

At Seven-Eleven, that is accomplished by 'itemized control' in which managers track each and every item of merchandise and change what is on their shelves to suit what their clientele needs. This is a focusing process rather than an expansion process. Department stores may try to deal with diversifying customer needs by carrying anything anybody could possibly want, but convenience stores only have 100 square metres of selling space. They have no choice but to engage in highly focused, accurate merchandising.

Lunch corners provide an example. If there is a boxed meal that the consumer likes, he will probably buy it without hesitation; if nothing strikes his fancy, he'll walk out the door regardless of how many lunches there may be left on the shelf. Popular lunches sell out quickly; unpopular ones are still there at closing time. In this case, consumption can be said to 'concentrate' in certain popular items. What consumers want is quality, which for lunches is equivalent to 'something that tastes good'. What they do not necessarily want is a wide range of choices. It is pointless to try to provide a plentiful selection just because this is supposed to be an 'age of increasing diversity'. It is more important to look for quality instead.

Explaining why Seven-Eleven expects managers to work on an item-by-item basis, Suzuki says:

When you don't have anything at all, that's what I call an 'age of diversity'. You're satisfied with substitutes. When you're starving, you may feel like a ham sandwich, but you'll settle for cheese instead. That's not the case today. People only buy what they really want to eat. So you have to focus on what they want, and check each and every item carefully.

Seven-Eleven's ordering process goes through three stages that can be likened to 'theory', 'experiment' and 'verification'. In the theory stage, current conditions are analysed, lessons from the past reviewed, changes in the surrounding area considered and a scenario drawn up. Orders are then placed on the basis of theory. The experiment begun, the company tries to verify whether or not the order was accurate and in line with what the market was looking for. It is a cycle of ordering what should sell, putting it in the store and seeing what happens. 'Shop-keeping is constant repetition of theory, ordering and verification,' Suzuki underlines. Orders are not placed because an item is sold out, but because the person placing the order has reviewed conditions and thinks he can sell x number of them in the future. One of Suzuki's most famous aphorisms is that 'ordering is a trial of managerial will'. It is in how he places his orders that a manager's skills are tested.

Seven-Elevens carry 3,000 items, but their customers usually only buy three or four at a time. Sometimes they may just buy a single sandwich, or if the sandwich they wanted is not available, they may leave without buying anything at all. That is especially true today when the sellers' market of the bubble has been replaced by a buyers' market. In a sellers' market, people will buy anything you offer, but in a buyers' market, putting something on the shelf is no guarantee it will be sold. Even if it is cheap, consumers will not buy it if it is not what they want. Suzuki muses:

> There are some out there who look at the growth of discount stores and conclude that prices are what drive today's consumer. But what are selling are not cheap products per se, but *quality* cheap products. Price is only one component of 'needs'. If anything, what drives today's consumer isn't price, but *value*.

That argues for even more stringent itemized control and more rigorous focus in the future.

In itemized control, managers need to be particularly watchful for merchandise that does not sell. As they fill out their order sheets, it is natural for people's attention to be drawn to the items that are disappearing from the shelves fastest. The idea is that 'we'd better order some more of this because we're running out'. But the reverse is also true: 'We're not running out of this so we don't need any more.' Unfortunately, few make the next leap to the idea: 'This isn't selling, so let's get rid of it.' Focus is lost.

Let's look at soft drinks again. When it starts to warm up, say early spring to May or so, fruit drinks are big sellers; when the early summer sun starts to beat down in May and June, sports drinks become more popular. In July, after Japan's rainy season is over and summer begins in earnest, people snatch up light, refreshing iced teas. Stores change their merchandise to reflect these trends, but there are limits to what they can carry. The refrigerator cases will only hold five or six 1.5-litre bottles of oolong tea in any single row. At the height of summer, a row of iced tea will be sold every 3 or 4 hours, and it takes about the same amount of time to get the next bottles cold, so there is little room for error. If some poor guy comes in 'ahead of schedule' and finds himself stuck with a bottle of lukewarm tea then in all likelihood he will give up on the store and shop elsewhere the next time he is thirsty. Consumers come to convenience stores for convenience. They want to drink cold oolong tea *right now*. How do you make sure they can? By getting rid of items that are not selling so that you have more room for those that are. In this case, by eliminating whatever it is in the refrigerator that is taking space away from big bottles of oolong tea. Convenience stores compete, if you will, in a very small ring. There is nothing more important for them than getting rid of non-sellers. This, of course, is a form of adaptation to change, or as Suzuki is wont to put it, 'The first step in itemized control is eliminating dead merchandise.'

By the same token, itemized control means never being out of something either. If the store does not have an item on its shelves, it means somebody forgot to order it, or did not order enough, or the wholesaler was out of stock or missed the delivery. There is a direct correlation between the out-of-stock rate and sales declines. A store that is missing 1 per cent of its items will loose 1 per cent of its sales.

After we installed Terminal Seven[2] in all our stores in 1978, we saw a sharp improvement in our wholesalers' missed delivery rates. Before that, we were using telephone orders, so we don't have any accurate data, but by our estimates we went from a 30 per cent missed delivery rate in processed foods to less than 0.5 per cent.[1]

Itemized control covers more than just focus. How merchandise is positioned on the shelves is also involved. In a buyers' market, Suzuki says, sales rates will change according to how you position your merchandise. Poor displays are a lost opportunity, because items that should sell will not. The only way to avoid this is to know what customers are and are not looking for. Seven-Eleven's thinking on this is clear. Rather than put things it wants to sell in places they are likely to be noticed, it puts things that are selling well in places where they are easy to buy. For instance, it is adamant that stores practise 'last in, first out' positioning rather than the more usual 'first in, first out'. Retailers normally put their oldest merchandise at the front of the shelves and their newest in the back because they want to get the older products sold and out. But consumers would rather have something that is fresher, and having worked out what the stores are doing, they will probably reach into the back of the shelves to get the newer merchandise. If that is the case,

Suzuki argues, then why not just put the new merchandise at the front and the old merchandise at the back. Isn't that what shop-keeping is all about?

WORLD-CLASS INFORMATION SYSTEMS

Suzuki has long maintained that 'we're not just in the distribution business, we're in the information business'. It is not surprising therefore that Seven-Eleven has been constantly building and upgrading its information systems. Today there is a sophisticated computer network at the heart of its operation that is able to track and immediately respond to increasingly complex and diverse consumer needs. It is unlike any other in the retail sector and it is what makes strict itemized control feasible.

The system does more than link Seven-Eleven's 5,475 stores with the headquarters, it also brings online 30 regional offices, 700 vendors, 200 manufacturers and 160 distribution centres. The result is greater integration between the manufacturing, distribution and sales arms of the business and the ability for all to share information in real time. Approximately 37,000 terminals are connected to the client-server network and it provides something for everyone. For manufacturers, the network lets them use ordering data directly from the stores as they are drawing up production plans; for vendors it means they are better able to schedule which products to deliver at what frequencies; and for stores it means being able to sell the merchandise they purchase with minimal losses.

In 1991 the network switched over from regular telephone lines to large-capacity Integrated Services Digital Network (ISDN) data lines. Seven-Eleven's point-of-sales (POS) data amount to more than 100 million records a week, and analogue telephone lines have been unable to keep up with the volume. In the past, stores have had to copy the data onto floppy disks and send them into the headquarters, which resulted in a 10-day lag as Seven-Eleven compiled and analysed its POS information. Now, POS data from each of the

5,475 stores come in and are processed in real time, at a rate of about 3 million orders a day.

Makoto Usui, general manager of the Systems Development Department, beams:

> The ISDN system uses a redundant, no-downtime design. We've set up the network so as to take full advantage of the potential that ISDN offers. For example, ISDN uses 64-kilobit lines, which is an enormous amount of data-carrying capacity. Normally, companies only use about 60 per cent of that, but the Seven-Eleven network uses 75 per cent. We've developed our own data exchange protocols to be able to achieve those rates. There are standard protocols for financial and distribution systems, but they aren't very good, so we developed our own. Instead of the 90 characters a second you get with conventional transmission speeds, we're going at about 480. That means we can send about fifty times more data. Another feature of ISDN is short connection times. It used to take about 30 seconds to get a response to a stock check. We've been able to shorten that to between 3.5 and 4 seconds, which means our costs vis-à-vis performance are about a quarter of what they used to be.

One of the things Seven-Eleven is most proud of is the fact that its ISDN network can have emergency messages out to all 5,475 of its stores in about 20 minutes.

As one would expect, the system is notable for its adaptability and emphasis on maximizing information use. Sales and customer data gathered by the POS systems in the store are first fed to the Store Computer for analysis before going to the chain headquarters for further analysis and application in marketing decisions. Seven-Eleven then supplies these 'basic data' to its manufacturers for use in their product development activities.

This POS-based store computer system is now in its fourth generation. The first generation was installed in 1978 when what were then advanced 'Terminal Seven' computers were used to replace telephone ordering. Terminal Seven was developed jointly by Seven-Eleven and NEC and this policy of working with manufacturers to develop its own, customized hardware and software is something that Seven-Eleven has followed throughout its history. Though a very simple system by today's standards, Terminal Seven was revolutionary for the time. Never before had headquarters been able to monitor stores' daily sales volumes and drawing power. Terminal Seven demonstrated the power and importance of information systems to this business, and touched off a computerization race in the convenience store industry.

The second generation came in October 1982 and was Japan's first POS system worthy of the name. POS systems had already been used in the United States, where they were seen as a way to cut labour requirements, improve accuracy and prevent pilfering. Seven-Eleven, however, had other purposes. It wanted information on what times of day which items were selling. The new system was also a boon to stock management, since it was powerful enough to be able to put out accurate information the next morning on how each individual item had sold during the previous day. These data in turn brought improvements in ordering precision, made non-sellers obvious and reduced out-of-stock rates.

Seven-Eleven then enhanced its system further with 'Electronic Order Booking' (EOB) terminals that were so easy to use that anyone could do store ordering. This combination of EOB and POS systems was a major step forward towards the realization of a Toyota-like 'just-in-time' system. It was now possible to send its stores the products that were selling best in the amounts that were needed at the times they were needed.

The next enhancement came in 1985, when two-way POS systems and personal computers with colour graphics were brought in. This was the start of the third generation. Two-way POS systems enabled stores to make inquiries of the host computer, which opened up new lines of business such as pre-ordered lunches, gift items and catalogue sales. This history-making evolution took another step forward when the fourth generation came online in July 1990. Usui says:

We recognized that the most important thing in shop-keeping is how you utilize information. That is why we placed so much priority on our computer systems. When we installed our POS system in 1982, we were the first in the world to use that kind of data for merchandising and marketing. But we still felt the system was not up to the level of precision we wanted for our ordering, which is why we began developing the fourth generation.

Generation Four is a combination of four terminals: the traditional POS terminal, a 'store computer' that serves as a kind of 'control tower', a 'graphic order terminal', and a hand-held scanner terminal to verify the merchandise that comes in. There were three requirements that it had to meet. Seven-Eleven wanted a system that was so simple to operate that anybody could do it, it wanted to have an accurate picture of consumer needs and merchandise stocks and it wanted absolute efficiency in the way stores were run.

The store computer performs eight functions simultaneously, including realtime analysis, information updates, ordering, data display and monitoring of other store equipment.

The graphic order terminal, one of the new members of the team, has opened new vistas in stock management. It is a portable terminal with a 9-inch display and a keypad, all together about the size of a sheet of A4 paper. The terminal reads in from the store computer what Seven-Eleven considers to be the minimum data needed for accurate ordering, so that the employee has these data in front of him as he or she inspects the shelves. Suppose, for example, you were ordering milk. It is not enough just to go over to the refrigerator and count how many of which brands are left. That only tells you what you have, not why you have it. The reason there are only a couple of cartons of a particular brand left could be because it is selling well, but it could also be because you only ordered a couple of cartons to begin with. And if a product sells out, you may forget it was even there. The Seven-Eleven terminal prevents that by giving you an array of charts and graphs on milk sales over the last 3 weeks: how many of which brands were sold, what percentage of stocks purchased were sold, any brands that have sold out and not been reordered, rankings of the top sellers, what days of the week milk tends to sell well on.

In the food and deli corner, you even get data on the time of day at which particular products are likely to sell, not just the day of the week. The terminal will, for example, tell you how many of a particular sandwich were ordered at what time on what day, what time on what day they were sold and, if they sold out, what time on what day you ran out of them. This information is further supplemented with a description of the item's characteristics, new product information from headquarters, information on what items are tending to sell well at other stores and seasonal advice and recommendations for particular events in the neighbourhood. Even a part-timer with almost no knowledge of the merchandise is able to place extremely precise orders.

The other new addition to the system is the scanner terminal, which has greatly reduced the time spent in delivery verification and stock management. Verification, most store-owners will tell you, is the most cumbersome task in retailing. Delivery trucks pile up box after box of merchandise, and it is no small job to check each of them against the invoices and make sure that the amounts ordered were correctly delivered. After checking, merchandise must be put on the shelves, but that is also far from simple. The scanner terminal relieves much of the stress and strain involved by reading bar codes on the shelves that tell it what the item is and how much it costs. Operators trace along the bar codes on each item delivered, from one end of the box to the other. The computer totals up the information and checks whether the quantities delivered match the quantities ordered. If they do, the merchandise goes on the shelves. The same process is repeated over and over again for the entire delivery. When the 'finish' button is pressed, the computer checks for missing items and if it finds any, the scanner beeps a warning and displays the name of what is missing, eliminating most of the stress involved in verification.

After verification, data from the scanner terminal are fed into the store computer, which updates its stock lists so that the newest merchandise appears first. There is a reason for juggling the order in which items appear on the list. If the list is in the same order as stock was placed on the shelves, then when it is time to book the next order, all employees have to do is check the shelves in the same order as they verified the last delivery and the information coming up on their graphic order terminal will match the items in front of them. That not only eliminates drudgery, it boosts precision. Previously, employees would have to go around the store looking for items in the order that they appeared on their terminal screens. The machine was calling the tune rather than the people, and stress would quickly mount if the machine was screaming for an item that just could not be found. More stress leads to more fatigue, which leads to carelessness and wrong orders that are placed without really checking stocks. The end result, of course, is to sap the store's efficiency and adaptability. The new equipment breaks that vicious circle and replaces it with a virtuous one in which efficiency and adaptability feed off and augment each other.

Toshifumi 'Mr System' Suzuki says:

It's not that we set out to build an information system at the beginning. It was something that came about because we had things we wanted to do and developed the tools to do them. I know absolutely nothing about computers. We don't even employ any programmers or systems engineers. When we build information systems, we out-source the entire project. In a way, these machines are like monsters. They're designed for top efficiency when they're running at full capacity. But when you reach full capacity, you find you need another machine too. They keep growing. Seems like a lot of waste.

The story of Seven-Eleven Japan's computerization is very much the story of networked distribution systems. Finance and transportation are the more usual examples of networked industries, but convenience stores, by virtue of also having networks, have been able to take over many of the functions of these sectors. Seven-Eleven has handled parcel delivery services since 1982, accepting packages on behalf of couriers. In 1987, it became possible to pay your electricity bill at the Seven-Eleven cash register; in 1988, your gas bill; in 1989, your insurance premiums; and in 1992, your telephone bill. That is how far the computerization of convenience stores has come.

SHARING INFORMATION BY DIRECT COMMUNICATION
Information is usually transmitted in companies along the chain of command, from top to bottom and from bottom back to top. Shop foremen talk to middle managers, who relay their ideas to the president, and vice versa. The president, sitting at the top of the pyramid, receives information from many different departments, but there is a distance between the ultimate destination of the information (the president) and its

ultimate source (the shop floor). It is not uncommon for information to become lost or distorted along the way. That may rob the president of the information he needs, which could lead to late or mistaken decisions. The reverse may also be true. Information from the top may never make it down to the bottom and, as a result, the company will fail to develop a set of common values and will fragment. Sharing information thus becomes an important managerial task.

There are two approaches to doing this: information systems and human communication. Seven-Eleven Japan uses both very skilfully. We have already seen the indirect communication that is possible with its computerized information systems. Let's look now at how it uses direct communication between people.

Whereas the computer system is concerned with transmitting data, direct communication is more of a 'human network' designed to let real people with real voices talk and bounce ideas off each other so that a common base of information is shared throughout the company. The staff are encouraged, for example, to bring problems at stores to the attention of top managers rather than brushing them under the carpet. The company has made it clear that it wants the bad news first, regardless of any obviating factors. This human communication proceeds wherever possible on a face-to-face basis so that it never becomes a one-way street. As one might expect of Seven-Eleven, it is also done very systematically.

At Seven-Eleven, it is the 'Operations Department' that takes care of the franchises. Its responsibilities include providing each and every franchisee with business consulting and supervision. The entire country is divided into ten zones and subzones, which are further divided into eighty districts. At the very bottom of the pyramid are approximately 710 'operations field counsellors', who look after seven or eight stores each and are required to visit them twice a week for at least 2 hours of counselling.

The counsellors report to eighty district managers, who are each in charge of one district containing seven or eight counsellors. This means the district managers must keep track of between sixty and seventy stores. Next are the ten zone managers who look after eight to ten district managers, or about 500 stores.

'Communication must be direct, and we must all share the same quantity and quality of information,' Suzuki declares. To do this, he has everybody in the Operations Department, all 780 counsellors, district managers and zone managers come to Tokyo once a week for a 'general conference'. This practice has continued throughout the 20 years of Seven-Eleven's existence and it illustrates the priority and enthusiasm the company has for direct communication with the people on the front lines.

Mondays and Tuesdays are the key days in this. Let's now look at how the schedule is set up.

Monday morning from 9.30 to 11.00 is the Managers' Conference. District managers will have already related any problems in their districts to their zone managers by the previous weekend, and this conference provides zone managers with a forum for reporting and discussion. The chairman and all executives are in attendance as well to ensure that they are kept up-to-date on what is happening in the stores. The chairman will often comment on reports and, if possible, the staff will provide answers on the spot.

From 11.00 to noon is the Executive Conference, which includes discussion and reporting on a preset agenda as well as time for considering and deciding on company-wide policy for issues that may have been raised at the Managers' Conference. Decisions are expected to be acted on immediately; the company has a deadline of 1 week for conformity.

After lunch, from 1.30 to 2.30, is the New Locations Meeting, in which representatives of all related departments – construction, training, operations, personnel, legal affairs, planning and distribution – gather to review prospective recruits. Having all there means everyone is informed of potential problems and ensures that they are not only moving in the same direction but moving there quickly. From 3.00 to 4.30 the Business Reform Committee meets. The group, led by the chairman and including managers from all departments, provides a forum for considering company-wide concerns and problems and is an important source of direction on major business issues.

At 5.00 the Merchandise Review Meeting begins, with district managers, zone managers and merchandisers from the Merchandise Department in attendance. This meeting has also been in existence since the company was founded. Its purpose is to avoid bias in the Merchandise Department's information by purchasing from outside suppliers merchandise other than what the department is recommending and evaluating it against what Seven-Eleven is carrying.

On Tuesday, the Operations Field Counsellors come to town for a meeting that includes about 1,000 people – the entire Operations Department plus all of the headquarters staff. The whole day is given over to the Field Counsellors' Conference. The morning is devoted to a general conference, the afternoon to zone meetings.

The General Conference, which runs from 9.00 to 11.30, begins with a short morning ceremony, after which the operations field counsellors and recruiting field counsellors proceed to the auditorium to hear the chairman review the previous day's managers' meetings and comment on any other issues or ideas he feels require direct communication. A shorthand typist is on hand to keep records of what is said for later distribution to the entire staff. Around the same time as the chairman's speech, the Merchandise Department distributes product information and recommended changes to all in attendance. All of the other departments also have an opportunity to relay any information they may want to put out, and all information to be communicated to stores is provided at this time as well.

After the General Conference, the Operations and Recruiting Departments separate for their own meetings.
Operations Department meetings are led by zone managers,
who discuss responses to issues that have arisen at stores in
their territory over the previous week and any other matters
of importance to their zone. This includes detailed introduc-
tions to each and every new merchandise recommendation,
discussions of items the company recommends dropping,
reviews of sales trends and any other information that needs
to be communicated to stores. Representatives from other
departments also come in to talk about changes to the
computer systems or new promotional strategies.

The Recruiting Department splits into two groups to
report on, check and supervise the progress made towards
new franchise contracts. The groups also look for reasons
why newly opened stores may not be meeting their sales
targets.

Tuesday afternoon has another round of meetings scheduled. In the Zone Managers' Meeting the ten zone managers
will meet with people from each of the other departments to
discuss problems and relay information. In the District
Meetings, district managers lead discussions of problems and
solutions on a store-by-store basis and make sure that field
counsellors understand what they should emphasise. This is
where much of the real work is done in transmitting decisions
from the top to individual stores and making sure they are
acted upon.

In short, top managers take up problems on Monday
and by Tuesday have provided stores, through their field
counsellors, with strategies for dealing with them. The
important thing in this cycle, according to Seven-Eleven,
is that everybody hears and shares the same information
directly.

Some may wonder if spending this much time and money
on meetings is not an enormous waste. After all, it costs the
company ¥1.5 billion a year to bring its field counsellors into

headquarters every week. 'Do the results really justify that kind of money?' Suzuki is often asked by journalists. He gives them all the same answer:

> You have to have face-to-face communication in order to really share the same information and thinking. You lose more if business decisions are not relayed accurately than you spend on meetings, so we do not spare any expense when it comes to communication.

Having spent Monday and Tuesday in Tokyo for meetings, zone managers, district managers and field counsellors get on their planes home between 5.00 and 6.00 on Tuesday evening. This 'human communication' system of weekly meetings has been with Seven-Eleven since the beginning and is now a permanent fixture in the company schedule.

CLEAN ENOUGH TO BUILD COMPUTER CHIPS

In the city of Kawaguchi, a community on Tokyo's northwestern border, is located the factory of Delica Ace, a company that supplies food to Seven-Eleven. It is owned by Ajinomoto, and provides precooked meals to 182 stores in four Tokyo wards (Adachi, Kita, Shinjuku and Bunkyo) and four Saitama Prefecture cities (Kawaguchi, Toda, Hatogaya and Warabi). On average, Delica Ace produces between 45,000 and 60,000 meals a day: 17,500 boxed lunches, 13,400 *onigiri* (rice balls), 6,800 burgers, rolls and noodle dishes and 8,500 sandwiches.

The popularity of a convenience store is said to hinge on how fresh and tasty its boxed meals are. Bad-tasting meals will not sell and, it goes without saying, hygiene problems can be deadly. Should there be just one complaint, the store develops a reputation for 'bad food' that can be hard to erase. If quality is poor, the damage could be fatal.

Quality control is something Japanese companies are famous for. It was here that the idea of 'total quality control' flowered. That same commitment to quality can be seen at Seven-Eleven too. More than anyone else in the convenience store industry, it is serious about making sure that its meals are fresh, delicious and trusted as 'something you can be sure is all right'. It has been successful in this because it has set up rigorous quality controls for the food products it carries.

From the outside, Delica Ace looks like just another unremarkable factory in an unremarkable town. As you step inside, however, you realize that its hygiene measures are every bit the equal of those in semiconductor plants. In order to be admitted to the factory floor, you are required to change into a freshly washed white surgical gown, white hat and special boots. All watches, rings and anything else that might carry germs or dust must be removed. You are not, in principle, allowed to bring anything with you inside. As you walk down the hallway that leads into the factory, there is a table on which several boxed lunches are displayed. They are samples of 'problem products'. The date and reason for return is recorded for each. Most of the complaints are minor, usually faulty packaging, but they are kept on display as a warning that minor problems, if left untreated, can become major.

There are still two gates to pass through. The first, which resembles an airport metal detector, is an 'air shower'. As you pass under it, you are hit by a blast of compressed air that blows off any dust or dirt that may have accumulated on you in the hallway. The white suit, the guide explains, is not enough. Some hair might have fallen on your shoulder during the walk over. The air shower prevents it from going any farther. At the second gate, you are required to sterilize your hands by inserting them in a bowl of cleansing solution for 3–5 seconds, which is apparently enough to kill any bacteria that may be on them. These gates cleared, you are handed a disposable mask and a pair of gloves and led on to the production floor.

These same rigorous hygiene standards are adhered to throughout the operation. The room is divided into four blocks that correspond to the meal-preparation process: cooking, cutting, topping (arrangement in the box) and sorting. Because they use water, cooking and cutting are known as the 'wet zone', while topping and sorting are performed in what the factory calls the 'pink zone'. Workers are not allowed to travel between zones without changing their clothing and shoes. Should they leave the factory entirely, no matter how briefly, the only way to gain re-entrance is to return to the very first gate and go through the entire process all over again. Even the toilets are set up so that the entrances and exits are physically separated and the exit leads back to the first gate.

However thorough this may be in warding off bacteria, it cannot provide complete protection against dust, dirt or hair. The topping process is particularly vulnerable because there are a lot of people who work there, and there have been a few cases in which dust or hair has got into food. Those, however, are the unwanted exceptions. The company has reduced the possibility of even those kinds of accident occurring by completely shutting off topping from the other blocks and pressurizing the room from inside so that when the door is opened, dust and dirt are blown out rather than in. It is almost like a semiconductor clean room.

While I was touring the topping room, music started to play and the entire production line shut down. I thought it was break time, but I was wrong. Once an hour employees spend between 30 seconds and a minute using rollers to remove dust and dirt from each other's clothing. Then, just as quickly, they go back to their jobs, arranging the food with practised hands. However, all those hands are enclosed in vinyl gloves. Nobody is allowed to touch food with their bare hands for any reason.

My guide, Delica Ace president Takehiko Tomita, explains:

When they start work on a new variety of meal, our employees must get clean masks and gloves and spray their hands with alcohol to sterilize them. That way, we prevent the sauce from one kind of meal ending up in another, and keep odours from travelling too.

The topping zone alone goes through 9,000 pairs of gloves a day.

NEXT-TO-ZERO STOCK

Freshness and flavour being the key to selling boxed meals, how does Delica Ace maintain them while trying to service 182 stores?

One way is by not having a warehouse to store inventory in. All it has is a small refrigerator and freezer near the food delivery bay. I was under the impression that boxed meals use mostly frozen foods since they will keep longer, so I was certain there would be a huge freezer somewhere, but the opposite turned out to be true. It was only about 2 metres wide and maybe 4 or 5 metres long and there were just a few boxes inside it. It seemed far to small for 60,000 meals a day, but the lack of a large freezer is actually the reason why Delica Ace's meals are always fresh. It carries next-to-zero inventory. The factory tries to purchase only the materials it needs for that day. It is Toyota's 'just-in-time' deliveries and '*kanban*' production applied to food processing.

In actual practice, Delica Ace gets its vegetables once every 2 or 3 days, but it only keeps a day and a half's worth of meat and fish on hand though such products could be stored for much longer periods in the freezer. Each day, 3 tons of rice are delivered and cooked, following the traditional wisdom that rice tastes best just after it has been milled. It thaws frozen meat and fish a day in advance so as not to harm the flavour. From the refrigerator it goes to the kitchen, and from there to cutting where it is chopped into the right size for arranging into a meal. Inside the kitchen is a special machine for frying salmon (a popular boxed meal in Japan), two large fryers for deep-fried dishes and a *yakisoba* noodle grill. There are two key points in the process: seasoning and temperature control.

Seasoning, obviously, depends on how the spices are mixed. Since inconsistency cannot be tolerated, it is all computer-controlled. Once order volumes and meal types are input, the computer automatically works out, for example, how much soy sauce and sugar are needed to prepare the boiled beef topping for the *gyudon*. As long as those volumes are used, the flavour remains constant.

The key player in temperature control is the vacuum cooler, which immediately cools food down to 20 °C. This temperature is not arbitrary. Research shows that it is just right for inhibiting bacterial growth while still retaining flavour. Anything warmer and hygiene would start to be a problem, anything colder and the food would not taste as good. 'We've found that 20 °C is the dividing line,' Tomita says. Strict temperature controls are also used in cooking the rice which, like the main dishes, is vacuum-cooled to 20 °C before being sent to the topping room.

In fact, food is maintained at 20 °C throughout the remainder of the process, from topping through sorting and delivery to the store shelves. All phases are equipped to hold a constant 20 °C temperature.

One of the things Seven-Eleven meals are known for is their rice, which is a 50–50 blend of Sasanishiki and Koshihikari, two popular varieties. Thanks to the just-in-time system, it is never more than 2 days out of the mill. Tomita boasts:

When you mill rice, it oxidizes, which harms the flavour. That's why our factory uses rice that has been ground within the last 2 days. It's the secret behind Seven-Eleven's meals. Compare that with what you get at home. Even if you buy the best rice in the supermarket, it takes at least 2 weeks to work its way through the distribution chain and finally arrive on the shelves. It's a minimum of 2 weeks old, then, just to start with. And you don't eat the whole bag at once, either. It may take you another 10 days or so to go through it, with more oxidation on the way. Here at our factory, it's never more than 2 days old.

Computers control the rice cooking as well. Cookers are brought under the silo, and the required amount of rice is inserted and washed. If something other than plain rice is required – *sekihan, onigiri or fukikomi-gohan* – the seasonings and other ingredients are mixed in. As with the main dishes, all the proportions are calculated by computer and the mixing is entirely automatic. The cookers move along a line to the cooking process, where they enter a 7- or 8-metre-long gas-heated tunnel. Twenty minutes later when they emerge from the other end, they are done and ready to move on to the settling process, which again takes about 20 minutes. The settling line twists around a number of times. Delica Ace explains that it uses the distance to ensure that enough time is given for settling in spite of cramped factory conditions. Only after it has passed through the line is the rice moved to a special rack to be cooled to 20 °C and sent on to the topping room. The entire process requires about an hour and is all managed by one person, a level of automation that rivals anything in the manufacturing sector.

The busiest place in the factory is the topping room. The operation is divided into four lines: *onigiri* (rice balls), sandwiches, boxed meals and *yakisoba* noodles. Most of the workers are women who, if they are working on boxed meals, are responsible for filling the containers with rice and accompaniments and wrapping everything up. The automation resembles a car factory; the line moves at a speed of 600–800 metres a minute. It is so fast that it often appears to new employees as if it were moving backwards, but the workers are surprisingly skilled at keeping up with it. Each wears a coloured ribbon to identify her experience and position, orange for general leaders, green for leaders, pale blue for sub-leaders and yellow for beginners. You will occasionally see general leaders helping slow beginners keep up. While this is going on, over on the *onigiri* line they are producing about 2,400 rice balls an hour.

Once finished, meals are put on racks and carried to the sorting area, where the computer takes over. It used to be that sorting had to be done by hand, with people checking order invoices from each store and filling their boxes accordingly. But that is a thing of the past. Today it is all done with scanners and bar codes. Each store has its own allotted space, next to which a display is mounted. Should a scanner pick up the bar code for 'ham sandwich', for instance, the displays will immediately flash how many their stores have ordered. Delivery people merely pull off the required numbers and put them in the box. Once the order has been filled, the 'finish' button is pushed and the computer checks for accuracy. Should something have been left out, the terminal flashes a message that 'you haven't finished with _____ yet'. Since introducing the system, Delica Ace says it has been able to eliminate mistakes in deliveries while seeing a tremendous boost in work efficiency as well.

THREE DELIVERIES A DAY
Seven-Eleven Japan began having its meals delivered three times a day in 1987. It was the first in the industry to do so and there is a complex distribution system that makes it possible. Distribution systems have been among Seven-Eleven's top priorities since it was founded. The company define their purpose as being 'to deliver to franchises on a regular basis the items they ordered accurately and with sufficient quality control'.

Having decided to go for freshness and flavour in its meals, it has developed a system that allows high-frequency deliveries while segregating items according to temperature ranges. It tries to make sure deliveries happen at set times that coincide with peak demand. Traffic jams, however, can get in the way. When the roads are clogged and lorries are unable to get through, the company turns to motorcycles, helicopters, aeroplanes and ships to make sure products are on time, all costs for the emergency measures borne by headquarters. It also tries to neutralize the impact of traffic conditions by reducing the distance its trucks must travel. Its distribution centres, which are usually only medium-sized, are designed for efficient delivery to a limited, predefined area. These smaller centres, it says, spread the risks around and have lower operating costs. Seven-Eleven has 117 in operation.

It used to be that merchandise was stocked three times before it reached the stores, once at the manufacturer's factory, again at the manufacturer's warehouse and finally at the Seven-Eleven distribution centre. Now the company can place orders with manufacturers in the morning and have the products manufactured that afternoon to be put on its national delivery network and brought to distribution centres during the night. Snack foods, for example, are delivered to stores twice a week, so under this system customers are assured that the potato crisps they buy are no more than 6 days old.

The effects of the system have been obvious and visible. In 1974, there were about eighty vendors per store with an average of seventy deliveries a week. When it inaugurated the joint distribution network in 1976, orders for seventeen companies could be placed with a single phone call and products were delivered together as well. That alone brought the average number of vendors per store down to fifty-three, and delivery lorries to forty-two. Today, delivery lorries are down to ten.

Even so, it was still not easy to put the three-deliveries-a-day system into practice. Adding the extra delivery meant forcing factories to stay open 24 hours a day, among other things. But the deli line is one of the mainstays of convenience stores. The focal point of competition in the industry is boxed meals. But until Seven-Eleven added the extra delivery, supplies were not prompt enough to maintain quality. Convenience store meals had a reputation for being 'bad', 'cold' and 'expensive'. Getting fresh food on the shelves three times a day, morning, noon and night, has erased that blotch.

Let's look at what the system means for production and delivery. Morning deliveries will have meals to stores between about 5.00 and 8.00. To make that happen, the factory has to begin work on them at about 1.00 the previous afternoon. The rice is cooked between then and 6.00, the main dishes between 6.00 and 9.00. From 9.00 until 2.00, is topping time. At about 2.00 a.m. the delivery centres begin their sorting work, loading the meals on to lorries so that they make it to the first store on their list by about 5.00 a.m. This is actually 'Delivery 2'. The first delivery occurs between midnight and 5.00 a.m., when evening snacks and breakfast food are brought by. (The food was cooked the day before, but is called 'Delivery 1' because it is delivered after midnight.)

Work on the food for Delivery 1 and Delivery 3 (dinners and evening snacks) proceeds simultaneously. The rice for Delivery 3 starts cooking at 11.00 in the evening while Delivery 2 is in the topping room. At about 4.00 the next morning the main dishes are cooked, with topping coming at 7.00, sorting at noon and delivery at 3.00 p.m., the same time topping starts for Delivery 1 of the next day. When Delivery 2 is reaching the first stores, at about 6.00 in the evening, Delivery 1 is in sorting, with the lorries scheduled to leave at 9.00 p.m. and arrive at their destinations around midnight. The factory stays open 24 hours a day to meet the three-delivery schedule. That, however, is to be expected. Most Seven-Elevens are open 24 hours a day round the year; it is only right that the factories work those hours too.

Orders are sent automatically by computer and follow an even tighter schedule. Orders for Delivery 3, the evening meals, must arrive no later than 10.30 that morning; orders for Delivery 1, which leaves the factory at 9.00 p.m., no later than 11.00 a.m.; orders for the morning shipment, Delivery 2, no later than noon. Everything, in short, must be decided during an hour and a half period in the morning.

Note, however, that the food for Delivery 3 has already entered the topping room by the time orders are due at 10.30. Likewise, cooking is almost ready to start when Delivery 1 orders come in at 11.00. The factory could not get the meals out on time if it waited until it had all the orders before it started, so it works on estimates, which will obviously have some discrepancies with the final numbers. Should orders exceed estimates, it rushes to make up the shortfall; if it overestimates, it takes a loss. The lost meals are disposed of because of quality concerns, so how well a factory can control its losses will have a large impact on profits.

Few realize that there is this level of computerization and sophistication behind the meals they pick up at their local store.

CLOSE TO THE PUBLIC

When Japan was playing catch up after World War II, its goal was clear. Growth. It imported models from Europe and North America, modified them to suit Japanese practice and established the 'Japanese-style production system' that has been one of its crowning achievements. But as growth gives way to maturity, this all-important system is finding itself at a dead-end. Faced with structural changes of historical magnitude, Japanese manufacturers seem unable to wean themselves from the catch-up, growth-at-all-costs mentality of previous decades. Seven-Eleven Japan has been one of the first to make the structural leaps required. Where manufacturers and big supermarkets tend to view the public as a homogeneous 'mass' to be satisfied with growth-era-style 'mass production' and 'mass consumption', Seven-Eleven has systematically analysed how public wants and needs change over the course of a day or a week, and has adapted splendidly to its findings. Those insights are its ultimate strengths.

Seven-Eleven's stores may be small and they may be limited to 3,000 items, but with a chain of 5,600 outlets, its sales of any one item are enormous. The company moves ¥253,321 million a year in fast food (boxed meals, sandwiches, salads), which makes it Japan's biggest fast food company. McDonald's, the industry leader, only generates ¥212,640 million. It also sells about ¥100 billion a year in books and magazines, which is more than Japan's largest bookshop chain, Kinokuniya. Estimates say Seven-Eleven is probably Japan's top retailer of soft drinks (920 million bottles and cans), batteries (56 million) and tights (20 million) too. Needless to say, this was only possible because of the itemized control system, which for Seven-Eleven functions much like 'pin-point attacks' did for the allies in the Gulf War.

Itemized control is also what gives Seven-Eleven Japan an efficiency that none of its competitors has come close to matching. It now averages sales of ¥680,000 per day per store, for an annual turnover of ¥250 million per store. The number two chain, Daiei's Lawson convenience stores, only averages ¥450,000 and ¥164 million respectively. Neighbourhood off-licences, which are among the prime candidates for conversion into convenience stores, only generate ¥59 million a year on average.

Building on its success with Southland, Seven-Eleven Japan is eying an Asia-based global chain. It is more than just a pipe dream. The Japanese-style convenience store system has the potential to take the world by storm. However, Suzuki demurs:

> We're not considering ventures in any other country but the United States. Whatever happens will happen.

I've never been good at developing long-term plans. I think it's a waste of time even thinking about them. Economists love to forecast exchange rates and economic indexes, but they rarely ever get it right. What's the point in developing a long-term plan based on forecasts that aren't going to come true? . . . Wherever we go, we stay close to the public. If you know what the public needs, it doesn't matter where you go in the world, it's all the same.

That is a managerial philosophy worthy of a global company in the twenty-first century.

CHAPTER 5

Creating Knowledge: Nintendo

IT ALL STARTED WITH DISNEYLAND

The Japanese are not known for their ability to have fun. If you were to ask them what they do on their days off, most would probably say they 'lie around the house' or 'watch TV'.

It was only in the eighties that the Japanese began to be interested in fun and leisure at all. During the high-growth period, work was the principle virtue and having fun was considered something of a vice or at least a very low priority. After the country began to achieve a measure of affluence in the late seventies and eighties, however, people began to be interested in entertainment, and just as in times past they imported manufacturing expertise from Europe and North America, the unplayful Japanese bought their fun from outside too. That was what the opening of Tokyo Disneyland in 1983 was all about – the wholesale importation of a Western theme park. The Magic Kingdom is a piece of entertainment culture that works anywhere in the world and its overwhelming popularity in Japan not only changed how people thought about fun, it turned the entire leisure industry on its ear. The 'Disney look', with its beautiful, spacious environments and pleasant sense of playfulness, represents a codified formula for producing a world that is delightfully out of the ordinary. The park's opening signalled a new genesis for entertainment in Japan. It was the beginning of the end for crowded, cramped suburban amusement parks as new Disney-esque theme parks sprang up across the country.

There is another reason for calling 1983 a new genesis for entertainment. By strange coincidence it was also the year that Nintendo launched the first of its 'family computer' video game systems, another global hit, and one that was particularly important because so little in the way of cultural information flows from Japan to the outside world, especially in leisure and entertainment areas. In the past, virtually the only 'fun' product that Japan could claim any worldwide recognition for was its animated films. Nintendo's video games changed that. They have been a smash-hit all around the world, including Europe and North America.

Over the past decade, the company has sold 18 million of its 'family computers', as the machines are known in the domestic market, and 41.75 million of its 'Nintendo Entertainment Systems' overseas. The 'super family computer' launched in 1990 has sold 7.39 million in Japan, and its corresponding international version, the 'Super Nintendo Entertainment System', 11.46 million overseas. These numbers depict an overwhelming success in foreign markets, especially when it is recalled that the Nintendo Entertainment System was only launched in the USA in 1986, 3 years after Japan, and the Super Nintendo Entertainment System only came on American markets in 1991, a year after Japan. Foreign markets, and especially the USA, have been instrumental in Nintendo's success. It is said that 'fun knows no borders' and that has been the case for Nintendo's game machines. They are entertainment that is recognized and loved the world over, indeed the first such entertainment product that has been accepted on a global scale since Disneyland itself. It is no exaggeration to say that the

Nintendo Entertainment System has become Japan's largest cultural export.

RETURN ON EQUITY

Nintendo is located in Southeastern Kyoto, about 10 minutes by car from the *shinkansen* stop, right next to the Toba Kaido station on the Keihan Honsen railway line. The five buildings that house its offices and factory are frankly unimpressive. None are more than two or three storeys high. It so much resembles a clutch of small urban factories, one would hardly guess that this was a company that during the year to March 1993 turned in current profits of ¥163.8 billion on sales of ¥562.8 billion, third in Japan only to Toyota Motor and NTT and outdoing even the giant consumer electronics concern Matsushita Electric Industrial. The sharp appreciation of the yen and the maturation of the domestic market cut into results in 1994 – only ¥121.0 billion in current profits on ¥467.0 billion in sales – but this group of grimy factory buildings remains one of the bluest of Japan's blue-chips.

Nintendo employs only 943 people, giving it easily more than ¥100 million per employee per year in current profits. One look at its return on equity is enough to convince anyone of what a gold mine this company is. In the past, it was common for Japanese firms to have about a 15 per cent return on equity, but in the eighties they dipped below 10 per cent and more recently returns have dropped to 3.84 per cent at Toyota and only 1.97 per cent at Matsushita Electric Industrial. Neither of those companies are exceptions, either. Most listed firms in Japan are now unable to produce more than about 3 per cent return on equity. Nintendo, by contrast, is at 27.0 per cent. With less than 1,000 employees, it not only rubs shoulders with the giants of Japanese industry, it stands above them. Its efficiency and profitability are unparalleled.

The company traces its roots to 1889 when Fusajiro Yamauchi, great grandfather of current president Hiroshi

Yamauchi, began to manufacture *hanafuda* playing cards in Kyoto. In 1907, Yamauchi's firm became the first in Japan to manufacture Western-style playing cards and that was pretty much its niche until Hiroshi, who had not yet completed his undergraduate studies at Waseda, was installed as its third president in 1949. Forced to take over the reins at 22 because of the untimely death of his grandfather, Sekiryo, the young president learned how to manage by a process of trial and error. Wanting more stability for his company, he began a diversification programme that led Nintendo far afield. Among his many ventures were 'instant rice' (just add hot water), 'Disney *furikake*' (mixes of dried fish, herbs and spices used to flavour rice – Nintendo included Disney characters on its packages) and a taxi company. The Disney *furikake* was actually something of a hit, but Nintendo was unable to capitalize on it because it had no distribution channels in the food industry. All through the fifties, Yamauchi was just another small businessman, hardly a likely candidate for an article in *Fortune* or inclusion in the ranks of the world's great industrialists.

There were three keys to Nintendo's success. First, it was able to create new demand. Second, it emphasized 'software values'. And third, it developed a highly profitable business system.

The term 'software values' deserves some explanation. For our purposes, 'software' does not refer to programmes that run on computers but to the opposite of 'hardware' or 'physical goods'. It is something more akin to knowledge and insight. If we assume that products have both visible and invisible components, software is the invisible, the added services, rather than the tangible goods.

Japanese companies have tended to favour growth over profitability. Management has been quantity-oriented, with greater market share the ultimate goal. This overwhelming concern with raw sales and share is what is behind the decline in return on equity. It encouraged companies to raise money with cheap equity financing and use it to expand capacity or gamble on the financial markets.

This will of necessity be changing. Now that the bubble has burst and continuous growth can no longer be taken for granted, management that is focused solely on share expansion no longer works. In the past, low-profit, high-volume businesses were able to survive because economic growth would provide enough of a boost in sales volumes to keep them above water, but today volumes are either not growing or not growing very much, so companies will per force have to emphasis profitability. In short, managers will need to do an about-face in their thinking, changing their goal from growth to returns. Nintendo, with its high return on equity, is thus something of a model for the post-bubble Japanese company. The keys to its success – creation of new demand, emphasis on software values, and highly profitable business systems – are the exact opposite of what most Japanese companies have been doing. Rather than create new demand, Japanese firms are more comfortable in 'me-too' markets in which everyone produces more or less the same products. Indeed, the resulting overcompetition has been the source of much of their vitality. Likewise, software values have never been a Japanese strong point – we have always concentrated on producing tangible goods. And we need not further emphasize our satisfaction with low-profit businesses. It is because of this that the Nintendo strategy stands out and provides an example of what our country must do in order to regain its strength.

THE IDEA OF THE GAME MACHINE

The days of being able to sell anything one churned out are over. Product cycles are growing shorter. Business is tough.

But not in video games. The popularity of game machines shows no sign of waning, and this is because their appearance did not try to poach on someone else's territory, it created new demand. Nintendo successfully pioneered a new market.

The roots of the family computer/Nintendo Entertainment System go back to 1976, when Rockwell Fairchild and Atari launched microprocessor-based video games on the US market. Similar games began appearing in Japan about that time too. Between 1977 and 1979, Nintendo launched such products as the 'Colour Television 6', 'Colour Television 15', 'Colour Television 112' and 'Block Toppler 6'. By the late seventies, colour televisions had already reached a 95 per cent penetration rate in Japan and people were looking for other forms of entertainment. Unfortunately, microprocessors were still not widely used and there was no separation of hardware and software so both the game and the tools for playing it had to come in a single package. No wonder it took more than a year to plan, design and market new products.

The first hit in this area came in 1980 when Nintendo launched its 'Game and Watch', a machine that could play different games when new cards were inserted into it. It was the first successful 4-bit microprocessor game machine to come on the market. The success did not last long, however. Roughly 2 years later, in June 1982, competitors began to sell copycat products that cut into Nintendo's share and the market itself eventually dried up. As we shall see, the reason for decline was in the software.

As Nintendo began to search for something to replace 'Game and Watch,' it started to become interested in the old home video games, says Masayuki Uemura, the head of Nintendo's Second Development Department and the father of the Nintendo Entertainment System. Uemura's team had four key concepts that it focused on in designing the games: 1) the machines must be priced so that anybody can buy them; 2) they must allow character designers full scope for creativity; 3) they must create expressive images; and 4) they must be able to be operated while looking at a television screen. These four concepts laid the groundwork for a new market. Let's look at them more closely.

The first, affordable pricing, recognizes that video games are after all toys and should not be priced out of that market. There are several reasons why game machines have been hits, and pricing is one of the chief among them. As the Japanese name, 'family computer', shows, the designers had the family market in mind. The product had to be priced so that parents would buy it. No matter how great the games, if mothers thought they were too expensive the machine would never take off. Nintendo therefore aimed for prices that children themselves could afford or at least would be able to convince their parents to lay out. And as Uemura says, 'If you just want to build something fun, there are limitless ways to do so and no bounds at all to the ultimate price.'

At the heart of the Nintendo Entertainment System are two custom large-scale integrations (LSIs), a central processing unit (CPU) and a picture processing unit. The most effective way to hold down prices is to reign in LSI costs. For Yamauchi, this involved the gamble of a lifetime. With no guarantee that his machines would sell, he had to bluff his way to lower prices, giving Ricoh an order for 3 million chips over the space of 2 years as a ploy to negotiate lower costs. Even if he had no intention of following through on the order, it was a bold gamble anyway.

Nintendo found itself in high-risk/high-return territory at a time when most Japanese manufacturers, believing that growth would continue forever, were content with low-risk/low-return businesses. Where the normal Japanese manager concentrates on surveys, studies and analysis, Yamauchi is a lone risk-taker. Perhaps because of his long years producing playing cards, he is the rare Japanese manager who has the courage to go for broke, and his company is one of the few that has enough entrepreneurial backbone not to be scared off by risks.

The second and third concepts have more to do with the basics of the games themselves. The innovation that video games brought was the ability to play in a visual world, and ever since the machines became popular, the fate of game software has hinged on its visual appeal. Games have to be able to interest both the person playing them and the people watching from the sidelines. Video games have an element of both solitaire and group activities about them. Even if you are locked in your room playing them by yourself, in the back of your mind there is always a gallery of friends and competitors watching you. This is especially the case for children. At first glance it may look as if video games close them off to the outside world, but in reality they are an important medium of communication. That is why it was vital that the designers be able to add depth to their visuals. They had to be expressive, so that both the players and the gallery could have fun.

The characters themselves also needed to be vivid and personal. Their expressions as they played different roles made it easier for users to transfer their own emotions to them. In the case of 'Super Mario Brothers', Mario is the perfect character for the kind of jumping that is involved, but in order for such characters to be possible, the designers had to have enough room to give them personality and appeal. That, of course, required higher-performance machines.

The fourth concept, being able to play the game while looking at a television screen, is fairly self-explanatory. The world of video games exists within the TV screen and that is where players' eyes are focused. The control had to be designed so that it could be operated while watching the screen, so simple that one did not need to look at it. Uemura recalls:

In the beginning, we wanted to add all sorts of bells and whistles to our game machines, but we realized that in Japan, anyway, most people would probably be lying on the floor or snuggled up inside the *kotatsu* (foot warmer with a quilt over it) when they played, not sitting in front of a solid, stable desk. 'Game and

Watch' was a hit because you could play it in any position, and we decided to adopt that same form for the Nintendo Entertainment System and Super Nintendo Entertainment System.

Failing any one of these four concepts, the Nintendo Entertainment System would never have become a super hit. Uemura says:

From a technical standpoint, semiconductors made it pretty easy to create the kind of fun games that people wanted. What happened was that we were able to successfully transfer chip-based systems into the world of toys. Were it not for computer chips, game machines would never have happened.

Video games create an unlimited field of play inside a television screen. They, and the computers that run them, were thus successful in producing an entertainment space that had never before existed. They created an entirely new market.

In the good old days, Japanese children had fields and meadows they could run around in, but nowhere in our cities today will you find such places. As a consequence of development, our children can no longer roam freely. Nor is it just children who have been robbed of their play spaces. Adults have lost them too. Trying to get away from the city for a weekend of fishing, travel or camping is a daunting task. In the first place, you have to persuade your boss to give you the time off, and even in the unlikely event of his doing so, you are faced with traffic jams or crowded trains both ways. It is no longer a simple matter for people to 'play' with nature, and the more distant and farther-removed it becomes, the more need there is for new 'natural environments'. Game machines and their computer chips give immediate access to unlimited 'meadows', a new 'nature'.

In hindsight, the Nintendo Entertainment System was the

epitome of the eighties' design goal of developing goods that were 'light, thin, short and compact'. They were also one of the first products to make the transition from hardware-orientation to software-orientation. Nintendo's creation of a new entertainment market had great social significance as well. The 'family computer' was the first computer to have mass-market appeal and helped popularize computers in general. Indeed, in the process of applying high technology to mass-market entertainment, it redrew much of the industrial map.

THE WORLD'S LARGEST SUPPLIER OF GAMES
Its game machines turned it into a growth company, but when you ask president Yamauchi why they were such a hit, all you get is a modest 'we were lucky'. He claims he had no idea the Nintendo Entertainment System would be such a runaway bestseller, but I beg to differ. Nintendo's success was no accident. It was a direct result of the company's decision to favour software over hardware. And that brings us back to software values.

Most other manufacturers of video games are oriented towards hardware. It is the machine itself that is the focus of their strategy. Right from the beginning, however, Yamauchi was aware of the latent value of the game software and that is where he placed his priorities. Rather than machines, he decided to specialize in software development, and he devoted his business resources to that end.

Video games are computers. They run on LSIs. The Super Nintendo Entertainment System, for example, contains a 16-bit CPU and six other custom chips. With almost 2 million sold around the world every year, the number of semi-conductors involved is enormous. In spite of this, Nintendo has never tried to produce its own chips. It did not want to invest the capital required to do so. In spite of being a ¥500-billion company, its capital outlays for the past several years have been no more than about ¥10 billion.

It also farms out production of its game machines and software. The company does have a factory in Uji, Kyoto, but it is only used for quality inspections. Most of the hardware and all of the software is assembled by subcontractors. Nintendo itself is a factory-less company. It has no production capacity of its own. Asked why this is so, Yamauchi explains, 'Entertainment products are not necessities. You're heading for trouble if you start building your own factories and engaging in your own manufacturing just because there is demand.'

Because it does not have any production capacity, Nintendo is able to devote its resources to software development. Its foresight in recognizing the importance of software values is similar to that of Apple Computer or Microsoft and certainly one of the reasons behind its success. The validity of the strategy needs no other proof than the fact that Nintendo is now the world's largest supplier of game software.

'Super Mario Brothers', a game developed in-house at Nintendo, has sold about 6.2 million copies, which means you will find it on roughly 34 per cent of the 18 million Nintendo Entertainment Systems that have been sold so far. That works out at about one in three Nintendo owners having the game. At about 4 million copies each, other in-house titles such as 'Dragon Quest 3' and 'Super Mario 3' are on 22 per cent of the company's machines. All together, Nintendo titles account for 20–30 per cent of the game software market; the company claims a 57 per cent ratio of software to hardware sold, which means that over half the people who bought Nintendo machines also bought Nintendo games.

Results are similar in the US, where the best-selling Nintendo Entertainment System game is 'Super Mario 3' at 15 million copies. The game is so popular it even became a movie. Roughly one out of every four Nintendo game machines in the country has it. Other popular Nintendo titles in the US are 'Legend of Zelda' at 5 million and 'Tetris' at 4 million. As in Japan, the ratio of Nintendo software to Nintendo hardware is about 60 per cent, so the company is justified in staking its claim to being the world's largest supplier of games.

Hiroshi Imanishi, head of Nintendo's Administration Department, muses:

> A long time ago, we had a lot of success selling Disney trump cards. All we did was add Disney characters to regular playing cards and sales started to go through the roof. I think that experience was where Yamauchi learned how much value there is in information.

In one way, the playing cards that Nintendo used to produce are just another kind of game 'software'. The cards themselves, being made out of paper, are hardware, but they can be used for any number of different games depending on what you do with them – the 'software' you put in. By contrast, most toys are just hardware. You have to have a bicycle to go bike-riding and a swing to go swinging. But by the same token, if you have good 'hardware', then children can use it to create any number of new games.

What children look for in video games is entertainment and fun. They want to see new worlds and experience new thrills. The appeal of video games is not in the hardware, but in the software.

Yamauchi relates some of his ideas about software:

> If somebody goes to the store to buy 'Super Mario' and it's sold out, do you think they buy something else? Do you think they'll go for another game if it's cheaper? Absolutely not. They'll wait until the next delivery of 'Super Mario' arrives. What about if you're out looking for beer? If they don't have your favourite brand, you'll probably be willing to make do with something else.

That's not the way it works for game software. People know what they want to buy before they ever leave the house. It doesn't matter how wide a selection you have or how cheap other games are, they aren't going to buy unless you have the game they want. If you turn that around what you find is that you can sell all of the software you want as long as it's interesting. And that translates into growth for your hardware too. That's why you have to emphasize the development of unique, creative software.

According to Yamauchi, software that does not sell does not sell at all, while popular titles offer almost limitless returns. Obviously, rather than producing a hundred flops, it is better to spend the time and money to turn out one hit.

'When you're making game software, you have to aim for the top. If it's not going to be among the best twenty, you're better off not doing it at all. We're very demanding in that way,' says Shigeru Miyamoto, head of the Second Information Department of Nintendo's Information Development Section and the man who was in charge of developing 'Super Mario Brothers', a game that has sold more than 60 million copies and delighted the entire world.

The ability to supply new ways to play at the right time is what being a toy maker is all about. When people find a new way to have fun, they start off forgetting about everything else, but that enthusiasm eventually wanes and they begin looking around for something new. If you aim for the moment at which interest subsides to provide them with their next bit of fun, then you are all set. In other words, being a toy maker means being able to think at all times from the user's perspective. This is just as true for video games as for any other toy. Trying to decide whether a piece of software is really fun means having to think from the consumer's perspective using the consumer's logic. Generally, game software has a life of about half a year.

If title A is a hit, then 6 months from now you will need to have a new hit title B ready. According to Yamauchi, those are the kind of marketing plans that game machine makers have to have.

> Video games are far more dynamic than conventional forms of entertainment. I don't think this market will ever disappear, but that is conditional on our ability to develop software – one title every 2 or 3 months that will provide users around the world with creative fun, with enjoyment, and at times with some emotional impact as well. I don't care how many hundreds or thousands of titles there are out there, if they aren't fun, if they aren't interesting, the market will collapse and disappear.

Success in the video game business hinges on being able to produce a continuous supply of satisfying software.

> You don't want to eat the same food day in and day out. There are few people who can eat the same food and be aware of subtle differences in the way it was prepared. You have to change the seasonings or cook something else.

Yamauchi says that the game software market is unique in that you have 'one winner and lots of losers'. Unlike other markets, game software is not an area where differentiation and diversification will let everybody have a little slice. Only those companies that are able to develop unique, creative products will survive.

Needless to say, it is a fairly black and white decision for users. Software is either interesting or it is not. There is no middle ground. One of the reasons why Nintendo has been successful is that it has understood this and therefore pushed its software development almost to the extreme.

For Yamauchi, software is something of a religion, and his faith is apparent in Nintendo's strategy.

Nor has his faith waned today, as makers of game machines target multimedia for the home market and virtual reality for the commercial market. The competition to develop machines is intense, but Yamauchi is sceptical. He sees it as nothing more than a manifestation of manufacturers' preoccupation with gadgetry and hardware.

That preoccupation, Yamauchi argues, is the logic of suppliers, not consumers. Manufacturers try to push technology on their customers by showing all the 'great things it can do'. For suppliers, it is convenient to use the latest technology to add new functions. Doing so should enable software to provide new experiences and excitement that had not been possible before. But still, this is just supplier logic. During the bubble, all sorts of new products came out loaded with advanced technology and the latest bells and whistles, but they all flopped. They tried to do too much. They had too many functions. Nintendo's competitors, Sega Enterprises and NEC Home Electronics, have both released new CD-ROM machines that are more technically advanced than the Super Nintendo Entertainment System, but neither has necessarily been all that successful. Yamauchi would no doubt describe this as the 'failure of hardware-oriented thinking'.

Software-oriented thinking takes the opposite approach. It asks what kind of technology is needed to produce fun, exciting games. It develops the technologies that will enable hardware to run the kind of games developers want to make. The base point is software, not technology.

By fusing computers and toys, video games have placed themselves in much the same position as playing cards. The software is everything. The value of the machine is determined by the fun to be had from the game you load in. It has no intrinsic value of its own. Since he spent decades producing playing cards, this sort of thinking may have come naturally to Yamauchi. In any regard, by enabling his company to base its products on consumer logic it was one of the keys to Nintendo's global success.

WHAT MAKES FOR A FUN GAME?

The mere awareness of software values does not ensure that you will be able to knock together interesting games. What makes software development so difficult is that, unlike hardware, there is nothing in front of you that you can see. Imanishi explains:

> It's hard to express just how difficult it is to create game software. You have a scenario that you've decided on, and your job is to provide as much fun as possible within those constraints. The difficult part, though, is that you have to do so without making the scenario too obvious.

Just what is it that makes a game such fun that you become absorbed in it? Some might say it is the shivers that go up and down your spine, the fear of falling into a trap or the thrill to be had from winning. Its also important that the game be paced correctly, that it match the tempo of the player's breathing. A good part of the explosive popularity of 'Dragon Quest' was its tempo. Music is another important factor. The proper environment must be maintained if players are to spend hours on a game. Games like *Go* and chess are interesting for the logic they require. For video games, tempo and rhythm are the appeal. The pace of the game, the rhythm of the music, the movement on the screen and the breathing of the player must all match. Games have to provide a 'livable' world to enter. Miyamoto explains:

> The best thing is to create a kind of livability that makes people want to go back. Everyone wants to be in a pleasant environment. One of the reasons why kids

drop their books and immediately head for the game machine when they come home from school is that the game provides them with an enjoyable, livable world. The music and tempo are likable; you feel what fun the game is with your entire body.

Take the music. There are some rhythms and tempos that are so pleasant they make you want to return to the womb. If you experience that, then while you're at school or at work, you will want to return to that world. The game already starts from the moment you think, 'I want to play that again when I get home'. It's exactly the same for golf or fishing. Part of the fun is preparing for your golf match the week before and thinking through a strategy in your head. If a game has the kind of livability that makes kids want to play it as soon as they get home, it is a sure-fire hit. Creating it is the hard part.

Perhaps it is something like being a child and reading the same storybook over and over again. Every day, without ever getting tired of it, you open to 'Momotaro' (the 'Peach Boy') and read about how he leads a pheasant, monkey and dog to thwart the demons. Finally, you get to the part where the demons invade the island. Your pulse races. Your palms are sweaty. . . . It is the same characters, the same plot, the same ending every time, but children still feel fresh excitement at each turn of the page. The question is, why?

Perhaps it is because while they are reading the same old Momotaro children are actually creating a different story in their minds. No doubt they see themselves as Momotaro going out to battle against the demons, but their image of the demons may change or it may be a different island that is attacked. One time it might be a lonely island in the middle of the South Pacific; the next, a space station on the edge of the universe. The story does not concern past events; it is transformed into something that is happening in the here and now. Children play among the images that they create and use those images to build their own world. This is a 'software' world and that world is why children become so enthralled in video games.

'Mario' lets children play in a world of images. They embark on a quest to rescue the Peach Princess from the castle, kicking turtles along the way and creating their own world out of the adventure. Children's play is always repetitious, but the process of repetition enables them to build new worlds. What the game software does is to renew those images and give them tangible form. Though children play the same game, they want to try this next, and that later. Good software is software that has this sort of expansiveness.

Games provide children with a means of self-expression. They are not sitting in front of the Nintendo just because they want to play a game. Superficially the objectives of 'Mario' may be to kick turtles, eat mushrooms and topple blocks, but the purpose of the players is to 'find a new hole and explore underground' or 'learn a new trick'. That sense of discovery, of exploring new worlds, is what draws them back.

Novelty is another requirement for fun software. It must provide something different, but difference alone is not enough. It must be *interestingly* different. 'Interesting' in this case is defined as something that you can play for several hours or something that has an intriguing theme. Things like golf and tennis pass that test automatically since they are of proven interest, but there needs to be something else as well. Comments Miyamoto:

> One barometer of how interesting a game is is whether you, as a developer, are aware of being involved in something that has never been seen before, whether you're able to lose yourself in that sense of newness. That's the whole point of development. For 'Mario' the questions were whether there was physical pleasure in bumping into things and how well we could express the

sensation of falling. When you watch children playing the game, you'll notice that they usually move their bodies along with it. When that happens, you know you've got a winner.

'Mario' was a million-seller because of three innovations. First, it was the first game in which the screen scrolled sideways. Second, it replaced distant, aerial long shots with a camera that was trained in on the main character. Finally, the character was dynamic, thrilling and flexible when he jumped, fell or leapt across something. By including these three elements, the developers used images to create a new 'game space', a new 'information space'.

Nintendo uses 'monitor checking' to determine if its games are fun. People from outside the development team play the game and give their opinions. Testing is repeated until these players are satisfied. Once their approval has been given, the sales department has a crack at it. If the game passes their tests, a prototype version is created and handed over to an evaluation committee (the 'Mario Club') made up of Nintendo staff members and outside recruits. The maximum a game can get is forty points. If the Mario Club gives it anything less than thirty, it goes back for reworking or is scrapped altogether. Behind the rigorous checking process is Yamauchi's certainty that 'boring software will be the death of both Nintendo and the entire video game market'.

CREATIVE CORPORATE CULTURE

Fun games are not something that everyone can turn out. They require creativity, and not only on the part of the individual but on the part of the company itself.

In pursuing the efficiency required in this age of mass production and mass consumption, Japanese companies have favoured one-dimensional employees, the kind of people who could easily become cogs in the wheel. They had no use for oddballs and did everything they could to get rid of them. The necessary result of this has been to turn people into 'company men' with little personality of their own. Workers have been too dependent on their companies and companies have been too good to their workers. Especially in big companies, no one gets sacked. Everyone lives in company housing at ridiculously low rents. The company provides sumptuous leisure facilities and splendid funerals. As long as they belong to the company organization, workers are assured of generous protection and support. The company really is 'one big happy family'. Needless to say, this kind of closeness between companies and workers does not foster creativity.

Today, however, me-too management is being forced to give way to creativity, and for companies that means emphasizing individuals more than organizations, oddballs more than cooperators, and relaxation more than intensity. Only then will individual workers have the creativity that comes from independence, and obviously this requires organizations that are flexible enough to allow their people to be independent. Nintendo has achieved both requirements.

The company divides its research and development division into five sections: liquid crystal display (LCD) games ('Game and Watch', 'Game Boy'), video games, commercial amusements, software development, and hardware and mass production technology. The first three handle both hardware and software, but it is the fourth, the 'Information Development Section', that is responsible for most of the software development. The section is divided into two departments of about forty members each.

So far, this organizational chart does not look much different from organizational charts anywhere else, so where does all the creativity flow from? Despite its outward appearances of normality, Nintendo's organization is actually extremely flexible, and it is that that enables its employees to be creative.

NO MEDIUM OR LONG-TERM BUSINESS PLANS

For example, the company has no long-term business plan. Yamauchi explains:

> What game software requires is quality, not quantity. Any company that announces a 3-year plan for a five- or ten-fold boost in its software development force is just proving that it hasn't the slightest idea what the video game business is all about.

Medium- and long-term business plans are *de rigeur* in big Japanese companies. Long-term planning is, after all, what Japanese firms are supposed to be best at, unlike their near-sighted American rivals, and they do in fact place great importance on their medium- and long-term goals. Nintendo, however, will have no part of it. Comments Imanishi:

> I'm sure the president and directors have a vision of the company's future mapped out in their minds, but just as economic analysts are unable to tell where the economy is going, it's a waste of time and money to draw up business plans that you have no idea whether or not you're going to be able to fulfill.

Depending on your viewpoint, that makes for a very versatile attitude.

NO SIGNATURES, NO PLANNING DOCUMENTS

Nintendo does not believe in circulating approval forms for its development plans. In a normal company, before product development could begin you would first have to circulate an approval form and get everyone to sign it, then you would have to set a development deadline and a budget, and only then could you get to work. Nintendo does not require its developers to draw up approval forms. Unlike hardware, it says, software development does not lend itself to planning documents, market surveys, approval forms or decisions of the board. The only time top managers interfere in game software development is to set basic strategic directions. After that, everything is up to the people doing the development and they are given full discretion over what they do. Imanishi continues:

> Software developers have expertise and experience that you can't put into writing. That's what makes them confident in their own abilities. Requiring approval forms and planning documents only makes their work more complex and gives them a way to avoid taking responsibility for what they do. When there are no approval forms signed by top managers, all the responsibility comes back to the individuals involved, and when you personally have to take responsibility for your work, you can't be that cavalier about it. You work quickly and you work efficiently.

The main reason Nintendo eschews approval forms and planning documents is that it considers them a waste. Planning documents require that market surveys be conducted, the data analysed, the design concepts formalized, the investment expenditure, required development staff, development period and potential distribution volumes calculated and all of this brought together in a coherent proposal. But none of that labour will guarantee a hit product. The company's attitude would no doubt be different if sales of its products were directly dependent on the thickness of its planning documents, but they are not and Yamauchi sees no reason to waste valuable time doing meaningless work.

Speaking of waste, Nintendo also shuns another time-honoured practice at Japanese companies: quality control circles. Imanishi demurs, 'It's not that we don't engage in quality control activities, it's just that we go way beyond what they do in the normal course of our work'.

Quality control activities mean forming teams, submitting documentation and holding lots of meetings. That, according to Nintendo, is a waste of time. It may be helpful when you are turning out manufactured goods, but it is unnecessary if your job is to think up creative software.

What one can see throughout the Nintendo organization is a strong desire to eliminate bureaucracy in all its forms.

NO DEADLINES
Project teams are in charge of developing new software, but they are not given clear deadlines. Rather, they are allowed to spend as much time as they need to develop software that they are satisfied with. Some may doubt the cost performance of doing this, but Nintendo does not. Uemura says:

> If the development period is unnecessarily long, the people doing the project will get tired of it long before anyone else starts pestering them. When they get bored or frustrated, they abandon it on their own. Development periods are limited by the interest of the developers.

Project teams are given unlimited freedom, and that autonomy is the source of their creativity. Autonomy brings with it enough responsibility to keep Nintendo's development periods within reasonable bounds, generally 2 or 3 years.

GAME SOFTWARE AS ART
There is another reason why Nintendo does not impose deadlines on its developers. It would rather spend the time to produce an explosive hit than force a deadline and end up with software that does not sell. Investments are much more efficient that way. Behind this is Yamauchi's conviction that

'game software is art'. It does not matter how talented the developer may be or how long he has worked to polish the game, you never know if it will sell until you put it on the market. If it flops, all of your development costs and the time and efforts of your developers will have been for nothing. Even so, Nintendo is prepared to – indeed, insistent that it must – spend the time and money to come up with creative software. Yamauchi hates copycats. An anecdote should serve to illustrate the importance he places on individuality. When he was 50, he legally changed the character used to write his given name. The reason? When he looked through the telephone book, he found too many Hiroshi Yamauchis written with the same character as he had. That sort of obsession with individuality has gone a long way to setting the tone for the entire Nintendo organization.

RIGOROUSLY RATIONAL

Hiroshi Yamauchi is a rigorously rational individual. No matter what happens, he is not the kind of person to become bureaucratic. Nintendo has no company motto, no wise company sayings, no company song. Yamauchi is, after all, a rationalist. 'Company mottos, company sayings and all that stuff . . . I'd make them if they were required by law, but otherwise I see no reason to have things we don't need,' he laughs sarcastically. Yamauchi is not the type to hobnob with fellow industrialists either. Everyone has their own ideas and ways of living, he says, and criticizing him for not engaging in 'business community activities' as if everyone were somehow obliged to do so is itself rather specious. There arc forty-two listed companies located in Kyoto. Nintendo by itself generates more in current profits than the other forty-one combined. That translates into a lot of taxes. He says he was once gratified when someone told him, 'Mr Yamauchi, you're paying so much in taxes you've already done enough for society.' 'At last,' Yamauchi sighed, 'there's someone who understands.'

'It's hard for people in Japan to accept my way of living. It's not suited to this country,' he acknowledges, showing the backbone behind his rationalism. Nintendo celebrated its first centenary in 1989. Or rather, it did not. Ever the rationalist, Yamauchi planned no special events to mark the occasion. Though often depicted as an oddball or an eccentric, it is Yamauchi and his strong individuality that have made it possible for Nintendo's products to be as creative as they are.

CHARISMATIC LEADERSHIP

The sort of thoroughgoing rationalism that he practises gives Hiroshi Yamauchi an aura of charisma. Some might call him dictatorial, but it is the attraction of his charisma that has won his staff's obedience. They are confident when they follow Hiroshi Yamauchi that they will not be led astray. For his part, Yamauchi does not fawn over his employees. He is not the kind to visit offices and factories to pump employees up with pep talks and dreams of a rosy future. If anything, he is a rather faceless manager within the company. The only time he comes in contact with rank and file employees is at the annual New Year's meeting. Nonetheless, Yamauchi understands how to draw people to him, he knows quite dispassionately that results more than anything else are what gain you loyalty. Management, he says, does not consist of writing down your ideas and pinning them on the wall. Nor will rousing speeches do the trick. He has drawn a line between himself and the 'human feeling' that most Japanese try to portray, becoming the rare Japanese manager who insists on rationality above all else. At the risk of repetition, it is this unique management style that is the source of Nintendo's creativity.

THE POWER OF 'PLACE'

Japanese companies operate by placing employees in a set framework and closely controlling their actions. Factory floors are no place for misfits and malcontents, so management is necessarily strict. But the opposite holds true for software development. Strict control stifles creativity and results in boring products. Traditional Japanese management has no scope for hare-brained ideas, unexpected answers or ingenious concepts, but in order to successfully develop creative products you need both to encourage individual innovation and provide a way for new ideas to bear fruit. With their long history in manufacturing, that is something most Japanese firms find extremely hard to do.

CREATIVE PROJECT TEAMS

Game software is developed in 'project' form, but it is substantially different from the project formats used to develop other products or design, say, cars. The process begins by defining a framework for the software. 'There are lots of ideas for games, but few ever make it through planning and into production. They are selected according to rigorous standards.'

For example, developers might study market trends, determine what kinds of games were selling and use that to come up with a theme for their game. Once the theme is set, directors, designers and programmers are lined up, and they spend 6 months to a year working on the idea. Nintendo calls this the 'sketch' period. Only later is the basic design work done on the game and only if it looks as though it will take off is a formal project team organized. The director/producer is then placed in charge of developing the software.

The process actually bears a strong resemblance to film-making. Even the jobs resemble those of a film crew. The director develops an outline of how the game is supposed to run and checks on its progress. He has an assistant director to help out, a designer to handle the graphic content, a graphic designer to produce the actual computer drawings, a sound composer to do the music and a programmer to put it together. Most directors are in their thirties and come from design backgrounds, though there are some musicians who also direct. Teams may have anywhere from six to twenty members. The job of the designers, for instance, is to chart the overall content and develop time sheets describing how the images are to flow. For 'Mario' they made maps and topographical drawings showing where Mario was supposed to run from and to.

I talked to Miyamoto about how project teams are run:

Though there is a point at which logic fails to describe software design, you can't go at it without some sort of plan. That's the hard part. If you have even one person on your team who considers himself an 'artist', you're doomed, your teamwork falls apart. The key to successful software development is how well you can communicate with each other.

There are times when one of the members will think the software he has developed is wonderful, while everyone else finds it dull and boring. Miyamoto says:

It's always a problem. Once you make something, you lose the ability to look at it objectively. I'm constantly reminding my staff that 'aims are high but reality is low'. You have to have high aims, but reality may not always pan out that way. Maybe you know you're able to do something absolutely fantastic, but it doesn't turn out the way you thought it would. You have to be able to stand back and say, 'I know I'm capable of better, but that's the best I can write today'.

Game software has to be able to convince large numbers of people that it is fun and interesting, and it is important for members of the development team to keep in communication with each other so that they do not become self-satisfied. There must be an atmosphere of openness and freedom in which people are able to criticize each other frankly as they try to make the best products they can. In short, there must be good teamwork.

Many people labour under the misconception that great games are developed by a handful of geniuses. While it is true that many of the computer ventures attached to Apple or Microsoft earn their money thanks to a few technical wizards, that is not the case at Nintendo. It works as an organization and turns profits as a group. '[At Nintendo] you're not treated differently just because you happen to be the guy who did "Super Mario",' Imanishi says. For all its uniqueness, the company still retains the Japanese emphasis on teamwork.

NO WALLS
Nintendo emphasizes 'place' as a factor in maximizing teamwork. Organizations need locations, and the company has tried to implement several innovations to make them work more effectively. For instance, it has tried to eliminate walls. Hardware technicians and software designers all work in the same, very large, room. Imanishi explains:

> When you have hardware people and software people in the same room, it makes improvements easier. The software people can say, 'We'd really like this function' or 'Wouldn't it be great if we could do this?' and the hardware technicians can work on it. It fosters communication and saves development time.

Nintendo's 'big room' encourages employees to share information, which shortens development periods, eliminates waste and also adds more depth to its products. Discussions between the hardware and software sides can be stressful occasions, but the software people claim that that sort of stress is important to their work. They need to be able to transmit their stress directly to the hardware people, because there are some problems that just cannot be solved with software. The ensuing discussions lead to more innovations. Uemura says:

> Both sides talk to each other about the kind of products they'd like to build, and by providing a place for these discussions to occur, we've developed new software expertise. Criticisms are readily forthcoming and unexpected ideas often pop up. The 'power of place' is important in software.

Long discussions with other staff members enable software developers to expand on their ideas. Comments Miyamoto:

> For instance, as a team leader it's ideal if meetings just sort of happen before you're even aware of it. That's why we try to keep members of the same project team seated as close to each other as possible. Even if they are facing away from each other, we want them close enough to be able to talk. That way, meetings don't have to be painful, laborious affairs. We want people to keep smiling. We place a lot of emphasis on jokes – they're a great source of new ideas.

By eliminating distances, the 'big room' guarantees that information is shared, that cohesion is maintained and that talking is free and unfettered. Imanishi says:

> We call it the 'big room', but it's not as if we've got all this space with nice music playing in the background or any of the other things that are usually depicted as creative environments. We work in a regular, ordinary office. If anything, the 'location' grew up on its own and before we knew it, it became the right environment, provided the right energy, for making software.

THE COMPANY AS SPONSOR

Though it emphasizes creativity and individuality, Nintendo pays its people according to seniority. It still uses old-style wage scales rather than the newer divisions between 'base wages' and 'skill allowances'. The development, management and sales departments all have the same scales, too, and while there are slight differences in the pace at which people climb the ladder, there are no stars or prima donnas. Development of a million-selling game does not earn an employee any special wage treatment or any higher a position. In March 1994, Nintendo's average employee was 36.5 years old and made ¥357,917 a month. At Matsushita Electric Industrial, the average was 36.3 years old and made ¥386,562 a month, so Nintendo is not a particularly high-paying company. Still, the employees do not seem to be dissatisfied. Uemura explains:

> Making software requires a tremendous amount of labour and money and facilities. You could spend your whole life working on your own and still not be able to finish a single title, but if you work for Nintendo, we'll let you build game software until you're satisfied that you've done your best. That's something that you can't exchange for money. You can build what you want to, and if it's a hit, you can bask in the applause. That kind of satisfaction is everything.

In other words, Nintendo provides its employees with a system for self-realization. One of the most interesting things about Nintendo employees is that they view their company as a kind of sponsor. Imanishi muses:

> Our wages aren't especially good, but not many people leave. I guess you'd have to call it morale. People who build games are creators. I don't know if they really think of the company as their sponsor, but it certainly

feels that way. I think maybe they see Nintendo as a good sponsor.

The idea of the company as sponsor is something you will not find elsewhere in Japan. Yamauchi explains:

> The game business requires lots of different skills. You need programming talent, artistic talent, musical talent, scenario-writing talent. But talented people don't like to be hemmed in by organizations and rules. When they enter the framework of the company, they find their resources and talents stifled. But when all this started, Nintendo was still a small organization – and it was lucky that we were, too.

HIGH PROFITS

Behind Nintendo products is the 'Nintendo Business System' of licenced software production that is the secret of its consistent profitability.

The software for the Nintendo Entertainment System and other Nintendo games is produced by outside contractors that the company calls its 'software houses'. To develop games for Nintendo equipment, these firms have to sign licensing contracts that specify that the software house will let Nintendo mass-produce its creations, will buy all the cassettes produced and will pay Nintendo royalties as well as production costs. Critics of this system, and there are many, say that it is too good for the company since Nintendo makes money whether its hardware and software sell or not. Without this licensing system, however, it is doubtful whether the video game market would have flourished in the way that it has.

The reason is that Nintendo uses this system to exert control over the software produced for its machines. It sets limits on the number of titles software houses can launch in any one year and because production must be consigned to

Nintendo, the company is able to check software's compatibility with the hardware as well as its adherence to standards of good taste and morality. Nintendo inspectors will often erase women's nipples, improve games that have flopped or update older versions. Nintendo claims that this system has prevented the market from being flooded with inferior goods.

This strict practice stems from a number of bitter experiences, primarily the 'Atari Shock' in the United States. Atari's 4-bit TV games were a big hit when they were first released, but there was so much poor software produced for them that users became disillusioned and the market evaporated. Another experience closer to home comes from Nintendo's own 'Game and Watch' machine. It too was a hit, but it ended up spawning thirty different copycats that made the market so competitive that it collapsed. Imanishi recalls:

> They'd just make minor changes in the basic pattern of our product, but most of them were poor imitations and their designers had absolutely no concept of what software was all about. There were so many boring games out there that people stopped paying any attention to 'Game and Watch' at all.

Licensing provides a way to keep out inferior software and ensure that what does get to market is interesting. Imanishi explains:

> With personal computers, all you need is the hardware and you can build your own software, but with game machines you can't create software on your own. From the moment we launched the Nintendo Entertainment System we were obliged to provide software for it. There are over 100 million of our machines around the world and we have a duty to provide all of our users

with good games. If we let developers freeload on our hardware, we'd be so deluged with inferior products that we could no longer meet our obligations to our customers. The market would almost certainly collapse. We developed the licensing system because we care about the kind of software that runs on our machines.

CREATING KNOWLEDGE

Up to now, Japanese markets have been notable for having a lot of companies producing more or less the same products under conditions of fierce competition. This system is what has driven our economic development, and during the growth period, companies were satisfied with its results. The 'pie' kept growing, so all they had to do was understand what the market wanted and their own growth was assured. But when markets mature, the pie becomes limited and growth-oriented management becomes untenable. American economist Peter F. Drucker talks about the transition from a capitalist society to a knowledge society, a society in which knowledge is prized above all else. Unfortunately, knowledge cannot be churned out with the kind of mass production Japan has been so adept at up to this point. The managers of the future must be willing to take bold risks in creating new values (read 'knowledge'). Nintendo provides an example of the knowledge-oriented companies that tomorrow will require.

CHAPTER 6

The Drama of Globalization: Yaohan

GOING BOTH WAYS

Being poor in natural resources, Japan was quick to realize that its economic viability was tied to trade. Japanese firms have long been interested in foreign markets and have tended to look at their business from a global perspective. But that is not to say that their entire organizations have been geared towards exports. Rather, exports have traditionally only interested a few people in the export division or the international division, and among the top managers, the people charged with the international section of the business.

In fact, most Japanese companies have taken a rather passive attitude towards globalization. For instance, it is generally more efficient to manufacture products in Japan and export them to other markets, but import quotas and protectionism in other countries have forced companies to set up foreign operations. Many companies, in fact, have had to be dragged kicking and screaming to globalization by foreign pressure. Perhaps because of this, globalization in a Japanese context has been a one-way affair centred around Japan.

The attitude in most companies has been that foreign subsidiaries should do as they are told by the headquarters in Tokyo. They are neither asked nor expected to participate in or influence the decision-making process. Their role is to quietly follow orders and produce results. Part of the reason for this attitude is that foreign factories have on the whole been assembly operations, screwdriver plants that put together parts and raw materials shipped in from Japan. Local sourcing has been limited to simple materials and parts that have little impact on product performance and quality. Equipment, managerial methods and quality control methods are all supplied by the Japanese parent. Policy comes from the headquarters in Tokyo via locally stationed Japanese staff members. It is rare for local employees to have any part in its determination or transmission.

Foreign subsidiaries are often criticized, therefore, for being companies run by Japanese for the benefit of the Japanese parent. But not always. There is at least one company that has gone beyond this one-way globalization: Yaohan, an international distribution group that sees globalization as a two-way street.

By any measure, Yaohan is a global company. Its headquarters is located in Hong Kong and it operates in seventeen countries, mostly in Asia. Its group comprises a total of ninety-three companies, thirty-eight in Japan and fifty-five in other countries. In fiscal 1992, the group announced total sales of ¥338.5 billion, of which ¥193.4 billion came from Japan and ¥145.1 billion from overseas. It operates a total of 420 stores, 220 within Japan and 200 outside. This gives it a total of 773,638 square metres of selling space, 361,638 in Japan and 412,000 in other countries. Its staff of 20,600 is made up of 6,200 Japanese and 14,400 non-Japanese. It estimates that a total of 1.1 billion people visit its stores each year.

The most striking thing about Yaohan may be the decision it made to transfer its headquarters from Japan to Hong

Kong. Up until now, Japanese parents have controlled foreign subsidiaries, never the other way around. By moving its headquarters overseas, Yaohan broke with the normal Japanese pattern of globalization and took a major step forward on the road to becoming a truly international company. In this chapter, we will look at how the company was able to break through into uncharted territory and, more importantly, how it was able to be successful in the process.

I am of the opinion that companies need to have their own 'story', their own element of drama. And I think that is the case now, more than ever, when growth is low and goals tend to be lost sight of. If a company has its own story, people will rally round it, taking active part in the drama they see unfolding around them, orienting themselves in the same direction, and boosting the 'voltage' that the company has to draw upon. Yaohan fits that description to a tee. It is one of the most truly global companies in the world, a place that really does recognize no borders.

If companies are stories, then most Japanese firms tend to be parlour dramas. They may move overseas, but their perspective is still domestic. Yaohan, however, is an epic. Its distribution operations sweep across Asia. It operates and, most importantly, *thinks* on a grand scale. And it is because it is caught up in this epic that Yaohan has been able to achieve its global perspective.

HOW A COMPANY BECOMES BORDERLESS
How companies allocate their business resources is a matter of managerial 'will'. Whether or not to set up foreign operations hangs on the will of top managers. Even if there is demand in foreign markets, if the people at the top do not have the will to take advantage of it, the company will remain a domestic concern. That much should be axiomatic, but let's test it against Yaohan's experience.

Yaohan dates back to 1929, when the late Ryohei Wada, eventually the company's chairman, and his wife Katsu, eventually the 'executive counsellor', rented a bit of space under the eaves of the Tsuyuki Inn in Atami, Shizuoka, one of Japan's premier hot springs resorts. There they set up their greengrocery. Literally starting from nothing, in 3 years the grocery had become prosperous enough to open its own 'Yaohan Store'. Before long, it was the largest grocery in Atami, supplying vegetables to twenty of the city's inns. In 1951, their oldest son, college-educated Kazuo, joined the store with the idea that he would inherit the family business. In 1956, Yaohan Store changed its name to the 'Yaohan Food Department Store', gave up its business supplying the local inns on credit, and switched to a 'cash on the nail, no discounts' operation.

It was Katsu's idea. She and her husband had been selling to the innkeepers on credit for years, but never had any cash in their pockets and their store was always teetering on the edge of bankruptcy. In 1956, she attended a 4-day business seminar in the nearby mountain resort of Hakone sponsored by *Shogyokai* ('*Commerce*'), a Japanese business magazine. Not having reserved her place, she was initially refused entry, but she did not give up that easily. She begged to be allowed 'even a seat in the back corner' and promised that she would make the trek from Atami each day rather than stay in the hotel. She got her way, and while at the seminar she asked one of the lecturers how she could improve Yaohan's business. His advice was:

> If you're tired of being cheated on credit sales, why don't you start a cash-only operation aimed at the general population of Atami? Business means selling things that people are happy with. If you do that, you'll eventually develop a rapport with your customers and they'll come to trust you.

That was all it took for Katsu to decide that from now on, Yaohan would be a cash-only business.

Convincing her husband and son was another matter. She tried to explain what a great idea it would be to change to a cash-only, no discounts policy, but both Ryohei and Kazuo were opposed because it would mean giving up their business with the inns. Not one to let go that easily, she arranged for Kazuo to attend the same seminar she had, this time in Wakayama. He returned convinced that cash-only was the way to go and between the two of them, they finally got through to Ryohei. Kazuo recalls:

> We'd have family conferences every night and my mother would try to convince my father that she was right. Going over to cash-only meant giving up the 120 inns we'd been doing business with all this time, so it was not easy. And we went into the red at the beginning, so all the other grocers were criticizing us. But my mother kept faith. She was well over 50 by that time, but every morning she travelled into the market in Tsukiji, Tokyo (about 100 kilometres), to choose the vegetables herself and get them as cheaply as possible.

This was the beginning of the Yaohan style of business – sell as cheaply as possible to everyone, and hold profit margins to a bare minimum.

In 1961, Kazuo travelled to the United States to learn about chain stores. While touring American supermarkets he became convinced that was the way for Yaohan to go. With the permission of his father and the idea of developing it into a supermarket, he changed the store's name from 'Yaohan Food Department Store' to 'Yaohan Department Store', and was installed as the president and chief executive officer.

Search as you will, you will not find in this early history a single clue that Yaohan would turn into a borderless, international giant with operations in seventeen countries. How was it that a greengrocer in the provincial resort of Atami grew into a world-class distribution group? The quick answer is that its founder, Kazuo Wada, had the will and the drive to internationalize.

The Yaohan Department Store Declaration, written by Wada in 1965 and amended slightly as the company grew, states:

> By studying and practising the truth of life's philosophies, the Yaohan International Group of Companies strives to create a company which will render better service to people all over the world, and in so doing hopes to become a model for other companies.

Becoming a borderless company means setting up a coordinated global system that goes beyond the confines of any one country, and the key to doing this is to develop a clear, strongly stated business philosophy that can be accepted and adhered to by people around the world. Certainly, no one can quarrel with Yaohan's goal of creating 'a company which will render better service to people all over the world, and in so doing . . . become a model for other companies'. Nor is there much to complain about in the clean, clear, forceful way this goal has been stated in the company declaration. In addition to the original Japanese, Yaohan has produced official versions of the declaration in six other languages: English (reproduced above), Malaysian, Spanish, Indonesian, Thai and Chinese. The declaration is recited by all 26,000 of the group's employees, successfully instilling a set of shared values among the members of a global-scale organization.

The somewhat high-blown phrases about 'better service to people all over the world' and 'a model for other companies' can also be seen as the starting point for Yaohan's borderless strategy. It is remarkable, however, that Wada could have written such a strongly internationalist declaration almost 30 years ago. In his book *Yaohan's Global Strategy*,[1] Wada looks back on those years:

> In 1965, I was participating in the training programme for newly recruited staff at the 'Seicho-no-Ie' training centre when I was suddenly inspired. It was revealed to me that the business philosophy of Yaohan was not wholehearted devotion to the pursuit of profit but to serve all people in the world.[2]

As was the case with many young people of his generation, Wada was enamoured of Marxist philosophy while a student. Certain that Marxism could make people happy, he joined the Japan Communist Party, became involved in the student movement and was eventually almost expelled from the university. Worried about his future, his mother suggested that he study the beliefs of 'Seicho-no-Ie', a Japanese religious sect. This was to be a turning-point in his life. In fact, it is virtually impossible to talk about Yaohan without discussing the Seicho-no-Ie faith.

Seicho-no-Ie was founded in 1929 by Masaharu Taniguchi, to whom God revealed that 'matter does not exist, only truth'. After his conversion, Taniguchi taught that all religion stems from the same source and he attempted to synthesize the ideas of Buddhism, Christianity, Shinto and other world religions with the philosophies of Kant, Hegel and Freud into what he called the 'eternal life of the cosmos'. Having learned the Seicho-no-Ie 'truth of life's philosophy', Wada came to believe that his duty in life was to serve the people of the world and in 1949 he officially became a member of the faith.

He writes:

> The faith in 'Seicho-no-Ie' permeates my whole outlook on life, and it is this outlook on life which forms the management conception of Yaohan.

I can thank my mother for the introduction to 'Seicho-no-Ie'. Deeply distressed at my infatuation with Marxism and concerned for my happiness, she gently introduced me to the 'Seicho-no-Ie' faith.[3]

His faith in Seicho-no-Ie is the basis for the Yaohan declaration that 'by studying and practising the truth of life's philosophies, the Yaohan International Group of Companies strives to create a company which will render better service to people all over the world'. Seicho-no-Ie is what transformed Kazuo Wada into an internationalist and what provided the underlying principles for his company. The Yaohan declaration is both the backbone of its international operations and the energy behind them.

THE GLOBAL PERSPECTIVE
Yaohan first acted on its principles with a 1971 foray into Brazil, where it set up a store in Sao Paulo. The direct motivation, however, was as much practical as it was religious. The big distribution companies – Daiei and Ito-Yokado – had already set up national supermarket chains and there was no room in the market for Yaohan to break in. Says Wada:

> When I come to think it over, the fact that the first overseas store was set up in 1971 in Brazil, a place on the opposite side of the world to Japan, at a time when Yaohan was still a small local chain with a few stores based in the Izu Peninsula, was also part of the then-strategy for survival by seeking a way of relief in foreign lands. At that time, the big names in the Japanese distribution circles had developed powerful retail chains yielding a turnover of over ¥100 billion per year. While thinking there would be no other way for Yaohan to survive unless we managed to advance to Tokyo, but faced with the knowledge that we lacked both the capital and the staff to do so, I was literally wallowing

in a slough of despair, struggling to find a feasible strategy of survival. It was at this point that I learned of the Sony Corporation's 'gap theory', which was being widely publicized in magazines and newspapers. When Messrs Masaru Ibuka and Akio Morita of Sony were repatriated to Japan after World War II and attempted to set up an electrical home appliances company, the leading manufacturers in this field already possessed vast sales networks existing from pre-war times. Sony, perceiving the existence of an 'opening gap' in that none of these makers had ever thought of advancing overseas, promptly began to do so, with the result that the reputation the company acquired in foreign parts was fed back to Japan and enabled them to close the 'gap' between them and the existing networks of their competitors.

Following this example set by the Sony 'gap theory', I then sought to find a way to ensure Yaohan's survival by adopting an overseas advancement strategy.[4]

In the past, Japanese manufacturers sought new markets and new growth overseas when domestic markets became saturated or started to wither. Yaohan decided to do the same, search for new markets overseas. But breaking into foreign markets is easier said than done. When manufacturers want to establish a foothold in another country, their first step is to build up a sales network. Distribution companies do not get off that easily. They have to build stores, take on staff and manage the operation too. In short, they have to run a business, and to do so in another country and culture with all the problems that entails.

If truth be told, there was considerable opposition within the Yaohan organization to the idea of setting up in Brazil. True, there were lots of Japanese immigrants in the country, but many had their doubts that a small, local supermarket chain could go overseas and make a success out of it, and there was a lot at risk if it failed. But Wada stuck to his guns and eventually convinced the company to go along with him. He had always been enamoured of the idea of living abroad. When he was a student at the Yokohama Commercial High School, he fell in love with the international atmosphere of the city, one of Japan's leading ports, and dreamed of becoming a diplomat. However, it had been decided even then that as the oldest son, he would take over the family business.

> In my youthful days, I dreamt of becoming a diplomat. I thought that a job in which one would be acting as a bridge between Japan and the rest of the world would be a most befitting career for a man. Being the eldest son and the successor to my father, however, I had to give up this idea.
>
> Today, however, I have taken up residence as the chairman of a foreign company in Hong Kong which is developing various types of business deals in the United States, Canada, the United Kingdom and South-east Asia, so I imagine it can be said that the dream of young days has been realized in another form.[5]

This gives a clue as to how Wada developed into an international businessman on such an un-Japanese scale. His dream of becoming a diplomat meshed with his Seicho-no-Ie faith in helping the world to give him a powerful incentive and drive towards globalization.

> There are no internationally known business leaders whom I can regard as an example to follow. What I do have, however, is the philosophy that human beings are given unlimited potentialities' derived from the teachings of 'Seicho-no-Ie.' Day in, day out, I have continued to nurture the belief that I possess the wonderful power of an unlimited potentiality within myself.
>
> Once an individual has a firm belief, he will find that

certain changes occur within his inner self, in the same way as is found in Jesus Christ's words: 'By thyself as thou believe.' Or, as Mr Masaharu Taniguchi said: 'If you do a thing, you can do it'.

Once such a firm belief had taken root in my heart and mind, it goes without saying that the inner aspects of the top ranks in Yaohan would undergo a change, leading to changes in the officers and eventually to overall changes in the whole company.

'If I change, the world will change too.' This is my philosophy.[6]

Yaohan's foray into Brazil was fraught with difficulties, not the least of which was lack of funds and staff. At the time, the only Japanese companies with overseas operations were a few trading houses. It was an undertaking that required enormous resolve and courage. Wada says:

When we were setting up in Brazil, I asked the banks to loan us money, but they wouldn't even talk to us. So I turned to the government's Overseas Cooperation Fund. Talk about paperwork! The stack of documents we sent to the Ministry of Finance and the Bank of Japan must have reached the ceiling! I wrote about how the Japanese immigrants in Brazil would welcome a Japanese supermarket and got letters of recommendation from people of Japanese extraction in the Brazilian legislature. 'It will be for the good of Japan, too,' I told them. They finally lent me $500,000.

We were so strapped for money, we had to send our Japanese staff members by immigrant boat. They spent 45 days travelling to the other side of the world on the 'Argentina-Maru'! There were twelve of them and they went as families after signing a paper saying that they were prepared to live in Brazil permanently. They really were, too.

I wrote previously about the 'little grocery store in Atami taking on the world', but it was precisely because Yaohan was a small player that it could take the sort of bold steps that other companies would never even consider. Naturally, none of this would have happened had there not been a Wada to exert strong leadership and decisiveness. In fact, had it not been for Wada's own internationalism, Yaohan would probably still be a local greengrocer's in Atami. It is doubtful it would have ever ventured overseas, and almost certain that it would not have been successful if it tried.

When they have strong managers at the helm, it is far easier for smaller companies to do something daring like setting up an overseas operation than it is for consensus-oriented larger firms. Yaohan is the classic example.

LESSONS FROM BRAZIL

When Yaohan set up in Brazil, few Japanese companies were running foreign offices and it was an elite assignment to be stationed to one. For Yaohan employees, the pressure was even higher, since it was the company's first-ever venture overseas. The Brazil-bound employees were given a set of 'Ten Commandments for Success in Brazil', among which were:

1 Plan to be there permanently.
2 Consider yourself to be at work 24 hours a day.
3 Until the operation gets off the ground, employees' wives are to work as employees, and not just as employees, as executives and managers.
4 Think of your job first, your family second.
5 Consider it impossible to return to Japan, even for family weddings or funerals.

Today, the Ten Commandments are a historical document only and certainly not something Yaohan employees are expected to obey, but when the first Yaohan staff members set off for Brazil, they went at their jobs with the same energy, determination and resolve as *kamikaze* pilots on raid. That is the kind of commitment that was necessary back then for the Japanese to head halfway around the world to a foreign country. 'Everyone went to Brazil speaking no Portuguese at all. It was hard on them. Their wives used to strap their babies on their backs and go around checking what kind of products were being sold at competitors' stores,' Wada recalls.

The determination of the first wave of employees, their commitment to be in Brazil for the rest of their lives, later became the psychological backbone for Yaohan's moves into other countries and one of the reasons its operations have become so thoroughly and successfully localized. It was through this experience that the company's attitude towards foreign expansion was formed.

Luckily, their initial efforts met with success. The first store built in Sao Paulo started off with about 1,000 square metres of selling space, but by the end of its first year it was doing so well that the sales area was increased to nearly 5,000. In a short period of time, Yaohan was operating four stores in the country.

Then its luck turned. When the first oil crisis hit, Brazil's 'miracle' economy crumbled. Inflation shot to more than 60 per cent, imports were banned or subject to high tariffs and stores were ordered to close on Sundays. The business environment turned so bad, and it became so difficult to repay foreign loans, that Yaohan was eventually forced to pull out of the country altogether.

Wada, who kept his resignation in his pocket during the episode, explains:

Hyperinflation turned the money worthless. We were at the point where if we spent any more money on our Brazilian stores, we would undermine our Japanese stores. At the time, Yaohan only had a shareholders' equity ratio of 3 per cent. We were up to our eyeballs in loans and shuffling money around to pay what we could. Forecasts said it would take 5 years before Brazil's economy would recover, so we decided to pull out. It was the biggest managerial decision I ever made.

When the company went into receivership, Brazil Yaohan had about 1,500 employees and liabilities of approximately ¥5 billion. Leading the operation in Brazil was the family's fourth son, Mitsumasa, now president of International Merchandise Mart (IMM) in Singapore. He relates:

The thing that worried me the most was what to do about the employees. We paid back the debts by selling off our stores. We had 1,500 companies we were doing business with, so we had to sit down with each of them and negotiate a settlement. Brazilian law stipulates imprisonment with hard labour for managers who are not able to resolve claims within 2 years.

Wanting to avoid that at all costs, Mitsumasa spent the next 2 years in a flurry of negotiations, but was still unable to resolve all of the company's debts by the time the deadline arrived. He prepared himself to join the chain gang. At 9.00 on the morning of the deadline, he called the employees together to explain about the closing. Just 1 minute before he was to set off for prison, he received a call from his lawyer telling him to wait, he had an idea. The lawyers who had been working with Yaohan were so impressed with its determination to pay back its debts that they put up their own assets as collateral to secure a 1-year extension from the court. By a stroke of good fortune, Mitsumasa was off the hook.

A while later his mother, Katsu, came to Brazil to visit her grandchildren. In spite of her age and her language gap, when she saw how intractable the problems were, she went round with Mitsumasa to their suppliers, making apologies and asking for understanding. By the time the year was out, the debts had been resolved and the bankruptcy proceedings were over.

This baptism of fire taught Yaohan five valuable lessons about expanding overseas.

The first was to be aware of local risks. They had experienced for themselves how difficult it can be to set up operations in countries that are politically unstable and sitting on tottering economic bases. Second, Yaohan learned the dangers of borrowing in foreign currencies. Instead of borrowing in the local currency, the cruzeiro, it borrowed in US dollars, exposing itself to large exchange rate risks in the process. Third, it learned the value of trust. For merchants, losing the trust of your suppliers is far worse than losing the trust of your bankers. Fourth, it learned to care about its employees. Having to let go ten employees every day, managers were made deeply aware of their responsibilities both for running the company and for providing for their employees' futures. Fifth, it learned how dangerous contracts can be. Dissolving a company carries with it an enormous load of problems, not the least of which come from contracts. If contracts are not honoured, fines and punishments await, as Yaohan's managers found out.

Besides learning a few lessons, Yaohan also gained the confidence that it could be successful overseas. Wada explains:

> Brazil is a country of immigrants. There is an incredible variety of people, races and cultures there. Brazil Yaohan was able to recruit people of all races, teach them and run its stores with them. We found out that our managerial style would work in other parts of the

world. We had discovered that it was indeed possible to overcome national borders and racial divisions and be successful in business. That gave us immeasurable confidence later when we decided to go overseas again.

Setting up in a foreign country is more than just an expansion of territory. It means operating in a completely different business environment, where nothing, not language, laws, markets, cultures or even customs, is the same. That is where the difficulties in running a foreign business come in. Brazil was where Yaohan learned the basics of international management.

LEARNING TO BE LOCAL

Yaohan did not waste much time in applying the wisdom and confidence it gained in Brazil. Three years later, in 1974, it moved into Singapore, opening up 'Yaohan Orchard' on Orchard Street. In 1979, it was back in Latin America, this time Costa Rica. In 1983, it expanded to the United States; 1984, Hong Kong; 1987, Malaysia and Brunei; 1991, Thailand and China; 1992, Indonesia; 1993, Britain and Canada.

If the Atami grocery store was the 'first act' in the Yaohan drama and Brazil the second, the third act was the 'Singapore story'.

Yaohan went to Singapore at the request of that country's government. The government was engaged in a project to build large department stores in the city and had been trying to sign up Japanese retailers. Most balked because anti-Japanese sentiment was still running high in that part of the world. For Yaohan, which was still trying to make a go of its Brazilian operations, the Singaporean government's eagerness was a gift from heaven. The only problem was the location. Today, Orchard is Singapore's main street, filled with smart shops and classy hotels. Back then, it was brushland. Recalls Mitsumasa:

We were all against it at first. The location was horrible. It was vacant land with nothing nearby. And there really was a lot of anti-Japanese sentiment in Singapore at the time. But [Kazuo] has always been a quick decision maker. Even now, our partners in Singapore still talk about how quick Yaohan is in making up its mind. In almost no time at all, we found ourselves committed to the expansion.

Kazuo explains his decision:

Back then, per capita income in Singapore was only about $1,500, but there were forecasts that it would go to $3,000 in the near future and on from there to $5,000 and $10,000. Then Prime Minister Lee Kuan Yew was such a brilliant leader that we didn't have to think about local risks at all. But after our experience in Brazil, we decided not to borrow any money to do it. We would build our first store, and if it was a success we'd build another.

One of the secrets to Yaohan's triumph overseas is that it chose the fast-growing economies of Asia. Economic growth in places like Singapore, Taiwan, Hong Kong and South Korea has increased national incomes and resulted in an explosion in purchasing power. 'When a country's economy grows, national income rises, purchasing power is greater and distribution sectors flourish,' Kazuo says. Yaohan has been able to ride the wave of Asian growth, and as we shall see, this is also what is behind its China strategy. Wada says:

I guess you could say that heaven has been blowing us a tailwind. Economic growth in South-east Asia gave us enormous chances. Growth has been startling in the newly industrialized economies, and has raised wages and incomes and sent purchasing power through the roof. It was like that in Japan during the high-growth period of the late sixties. All you had to do was open a store and the goods would fly off your shelves. The same thing has been happening in Asia. When we really started to set up in South-east Asia, around 1988 and 1989, the 'dragons' were right in the middle of their growth spurt. There were shopping centres springing up all over the place, and developers were begging us to be the anchor store for their new projects.

When Yaohan arrived in Singapore, everything was done by barter. If children came, vendors would charge them more; when their friends came, they reduced prices. Yaohan's strategy for getting around these pre-modern business practices was to stick to its 'cash-only, no negotiations' policy and set its prices attractively low. It developed a reputation for being a store where anyone could buy things any time for the same low prices. It also gained customers by staying open Saturday afternoons and all day Sunday, something Singaporean retailers would not do, and setting its business hours from 10.00 in the morning to 10.00 at night. Kazuo recalls:

Singapore is a hot country. If they had their choice, people would have really preferred to do their shopping at night, but around six o'clock everybody started shutting their stores. We were a hit because we stayed open to 10.00 and we kept the air-conditioning running.

Yaohan was the first to bring a modern distribution system to Singapore. Today, it operates thirty stores in the city: four department stores, six appliance outlets and twenty sporting goods shops. Including the International Merchandise Mart (IMM), it employs about 1,800 people. One thing to remember about Yaohan's expansion to

Singapore is that it built one of the best distribution centres in the world there. It has been true to its promise of becoming 'a model for other companies'. For all its growth, Asia still lacks adequate distribution infrastructure. Far from having distribution centres, many places do not even have decent wholesalers. Mitsumasa reveals, 'One worry we always have is that we're going to have the store built, and when we come to put products on the shelves, we're not going to be able to get our hands on any.' As an example of how difficult it can be, big stores like the first one it built in Malaysia (16,500 square metres of selling space) may carry as many as 100,000 different items. In Japan, about 60 per cent of them could be found just by having dealings with the 200 or 300 largest wholesalers, but in South-east Asia it is not that simple. The Malaysia store originally had to deal with 10,000 different suppliers. 'We wanted to build our own distribution centre' to avoid all the complexity and trouble that entails, Mitsumasa says.

In April 1988, Yaohan went in with two Japanese wholesalers and the government of Singapore to establish the IMM. The International Merchandise Mart began partial operations in 1990 and was fully opened in 1992. With five storeys and 172,300 square metres of floor space, it is one of the largest distribution centres in the world.

The centre has 8 different divisions: 1) cash and carry; 2) product development and wholesaling; 3) brand centre; 4) unified international distribution; 5) international information; 6) international events; 7) retailer support; and 8) interior design. The main part of the operation is the cash and carry division, which occupies the first and second floors. The division imports everything from foodstuffs to precious metals. Its suppliers are located in forty-five different countries and its customers range from buyers for large department stores to street vendors.

The retailer support division sets the centre off from others of its kind and is the prime reason why local companies have not protested against the IMM's existence despite its size. Mitsumasa explains:

> A lot of Japanese retailers have moved into Singapore. The locals say that they are welcome to come, but the fact is that they have crowded out a lot of the smaller local shops. The government asked us to give them some back up so that they could become strong enough to compete on their own, so we started the retailer support division.

The division's job is to pick out promising local retailers, forge business and capital ties with them, and provide opportunities for them to set up shops or market products in IMM or Yaohan outlets. Those who grow strong enough are also given support for expansion into neighbouring countries. Nestled between Singapore's skyscrapers are hundreds of small retail stores with neither the capital nor the know-how to grow any larger. Yaohan has helped many of them convert to convenience stores, giving them managerial expertise and supplying their full line of products in the process.

Having learned the basics of international operations in Brazil, Yaohan mastered the art of localization in Singapore.

ON TO SUBURBIA

Singapore was not even Yaohan's greatest success. That came in Hong Kong, the setting for act four and the springboard to act five – China. The first Yaohan there opened in 1984.

Hong Kong offers many attractive tax advantages. Where Japan takes 50 per cent of all corporate profits, Hong Kong only wants 16.5 per cent. Where Japan taxes foreign business, Hong Kong does not. Yaohan had long eyed this tax haven as one of the prime locations in the retail market.

The company timed its entry perfectly. When China and Britain began to negotiate the colony's return, land prices in

Hong Kong plummeted, eventually reaching about a third of what they were when Yaohan was first approached about setting up there. At those levels, the company was confident that it could build a store and still be able to recover its capital before Hong Kong reverted to China in 1997. Kazuo says:

> The government of Hong Kong was in trouble. They were building 'new towns', and they needed some shopping centres to put into them. After all, the people living in the new towns had to have somewhere to do their shopping, and the government needed somebody to build and run them, so they were willing to agree to our demands. We worked out there was no point in setting up there if we couldn't recover our investment by 3 years before Hong Kong reverted to Chinese control. We calculated what our investment would have to be in order for it to be profitable, and then told the government what we needed it to do. They were willing to do everything we asked, so we decided to go for it.

There were many factors in Yaohan's Hong Kong success, but the most important may have been the fact that it had a 'suburban strategy' that allowed it to apply the managerial expertise it had gained in Japan.

When Yaohan opened its Ito store in 1966, its motto was 'stores with a view of Mount Fuji'. Japan was in its high-growth period, and the company focused on new openings in busy commercial districts where the mountain could be seen. By 1972, it was doing about ¥10 billion a year in business and it decided to switch its focus from food-centred supermarkets to shopping centres and general merchandise stores. But just as it did so, the oil crisis hit. The downturn in Japan combined with the debacle in Brazil to put Yaohan at the brink of crisis.

Terumasa Wada, the family's second son and the president of Yaohan Japan, recalls:

Business conditions were good, so we were expanding, adding on to our smaller stores and opening new ones. Then we were hit with a double punch. Between the oil crisis and the pull-out from Brazil, we were strapped for cash. At the time, our debt was almost the same size as our sales.

The company was very close to having its cheques dishonoured, which could have plunged it into bankruptcy in Japan as well as Brazil.

At the time, Terumasa was vice-president in charge of finances at Yaohan Department Store, and spent his days trying to round up enough cash to keep the company afloat. Payments to Brazil and operating funds for the head office were among his major headaches. He asked the Shizuoka Branch of Sumitomo Trust and Banking to lend the company ¥300 million. The branch manager and loan officer were very positive, having high regard for what Yaohan had achieved domestically. But the company's bills were coming due and there was still no answer. Terumasa visited the branch almost everyday, and saw very little progress for his efforts. Finally, he had just one day before he had to settle his bills. He went to Sumitomo Trust only to be told that the loan officer had gone to Tokyo to try to arrange it with the head office, but the director in charge would not give his approval. The loan officer ended up following the director home. 'Look,' he said, 'if you won't trust Yaohan, I'll offer myself as collateral.' Finally, the okay was given. It was well into the night, but Yaohan escaped having its cheques dishonoured by a hair. Today, Sumitomo Trust is Yaohan's main banker.

One of the things Yaohan learned from this experience was that it was getting too low a return on its investments. Time for 'Strategy B' – for 'bowling'. During the seventies, there was a boom in bowling across Japan and bowling alleys sprang up in the suburbs. When the boom fizzled out in 7 or 8 years, many of the bowling alleys went out of business, leaving behind big, empty buildings and lots of surrounding land, perfect for the kind of suburban stores Yaohan wanted to build. The company leased the old alleys, refitted them as supermarkets and began to expand its chain again.

Strategy B and expansion to the suburbs coincided with the motorization of Japan, and one of the prime reasons for its success was that Yaohan could provide plenty of parking. Its profits from Strategy B and its concentration on its domestic operations were enough to qualify Yaohan for listing on the Second Section of the Nagoya Stock Exchange in 1982. In 1986, it was listed on the Tokyo Stock Exchange, securing for itself a stable position at home.

When he accepted the government of Hong Kong's invitation to build a supermarket in the new towns, Kazuo was calculating that Hong Kong would follow much the same course of development as Japan. As the city grew larger and more expensive, he foresaw the population spreading out to the suburbs and commerce following close behind.

Terumasa says, 'The people in Hong Kong and the banks couldn't understand why we wanted to move into a new suburban residential area that wasn't even built yet, but [Kazuo] didn't let them get to him.' He had seen his suburban Japanese stores succeed, he did not need to pay attention to disparagement.

Yaohan now operates nine stores in Hong Kong, all in new town areas: Shatin (1984), Tuen Mun (1987), Hung Hom (1988), Tsuen Wan (1991), Yuen Long (1992), Lam Tin (1992), Macau (1992), Tin Shui Wei (1993) and Tseung Kwan (1994). Its concentration on the new towns is now commonly acknowledged as the chief reason for its success in the colony. Its first Hong Kong store, in Shatin, was turning an operating profit in its second year, and by the third had been able to clear its balance sheet of debt.

Zensuke Yamada, managing director of Yaohan International, says:

> Usually, your business territory spreads horizontally, but in Hong Kong it spreads vertically – towards the sky. Land is scarce, so people live in high-rise buildings. The city expands upwards. Ever since we opened our first store, we've regularly chartered helicopters to fly by the buildings at night and take pictures. We blow these up and count each of the lights in the windows so we know how many people are living there and how our business territory is growing. In places like Shatin that are located in new developments, we wait until we can confirm a certain level of population from the lights in the windows, and when they reach that level we may, for example, add more space to our furniture department.

Another key factor in international success has been learning how to dominate markets. Yaohan's strategy is to concentrate its stores in certain areas until it achieves a dominant position. That was why Kazuo Wada originally developed the Yaohan Department Store chain around the idea of 'stores where you can see Mount Fuji'.

'Mount Fuji is a symbol of Japan and a symbol of Shizuoka. Dotting the area with stores became a kind of slogan for us. It was a simple, easy-to-understand reason,' Terumasa Wada recalls. Instead of becoming a national chain, the store concentrated on a specific theme and area. Overseas, Yaohan has adopted the same technique.

It does not try to have a store in each major city – the company considers that a needless widening of its territory. Instead, when it moves into a country, it builds lots of stores there and tries to become the top chain. That is why it has nine stores in Hong Kong, five in Malaysia, four in Singapore and three in Thailand.

'Our idea is to become number one in all of those countries', Terumasa says.

USING LOCAL STAFF

When it moved into Hong Kong, Yaohan started to make active use of mergers and acquisitions to expand its empire. It became a player in the rapidly internationalizing money system, and as a result became more international itself. Its first acquisition was Reed Company, a firm that ran Chinese restaurants which it purchased in 1988. In 1990, it bought another eight Chinese restaurants and two bakers to form Yaohan International Caterers. To this was later added an importer of frozen meat, a major cake chain, a maker of processed ham, a ham processing company and an amusement company. Today it owns thirteen companies in Hong Kong, together operating more than 100 stores.

Yaohan had four objectives to its Hong Kong mergers and acquisitions push: 1) to build large, internationally oriented stores; 2) to develop an international restaurant chain; 3) to expand its shopping centre development business and specialty stores; and 4) to gain a foothold in China. For instance, its restaurant chain, which serves mostly Chinese food, is preparing to expand from Hong Kong into China. The company is already the third largest chain in the colony, but most expect it to be number one within a few years.

Another key facet is its development projects, which were only possible because it bought its land early. 'When prices were low, we bought enough land to open four stores,' Zensuke Yamada says. With 6 million people living in an area of about 1,000 square kilometres, Hong Kong suffers from a structural shortage of land. Prices are, by rights, high. Rents at the Shatin location are now five or six times what they were when Yaohan first signed the contracts for it. Rents at Lam Tin soared 3.5-fold in one year. Now that land prices are booming, Kazuo says, Yaohan wants to 'set a model for development projects'. The company plans to join forces with other developers to build more shopping centres in the future.

Kazuo writes:

> Since we moved to Hong Kong, I've charted a course for the Yaohan International Group as a 'distribution conglomerate'. The first phase of our strategy is to acquire promising companies in distribution areas that are strong financially.
>
>   The second phase is to list the companies we acquire on the stock exchange and use the proceeds from the listing to fund new acquisitions. Listing lets us recover our capital quickly, and so it accelerates the next round of mergers and acquisitions. We plan to eventually use the profits from listing to list Yaohan International Holdings itself, which will give us a foothold for our move into China.[7]

As long as foreign subsidiaries are managed by Japanese staff for the benefit of the parent company in Japan, talented locals will not sign on. No one is attracted to a workplace where they will have few opportunities to use their abilities. Indeed, morale in the offices of the foreign subsidiaries of Japanese companies is not necessarily high. There is a good deal of complaining and dissatisfaction among the local staff and frustration that their abilities cannot be put to use. And to be honest, the people taken on were never first-rate to begin with. One of the strengths of multinational companies, however, ought be their ability to use talented people from around the world. Yaohan's awareness of this can be seen in the fact that all the companies it has acquired in Hong Kong are managed by the talented locals who were managing them before. The results have been much better than if they had been turned over to Japanese.

Yaohan Japan produces a net, after-tax profit of about ¥3 billion. All together, the Hong Kong group has net profits of ¥4 billion. Obviously, taxation differences are a big part of this. Hong Kong corporate taxes are only about 17 per cent, compared to Japanese corporate taxes of 50 per cent. Still, our operations in Japan have been around for 60 years, while we've only been in Hong Kong for 3 years. It's hard to believe that companies can generate this much profit this quickly. This tells me that our strategy of acquiring companies in Hong Kong and letting local managers run them has been a great success.[8]

When US companies move overseas, their local subsidiaries tend to have higher profit rates than the American parent. Japanese companies have experienced just the opposite. Few if any have made money overseas. Yaohan has been the opposite of the opposite – the rare Japanese company profiting from its foreign operations.

Though it runs stores in seventeen countries, it only has about 230 of its Japanese staff stationed overseas. Hong Kong Yaohan employs 920 Chinese and only eighty-six Japanese. But in spite of the low numbers, almost 30 per cent of the Japanese staff has experienced working overseas and 70–80 per cent of the new recruits say they want to be sent abroad. These numbers give some idea of how well Yaohan has globalized its personnel. There is an anecdote in the company about one Japanese staff member who had spent several years in Hong Kong. When he was sent back to Japan, he did not describe it as 'going home' but 'being transferred'. For Yaohan, Japan is just one of many countries.

Mitsumasa says, 'We have about 1,800 employees in Singapore, only thirty of which are Japanese. But some of those are from our joint venture partners. Of our own people, there are probably no more than twenty Japanese.'

When a foreign store first opens, the executive staff comes from Yaohan Japan to oversee the start-up, but custom dictates that the branch manager is local and the local staff has responsibility for day-to-day operations. Yaohan has no qualms about moving non-Japanese around is empire, either. It has, for instance, transferred local people from Singapore to its London store. As we said earlier, the ability to draw on talented people from around the world is one of the strengths of global companies, and Yaohan is taking advantage of it.

'We call them all "Yaohan",' Mitsumasa says, 'but we think of each store as an independent entity – Singapore Yaohan, London Yaohan. Each of them operates on the idea that it will become a model company for its country.'

Yaohan has been active in training its local staff. For those on management tracks, the company provides training in making the quick decisions required of leaders. Those destined for top managerial positions are, wherever possible, given one-to-one training in making big, far-reaching decisions. Mitsumasa says the company 'wants to use its training programmes to develop business people who are able to react to events from a global perspective'.

Obviously, operations in seventeen countries means that its staff includes people from a variety of ethnic and religious backgrounds with a variety of customs and ways of life. I asked how the company dealt with those differences in its training programmes. The secret, I was told, comes from Seicho-no-Ie.

Our business principles are founded on 'the truth of life's philosophies'. In simpler terms, that means showing gratitude and service to our customers. We emphasize over and over the need for gratitude and service. Seicho-no-Ie has always believed that all religions are one, that the teachings of Islam, Christianity and Buddhism are fundamentally the same. When you climb Mount Fuji, you can start off in Shizuoka or Yamanashi, but either way your objective is still the same – to get to the top. What is at issue is whether or not people can be happy. That's what we teach in our employee training programmes.

(Yukio Kayama, secretary, Yaohan Japan)

The 'truth of life's philosophies' does not involve difficult dogma, it is just a recasting of the old Asian concept of filial piety. Yaohan teaches its employees values that are understood and shared by people around the world. The basic principle is to show respect for your parents, which leads to respect for those above you, your supervisors and others you come in contact with. From there, you feel gratitude towards people and objects. It is the traditional teaching that 'God is not pleased with those who will not show thanks to Him and gratitude to their parents'. One manifestation of this teaching comes from the Singapore store, where all of the employees line up in front of the store in the morning and greet their customers with applause and a rousing 'Good Morning! Welcome!' At closing time, the staff again lines up and sends out the last customers with a 'Thank you and good night!'

Seicho-no-Ie is a religious organization, but Yaohan employees are not forced to convert or proselytize. Both in Japan and other countries, Yaohan does have a weekly 'morning ceremony' in which the entire staff is asked to recite a slogan. The ceremony ends with a prayer, but it is usually something very simple, along the lines of 'Thank you, Father. Thank you, Mother. . . .' Kazuo writes:

> The basic concept in educating staff is not to forget that those one is trying to educate are human beings. It is necessary for a person in charge of staff education to possess a sort of gut feeling, to regard them as friends, I believe. This attitude is particularly prevalent in Asia, I think.

For instance, at morning gatherings, we adopt a unique practice of all joining hands and shouting: 'Let's try our best today too!' as a means of encouraging morale. Taking Singapore as an example, however, normally Malaysians and Singaporeans, or Chinese and Malaysians, never join hands. In fact, the antagonism between them is so deep-rooted as to make them reluctant even to touch each other. However, at morning gatherings in Yaohan, the Malaysians, the Singaporeans and the Chinese all join hands and shout the slogan, thereby mutually boosting each other's morale. This kind of scene is indeed the fruit of education.[8]

As we will see, Yaohan plans to build 1,000 supermarkets in China. It cannot afford to send expensive Japanese managers to each of them. Kazuo says:

If we had Japanese mangers in charge of each of them, half our costs would be for salaries. What we have to do is teach the Chinese how to run supermarkets – train local people who are able to function as store managers.

The company will be building a school in Shanghai to give employees intensive training in retailing practices, Japanese language and distribution terminology. It also plans to build a 'Yaohan Distribution College' in Hong Kong.

RUNNING A JAPANESE COMPANY FROM HONG KONG

In 1989, when Kazuo Wada was about to turn 60, he declared that it was time for 'myself and the company to "shed our skins"' and announced that the Yaohan headquarters would move from the provincial Japanese city of Numazu to the international metropolis of Hong Kong. He resigned as president of Yaohan Japan and installed his younger brother, Terumasa, who had served as vice-president, in his place. Kazuo became the chief of the international distribution group and he and his family migrated to Hong Kong.

In the eighties, it was common for Japanese companies, backed by the strong yen, to expand overseas, but none of them went as far as Yaohan and actually transferred their headquarters. Nor was there any precedent anywhere in Japanese business history for the top manager himself to move overseas and run the company from abroad. With the Japanese parent company and the top management in Hong Kong, management driven by purely Japanese interests disappeared. No one could ever accuse Yaohan's foreign operations of being 'run by Japanese for the benefit of the Japanese head office'.

Migration to Hong Kong is an example of Kazuo's penchant for 'subsuming the self to fulfill a dream'. At the heart of his management style is the idea that personal considerations should take second place to larger goals. He thinks nothing of self-sacrifice, of treating himself as if he were nothing. Why should he? He experienced the Great Atami Fire.

The fire struck on April 13, 1950 and destroyed 1,015 of Atami's best inns. Yaohan was burned out too. It was the day Terumasa began his studies in the Economics Department at Yokohama City University. The entire family had gone to the welcoming ceremonies except Kazuo, who stayed behind to mind the store. When the fire struck, he was unable to save anything, and he felt responsible for the loss. That was when he decided that he would follow in his father's footsteps and take over the family business.

I was in my final year at college. Until that time I had this vague idea that all I'd have to do was keep on good terms with the customers that my father had gained. But then the fire happened. We lost everything, and I was the one responsible. My younger brother told me,

'You've only got a year until graduation. Go to school and get your diploma. I've only just entered so I'll get a two-year deferral and help rebuild the store.' But I couldn't let him do that. I helped build the store and only went to school to take my finals. Somehow, I graduated. My brother did take a year off from school, and it was from that time that we learned to work together to accomplish things.

There is a Buddhist proverb that 'when you have nothing, you have an inexhaustible treasure'. That was Yaohan's situation. The fire had turned the Wada family penniless. There was nothing more to lose. It is often said that no ambition and overweening ambition are similar phenomena. Perhaps it was because Wada has been able to subsume himself to larger causes that as a manager he has never feared failure and as a person he has become an internationalist on a scale seldom seen in Japan. Speaking on his own managerial philosophy, Kazuo says:

When you try to use everything as a manger, it is the same thing as sacrificing yourself. When you sacrifice yourself, everything else comes alive. When you eliminate the self, the ego, when you reduce yourself to zero, you can understand who the people you are dealing with really are. Only then do you know what it will take to make them happy. If you aren't in this state, then all you do is try to push your own desires on to other people. But if you try to work out what the other person is thinking, then he'll begin cooperating with you on his own.

By moving the Yaohan headquarters from Japan to Hong Kong – by 'sacrificing' Japan – he was able to obtain that state of nothingness and as a result gained the opportunity to build a world-class company, he explains.

If we had gone with the idea that it didn't matter if we failed in Hong Kong because we could always go back to Japan, I don't think we would have been successful. You can't do business with the Chinese with that kind of attitude. Lots of Japanese businessmen try to approach the Chinese, but everyone knows they'll be back in Japan in a few years so the Chinese don't really regard them as serious business partners.

Indeed, no Japanese businessman has been as successful as Wada in carving a place for himself in Chinese society. Foreign subsidiaries have a dual character. On the one hand, they are subsidiaries of a parent company in another country, and on the other, they are independent companies with their own stock and capital. Up until now, the emphasis has been on the first part, on being subsidiaries of a foreign parent. As a result, foreign subsidiaries have not been taken seriously as companies in their own right. Management has centred on Japan, and the information has only flowed in one direction.

But economies are becoming borderless and I think it is time to emphasize the other aspect of foreign subsidiaries, that of independent companies. Rather than being managed by Japanese in the interests of the Japanese parent, they should be managed independently by local people. Yaohan has gone a step farther. Not only does it have local people managing its companies, the owner of the parent company himself has migrated overseas. No globalization has ever been so dramatic. Wada continues:

You can shout all you want about being an international company, if your headquarters is in Japan, your employees are never going to be able to abandon the idea that this is a Japanese company. As long as their focus is on Japan, you won't be truly international. To 'shed your skin', to make the leap from Japanese company to international company, you've got to change employees' attitudes. The quickest way for us to do that was to move our headquarters overseas. If your headquarters is in Hong Kong, your employees stop thinking about going back to Japan.

The top management committee of the Yaohan Group has five members: Kazuo Wada, Terumasa Wada, Mitsumasa Wada, Shoichi Tajima and Zensuke Yamada. Kazuo Wada is the eldest son of the Wada family. Terumasa is the second son, Mitsumasa the fourth. The third son, Naomi, who was vice-president of Brazil Yaohan, now runs a ranch and plantation in Chile. The fifth son, Yasuaki, married the daughter of the owner of 'Izumi', a local supermarket chain with ties to Yaohan. This is very much a family company. The brothers divide up their responsibilities. Kazuo is in charge of overall strategy from the group headquarters in Hong Kong. Terumasa has stayed in Numazu, where he runs the Japanese arm of the group. Mitsumasa is in Singapore and handles most of the foreign operations. Mitsumasa enlarges:

All three of us live in different parts of the world. I spend about half the month in Singapore, maybe 5 days each in Hong Kong and Japan, and the remaining 5 days in Indonesia, Brunei, Canada or some other country. Kazuo currently divides his time between Hong Kong, China and Japan. We may have scattered ourselves between Hong Kong, Japan and Singapore, but we keep in close communication and talk on the phone every morning. Each morning without fail I call Kazuo at 5.45. It's funny, when we're all together we get sort of vague and have a hard time communicating!

When the headquarters was still in Japan, the management committee would only meet two or three times a year and those who were overseas could not attend. Since moving to Hong Kong, the management committee has met twice a month for a full day each time, and all five of the top managers are there, together with executives for Japan, the United States and the South-east Asian countries. Hong Kong is where the information comes together and decisions are made.

'We put all the information we've obtained up on the board. When you start comparing items, you come up with these incredible strategies that you never would have thought of in Japan,' Kazuo relates.

For example, Yaohan opened a supermarket in Vancouver, British Columbia, about a year ago. It also bought 21,000 square metres of adjacent land, a decision that came straight from the Management Committee. The US manager who was in charge of the Canada project came to the meeting with information that the land was for sale. Kazuo immediately decided to buy it. He had information that Hong Kong developers wanted to buy shopping centres, Chinese restaurants and hotels in Vancouver, but that they had to come with land. Kayama explains:

> When [Kazuo] was running the group from Japan, information from overseas would come in by fax and we'd use that as the basis for discussion in the Management Committee. That took too much time, though, and we really couldn't get that good a grasp on what was happening elsewhere. Take land prices. They're completely different in Japan from what they are in other parts of the world. Prices are so high here that we're likely to find local prices cheap and buy the property without thinking. Now that we're in Hong Kong, where you can get information from all over the world, particularly Asia, we're not that easily misled.

Kazuo says that what sets Hong Kong business apart is quick decision making. Many of the people in Hong Kong fled there from the mainland with only the clothes on their backs. According to Kazuo, 'they look at business as a short-term contest'. He himself has much the same style. Once he has made a decision, he does not back down. Perhaps that is what being a manager is all about.

THE CHINA CARD

When Yaohan decided to transfer its headquarters there, most people thought Hong Kong was a risky investment. It was already set to revert to Chinese control in 1997. In fact, since it became known that the colony would definitely be going back to China, many Hong Kong people have left it for the United States, Canada and Australia. No wonder Yaohan's announcement came as such a shock. It goes without saying that all the company's bankers were against the idea.

But Wada stuck to his contrarious position and moved the headquarters. There was a reason for his determination. He had his eye on the latent potential of the giant Chinese market in the Hong Kong hinterland. Yamada explains:

> He had expansion into China in the next century in mind and calculated Hong Kong, which is right next door to it and shares a land border, was the best place to put down roots. People say you can't move into China unless you know Hong Kong, so one of the ideas behind our moving was to set up a kind of 'antenna shop' [that would give us information about China].

Yaohan made its decision in 1989, the same year that China's relations with the West reached a low ebb in the aftermath of the T'ien-an-Men Square incident. Most Western companies were pulling their capital out of the Chinese market.

Wada, however, had a different vision. Unlike most managers, he saw China achieving rapid economic growth that would bring it to the centre of world politics and economics at the beginning of the twenty-first century. The main growth would come from the coastal regions that stretch from Tianjin in the north to Hainan in the south. He was confident that a gigantic market would emerge there. The coastal regions are already home to 120 million people, roughly the same number as live in the 'Tokaido Megalopolis' in Japan. As the economy developed, he foresaw the cities swelling with people who had moved in from the countryside, boosting the population to a staggering 300 or 400 million. When that happened, there would be a time when 'you could build all the stores you wanted and there still wouldn't be enough', Kazuo predicted. He says:

My dream is to be a comprehensive developer. Yaohan will build shopping centres in China, but we'll also put up Chinese restaurants and department stores. I moved the group headquarters to Hong Kong in order to make this dream come true, and that's why I myself migrated there.

On September 29, 1992, Yaohan broke ground on its first Shanghai store, 'Yaohan Nextage', a joint venture between it and the Shanghai Number One Department Store. It was the first-ever foreign investment in the Chinese distribution industry and became a symbol of the country's policy of 'economic openness'. It was no coincidence that the day of the ground-breaking also marked the twentieth anniversary of the restoration of diplomatic ties between China and Japan.

Wada told the Chinese government officials and the people of Shanghai who gathered for the ceremony:

In May 1990, I moved the headquarters of the Yaohan Group to Hong Kong because I wanted to contribute to the development of China. Thanks to you, we have been able to commence work on the largest department store in Asia here in Shanghai. Our group will be doing everything in its power to ensure that this project is a success.

So far, Wada has been right. While the rest of the world economy stagnates, China has been growing at dizzying rates. In 1992 its economy expanded by 12.8 per cent in real terms. Permission to carry on side businesses in the cities has boosted agricultural production, and the Chinese population is undergoing something of a consumer frenzy. Even more telling, however, is the Communist Party's adoption at its 1992 convention of the idea of a 'Socialist Market Economy', an economic policy with strongly capitalistic overtones. Kazuo notes:

I've watched the changes taking place in China closely. I didn't think its markets would really start opening up until about 2000, but Deng Xiaoping's openness policies have spread rapidly. For people like me who are living in China and doing business there, it's hard to know how to express our gratitude for these developments.

Act five, the China story, is about to begin. But expanding into China is not easy. The hardest part is getting a business licence. Foreign firms wanting to do business in China are required to get a 'People's Republic of China Corporate Business Visa' issued by the State Council. In September 1992, Yaohan became the first foreign firm to be issued a licence.

'Distribution companies all over the world would love to get their hands on this visa. Just after we got ours, the Hutchison Whampoa Group from Hong Kong became the second to get one,' says Shoichi Tajima, vice-president of Yaohan Japan.

The reason Yaohan was the first to get a foreign company visa, of course, was that it had moved its headquarters from Japan to Hong Kong and was therefore given 'national treatment' as a Hong Kong company. In March 1993, the company established the 'Yaohan China Development Company, Ltd' to run its China project. The office targets six businesses in China: 1) department stores; 2) retail; 3) manufacturing; 4) restaurants; 5) wholesaling; and 6) amusement. In its core business, department stores, the government of China has already given it permission to set up operations in six independently administered cities (Beijing, Shanghai, Dalien, Tianjin, Qingdao and Guangzhou) and five special economic zones, including Shenzhen, Amoi and Hainan. For each, it will be forming joint ventures with one of the major department stores in the city.

Tajima, who is also president of the China Office, says, 'The central government has given permission for two foreign-owned department stores to be set up in each of these eleven cities. Yaohan has one of those slots in all eleven.' Its Shanghai store, 'Yaohan Nextage', will have sales space of 122,000 square metres, about 50 per cent larger than the largest department store in Japan. It is scheduled to open its doors in December 1995. Wada exults:

Everybody's worried that the store is going to be too big, but moving out from Shanghai along the banks of the Yangtze River, there are 300 million people. If even 1 per cent of them wanted to come shopping at a Shanghai department store once a month, that would mean we had 3 million customers. Even with only 0.3 per cent we'd still have 900,000. At the store we manage in Beijing, we get about 150,000 people on Sundays alone. It's so crowded, you really can't shop at your leisure. The Chinese market has an inexhaustible supply of power waiting to be uncovered.

The Number One Department Store in Shanghai produces sales of between ¥25 billion and ¥30 billion a year. If each of Yaohan's outlets in each of the eleven cities did that well, it would mean sales of ¥300 billion. That is before the supermarket division is included. Yaohan plans to open more than 1,000 stores around China by 2010 in a joint venture with the state-run CVIC (China Venturtech Investment Company) conglomerate. Tajima says:

> We say 1,000 stores, but if they were all supermarket size, I don't care how cheap things are in China, we're still talking about an incredible amount of money. It won't be that easy. I think we'll start with smaller convenience-store-type outlets of maybe about 500 square metres, with the idea of doubling them at some point in the future.

The supermarket business has enormous potential. A store of about 500 square metres can be expected to produce ¥500–600 million a year in sales. With 1,000 stores, that is ¥500–600 billion a year. If the business grows smoothly, the supermarkets alone will be worth more than ¥1 trillion in annual sales.

The restaurant business is also promising. Yaohan will be launching Chinese restaurants, but it also has plans to work with MOS Food Services, a Japanese hamburger chain known for its 'Teriyaki burgers' and oriental flavours, to develop a chain of 3,000 stores. That is an ambitious goal. MOS Food only has 1,200 stores in all Japan.

Running department stores and supermarkets in China also means running a distribution network. The country has manufacturers and retailers, but not much of a network to link them. Yaohan plans to build its network from scratch, setting up large wholesaling centres in Beijing and Shanghai similar to its IMM facilities in Singapore. Kazuo says:

I met the mayor of Beijing last December and he asked me to build something like Singapore's IMM in his city. I was quite in agreement with the idea, so I asked if he would help us get all the business permits and land permits that we needed. He said okay right on the spot. Beijing is an independent administrative district, so the mayor can make decisions like that on his own. I think that if we build an IMM in Beijing, it will serve as a model for wholesalers all over China.

In manufacturing, Yaohan plans to use joint ventures with other Japanese companies, since it has no manufacturing expertise of its own. There is talk of setting up a toilet paper company, for example, and Yaohan is now trying to decide which Japanese toilet paper company it wants to work with.

In food processing, its Hong Kong subsidiary, Yaohan Food Manufacturing Ltd, has already decided to expand into China and has purchased a factory in Shenzhen. Amusement will be handled by another Hong Kong subsidiary, Yaohan Whimsey.

Yaohan started off as a Japanese company, but moved its headquarters to Hong Kong. When Hong Kong reverts to China in 1997, it will automatically become a Chinese company. It would not be surprising to see it move its headquarters to Shanghai at that time. In fact, the day it moves to Shanghai will mark the final chapter in the 'China story' on which Yaohan has pitted its survival in the twenty-first century.

Epilogue: The Path to Survival

After the war, Japan's manufacturers became fierce competitors on the international scene. What were to become known as 'Japanese-style' systems of running economies, markets and companies provided them with a base from which they could polish technology imported from the West, slash costs and achieve a quality and price that few could match. Those same manufacturers who terrorized the world, however, are now throwing up their hands in the face of a trade surplus that refuses to budge and the exchange rate spiral that it has created. The yen was worth about ¥150 to the dollar in 1990, but since that time has increased in value at a breathtaking pace. On June 27, 1994, it crossed the ¥100 to the dollar line. It had only nudged its way past the ¥110 to the dollar mark a year earlier, and few managers in Japan thought another ¥10 would be gained so quickly.

As I have said throughout this book, this is a time of great trials for Japanese manufacturing. Cold War structures have eroded, leaving the world to grope for a new political and economic framework. Industry has not been immune to these historical changes. Japanese manufacturers have not been slack in their efforts to cure what ails them, whether it be the prolonged recession of the nineties, the high exchange rate, the increasingly vitriolic nature of trade friction or the eruption of all the distortions in the economic system. But despite their restructuring, workforce rationalization, attempts to chop even ¥1 off their costs, managerial reforms and transfers of production overseas, they have still watched their international competitiveness be undermined by the strong yen. Some are even wondering out loud if they will be able to survive. It is time to ask ourselves that same question: will Japanese manufacturers be able to survive? If so, how are they to pull out of this crisis?

Let us examine these questions by looking at several companies who are struggling valiantly to deal with an exchange rate crisis of unprecedented proportions.

WHAT DILIGENCE AND PERFECTIONISM EARN YOU
Times have never been this tough for Japanese car manufacturers. Toyota Motor, one of the leading companies in the country, saw its sales decline to a 7-year low of ¥8,154.7 billion during the year to June 1994, 9.7 per cent less than the previous year's figure. Current profits were even worse, plunging 25.3 per cent to ¥214.0 billion, while operating profits, which are an indication of how much the company made in its core businesses, were down 25.9 per cent to ¥76.7 billion. But if you look more closely, you will notice something surprising about the second half of the year – recovery! Operating profits surged nearly seven-fold from the first half to ¥67.4 billion. Commenting at a press conference after the results were announced, company president Tatsuro Toyoda displayed confidence in Toyota's ability to recover, saying that he wanted to 'move *with haste* towards the bright signs'. Toyota will be changing its settlement term to March, so it will only have a 9-month business year, but translated into 12-month figures it forecasts operating profits of ¥150 billion on sales of ¥8,200 billion. Not only will profits themselves double, the ratio of profits to sales will also double to 1.8 per cent.

As we have already seen, there are two factors in Toyota's

new lease of life. First, its efforts since 1989 to overcome 'big company disease'. Faced with fossilized organizations and declining productivity, the firm shook up its management, flattening out bureaucracies, boosting the portion of pay accounted for by merit ratings, reshuffling the product development teams that function as its 'brain and spinal cord' and developing a 'new Toyota production system'. All of these moves had indirect benefits for the company.

Of more direct impact was Toyota's traditional emphasis on squeezing costs – surgery. Hiroshi Okuda, director and vice-president, explains, 'In manufacturing, the only way to get yourself out of crisis is to cut your costs.' Indeed, that is the way Toyota always does pull out of crisis. This time, it is asking its parts suppliers to slash their costs by 15 per cent over the next 3 years. But how far will cost-cutting take you when the yen is trading at less than ¥100 to the dollar? Unless they proceed with greater speed than the exchange rate, cost cuts will not have much overall effect. It is a dreary business to be shaving ¥1 or even ¥0.1 off the price of a screw, but the effects eventually add up. Toyota is second to none in its ability to do this sort of plodding towards its goals. It is that kind of hard work and perfectionism that is behind Toyota's success and indeed that of Japanese manufacturing in general. Okuda says:

> If we put our minds to it, there are limitless ways [to get over the crisis]. Even if it's just a single yen, if you spread that over tens of thousands of parts, the combined effect is enormous. There are all sorts of things we haven't tried yet, like rethinking our quality concepts.

One of Toyota's biggest problems was that it forgot the principle of 'appropriate quality' during the bubble. Rising development and production costs have become one of the largest pressures on its earnings structure. Okuda goes on to say:

'Appropriate quality' takes in many things, including the quality of the hardware in the car, the quality of your management and the kind of quality recognized by consumers. Up until now, we've always seen customer satisfaction as our main goal and have spared no effort in manufacturing 'good' products. But in reality, maybe we were more concerned with satisfying our engineers than with satisfying our customers. We tended to gauge our new models by how many world-first or Japan-first technologies we could claim for them, and that produced a lot of devices and parts that consumers didn't really want. What we need to do now is rethink what 'best quality' is from the consumer's point of view. That will obviously mean rethinking the materials and production processes we use too, so there will be cost savings that come out of it.

For Toyota, the keys to overcoming high exchange rates are managerial reform and cost-cutting. In them it believes it has found a path to recovery and future growth. Obviously, however, the same thing will not happen at every Japanese firm. Times of historical transition are sifting periods for companies. Some will survive, some will not. One trait of survivors is that they are able to change themselves. Some, like Toyota, may do so seriously, rigorously and single-heartedly. Others, like the newly privatized JR East, may blaze with reformist zeal. Still others will be like Seven-Eleven, constantly adapting to an ever-changing environment. The thread that links them is dynamism.

MAKING MONEY BY DOING WHAT OTHERS CANNOT
The higher exchange rate has had less of a visible impact at Canon, which saw its current profits zoom 84 per cent to ¥28.54 billion during the year to June 1994. Office machines, which account for 84 per cent of total sales, were up 4 per cent. The rises were slight for copiers, faxes and

laser printers, but bubble jet printers scored a 40 per cent increase.

Canon's strong performance rests on its unique product lines. Indeed, developing products that are available nowhere else pretty much sums up the company's strategy for dealing with the exchange rate. Laser printers saw it through the appreciation of the yen in 1985; bubble jet printers are doing much the same for it this year. Vice-president Fujio Mitarai says, 'The biggest factors in our international competitiveness are original patents and original products – and of course, attractive products too.'

Canon claims a dominant 60 per cent share of the world laser printer market and is now fighting it out with Hewlett-Packard of the US for the top spot in bubble jet printers.

'The significance of getting a top share in an original product area is huge. When you've got the top share, you're the price leader,' Mitarai goes on. Original products keep companies competitive by giving them 'founder's profits' and enabling them to stay on the leading edge by releasing improved versions. That competitiveness feeds back into new product development and enables the company to produce yet another round of high value-added products. On the surface, it may appear less risky to jump into existing markets, but existing markets have their own inherent risks, not the least of which is price competition. Creating new markets like Canon may be more risky initially, but the payoffs are enormous if you are successful, for you have become the leader. In the Canon philosophy, you do not expect to make money doing what everybody else is doing, you expect to make money doing what everybody else is not.

Certainly, it is no easy task to develop an original product that no one else can copy. At the risk of stating the obvious, original products require original technology, which means being constantly involved in the search for new technologies. A brief review of Canon history should illustrate this. During and after the war, Canon used optical mechanisms to develop cameras; in the sixties, it used electronics to make calculators, chemical technology to make copy machines and telecommunications technology to make faxes. This fed into the development of the laser printer in 1979, the bubble jet printer in 1985 and the full colour digital copy machine in 1987, all original products.

The bubble jet printer started off as a mistake. Seventeen years ago, a Canon engineer's hand slipped, causing a soldering iron to hit a hypodermic needle. He watched the ink inside the needle spurt out and got the idea for heat-propelled ink jets. Canon has been perfecting the concept ever since, and the bubble jet's appearance on the market turned printer technology, which had been based entirely on electrophotographic techniques until that time, on its ear. With its original bubble jet printers, Canon pioneered an entirely new market.

Canon's obsession with originality is summed up in its five famous 'Research and Development Principles', two of which are of particular importance for our purposes: 'Canon will create technology and product genres that have never been known before' and 'Canon will respect similar technology and product genres at other companies'. One manifestation of this has been the company's policy of ploughing 10 per cent of sales back into research and development. The investment has paid off. For the past decade, Canon has been one of the five top patent awardees in the United States. In 1993, it was ranked third behind IBM and Toshiba with 1,308 patents. This tireless search for new technologies is one of the keys to survival for Canon and for Japanese manufacturing in general. Mitarai enlarges:

If you want to build a strong earnings structure, you can't just rely on a single technology for your growth. You've got to have many layers, like a fancy pastry. Failure is a part of development, but the experience and technology stay with your people. Even if one technology runs into a dead-end, if you're patient, there will be a way to capitalize on it, though you might have to change your direction or fuse it with another technology in the process.

Its accumulation of new technologies has diversified Canon's business and transformed it from a low-value-added to a high-value-added company, one that is strong no matter what the exchange rate does. In that, Canon illustrates another key to survival: originality. Nintendo, the creator of the video game market, is another example.

STRUGGLING TO COME BACK
Japan's semiconductor industry began to grow rapidly in the late seventies and took off in the eighties as consumer electronics and audiovisual manufacturers began to stuff computer chips into their products. Currently Japan enjoys a share of just under 50 per cent of the world market. But after more than a decade of steady growth, semiconductors have reached a turning-point, according to Michiyuki Uenohara, special advisor to NEC:

There are two hurdles we're going to have to cross in order for semiconductors to keep expanding into the next century. The first is to develop a method for verifying and accumulating production technology. We have to become stronger in the memory chips that have been our strong point all along. We're at the stage where chips of up to 1-gigabits are profitable to produce, but when you get up to the 4-gigabit and 16-gigabit levels where greater degrees of miniaturization and integration are required, we may be able to produce them in the laboratory, but I have my doubts about whether we will be able to bring costs down far enough for them to be commercially viable. In other words, we know we're okay on 1-gigabit chips in the next century, but we don't have much confidence in 4- or 16-gigabit chips. The other hurdle we need to cross is finding ways to pool our knowledge to develop higher-value-added products such as microprocessors. Compared to America, Japan is way behind on basic software and architecture.

Japanese semiconductor manufacturers have so far concentrated on producing memory chips. Today, a lot of attention is given to the microprocessors that are at the heart of computers, but back in the early eighties, microprocessors were 'giveaways' that were used to sell memory. Sales from microprocessors were minuscule by comparison, since they were not used very much at the time. But today, thanks to the spread of the personal computer, microprocessors are at the top of the heap in the semiconductor market.

Japanese chip companies have lost ground in the microprocessor competition. Fujitsu was allowed to produce them under a licence from Intel until the mid-eighties, when it was suddenly cut off. NEC, meanwhile, was taken to court by Intel under charges that it illegally copied Intel designs. Hitachi also found itself in court for alleged infringement on Motorola's microprocessors. The litigation has had a pronounced impact on their strategies for this market. It has made them content with low-profit memory chips and they have ceded the high-profit microprocessor market to America. Even in memory chips, however, it is under attack from upstarts like South Korea, Singapore and Taiwan, hemmed in as it were by Silicon Valley on one side, Seoul on the other. Uenohara says:

> Unlike memory chips, microprocessors require large investments. You have to develop everything from the tools to the basic software and operating system, and that costs a lot of money, so if you don't get a fairly large share of the market, it doesn't pay to produce them. Intel of the United States is far and away the

leader in microprocessors, and it will be no easy task to break into its territory.

Microprocessors will be at the heart of the multimedia age, and Intel has a 74 per cent share of the market. Coming back, as Japan's chip makers are finding out, will be no easy task.

BEING CREATIVE

What are Japanese semiconductor manufacturers doing about software? And what *should* they be doing? I went to Fujitsu to find out. Fujitsu was once known as a haven for individualists and renegades. The late Toshio Ikeda, who committed his entire life to computer development, was an odd man who had a reputation for never coming to work during the day, but being in the office all night. It didn't matter what time it was, when Ikeda had an idea, he would call all of his colleagues together to discuss it, often at his own home. He devoted his life to building computers, and it is because of Ikeda that Fujitsu has become what it is today.

But along the way it got big, and size robbed it of the flexibility it once enjoyed. Old-timers often lament the fact that 'young people don't want to do things on their own'or that 'nobody has much enthusiasm'. President Tadashi Sekizawa has tried to turn the company around by looking for 'in-house entrepreneurs' in a 'venture programme' that he inaugurated in July 1995. Under the programme, the company will match the investments of employees who wish to start their own businesses. If they are successful, Fujitsu will buy out the employees' shares too. It is a chance to do something for people who are unable to make full use of their abilities within the confines of a large organization.

Fujitsu has also shaken up its research and development organizations. The laboratories used to be divided by location: Kawasaki and Atsugi. Now they are divided by function: multimedia systems, personal systems, electronic equipment, basic technology, information society studies and special projects. The last is worthy of note, since it works outside the traditional organizational framework in teams that may have anywhere between ten and fifty members depending on the assignment. One example is the 'P Project' team that is developing what it hopes will be the most advanced processor in the world. Another new feature in Fujitsu's research division is the establishment of a 'My-Way Project' in which selected researchers are given 3 years to pursue whatever research they are interested in, including trips overseas, additional education and time at laboratories other than their home base. Vice-president Mikio Otsuki says:

> We hope that this kind of flexible research system will produce something, and it really doesn't matter to us what. We need cooperation and creativity to pull out of the slump. Part of that is coming into contact with different cultures, obtaining new information from them and building new products from it. It's that kind of 'cooperative creativity' that's important. That's the sort of thing that will enable us to apply our technology to areas that we previously thought we couldn't, and new things will come out of that.

Mass production has always been one of Japanese companies' biggest strengths; creative development, one of their stumbling-blocks. Like Fujitsu, however, they are now becoming aware of the need to foster and encourage creativity.

BUSINESS WITHOUT BORDERS
Mabuchi Motor is one company that is having a field day on world markets while the rest of Japanese manufacturing has been sidelined by the high yen. The company makes the tiny motors that are used in audiovisual equipment and car electronics. Its 55 per cent share of the market makes it

something of a Gulliver in the Lilliputian world of small motors. Mabuchi expects sales to decline 10 per cent to ¥60 billion during the year to December, but current profits will be up 4.3 per cent to ¥11.8 billion. Management says it is virtually assured of reaching its production target of 1.1 billion motors for the year. Thanks to recovery in the US and the explosive growth of Asian economies, Mabuchi reports that it is all it can do to keep up with demand, a complaint that other Japanese manufacturers can only envy.

Backing these results is a strategy that some find unique, others extreme, and many consider similar to Yaohan's. Mabuchi has located all of its production overseas. For it, the strong yen means strong business.

Mabuchi's basic philosophy has been that it does not really care where it goes as long as it is able to turn out good products as cheaply as possible. Under that idea it has spent the past several years moving overseas in search of cheaper costs. It built its first overseas factory in Hong Kong in 1964 back when the yen was pegged to the dollar at ¥360. In 1969 it set up another plant in Taipei, Taiwan, followed by one in Khaosiung in 1979, and a further one in Dalien, China, in 1987 (with which it became the first Japanese company to have a wholly owned Chinese subsidiary). In 1989, it built another plant in Malaysia, and in July 1995 began production in Jiangsu, China. The history of Mabuchi's overseas moves is the history of its search for cheaper and cheaper labour.

Today, Mabuchi engages in no production whatsoever in Japan. Everything is done overseas. All that is left in Japan are the headquarters functions – research and development and administration. It has about 1,000 domestic employees and 30,000 foreign. Its markets are spread throughout the world, 75 per cent of sales coming from Japan, North America and Europe, the remaining 25 per cent from Asia. That is one of the reasons why Mabuchi is recession-proof. Says Vice-president Akira Onishi:

It matters very little to us if Japanese car manufacturers are beaten by American car manufacturers. All that means is that demand from America will increase, so the effects on us are almost nil. If the opposite happens, the effects are still nil.

Mabuchi is trying to further insulate itself from the exchange rate by reducing its yen-denominated transactions. The company estimates that every ¥10 gained against the dollar costs it ¥5 billion in sales and ¥1 billion in profits. The only way to reduce the foreign exchange losses is to reduce the portion of costs denominated in yen. To do that, Mabuchi has pulled out of the business of exporting parts to its subsidiaries, something that used to go through the head office. Instead, it allows its subsidiaries to deal with each other directly. The result has been to reduce yen costs from 50 per cent of the total to 38 per cent, and before the year is out, Mabuchi wants to have them down to 25 per cent. Onichi explains:

Most domestic manufacturers have rationalized to the point where further rationalization is almost impossible, but we've been lucky. By being among the first to move overseas, we've been able to attract cheap labour for the asking. That means we still have a lot of room to rationalize and improve productivity in our overseas factories. Rationalization is something we're just starting to work on. One of the ideas we're looking at now is to transfer managerial expertise to our foreign operations along with technology. Teaching management – how to run personnel departments, for instance – is a lot harder than teaching technology in a lot of ways, but we think that is the direction to go in improving our overall efficiency.

The only other company that even approaches Mabuchi in the extent of its globalization is Aiwa, a consumer electronics company that now has 80 per cent of its production located in low-cost South-east Asian countries. Some, however, may wonder if this sort of excessive shifting of production overseas will not result in a severe hollowing out of Japanese industry. Indeed, there are worries that Japan may be in for the same sort of hollowing out of jobs and industry that occurred in the United States during the eighties, and that it may even see domestic manufacturing extinguished altogether. Were Mabuchi to boost its capacity and take on more staff, for example, it would not result in any more Japanese jobs. Does it think nothing of these sorts of issue?

> We do not see any sort of hollowing out of technology that would directly affect our business core. Both Taiwan and China are close; you can get there in 3 hours on an aeroplane, though there are lots of places in Japan that you can't get to with a 3-hour flight. I don't understand why people get so worried about 'hollowing' just because we've moved our factories to Taiwan and China. All of the important stuff – quality control, decisions on which parts to use and where to source them – is handled in Japan, so there's no problem. We sent a total of 440 employees from Japan to foreign factories last year alone. That works out at about half of all our domestic employees travelling abroad. With employees travelling that frequently, there is no way that hollowing out can occur,

replies Onishi, dismissing the issue entirely. Active transfers of production technology to other countries, he says, result in more technology being accumulated at home, too.

> When we were manufacturing in Japan, we passed down technology with a lot of unspoken understandings, but that doesn't work in foreign factories.

Engineers have to write their own manuals and give thorough work instructions. Those manuals have to be as easy to understand as possible, so you're faced with the task of putting into the book everything you have learned about technology, about how to operate and maintain the equipment and about any other phase of the operation. And you have to do it in a way that the people reading it will understand. You end up gaining expertise in the process.

With the yen now going for less than ¥100 to the dollar, many Japanese companies are accelerating their shifts overseas. Certainly, companies like Mabuchi Motor with its zero domestic production or Yaohan with its overseas headquarters offer one option for dealing with the new environment. They are living proof that borders are increasingly irrelevant.

WHERE TO GO FROM HERE

The current yen appreciation is so serious that the spiral of the late eighties triggered by the Plaza Accord pales by comparison. For most managers, it represents their worst nightmare come true. Some are confident that they can continue to grow even with the yen going for less than ¥100 to the dollar. They are the companies that have used original technology to attain absolute dominion over their markets, the companies who have succeeded in cutting their costs even faster than the yen has risen, the companies who have avoided exchange rate risks altogether by moving their entire production base overseas – in short, the companies that have something in reserve. We have truly reached the point where only the strongest firms will survive.

Keizai Doyukai (an organization for business managers) conducted a survey of corporate managers in June and found that ¥113 to the dollar was the limit for most manufacturers beyond which they could not maintain their international competitiveness. Six months earlier, those same managers gave ¥119 as their breaking point, which indicates a 5 per cent rationalization in just half a year. Even so, the yen is trading at less than ¥100 to the dollar, and that level is beyond the capacity of the average firm to deal with.

Obviously, half-hearted efforts will not be enough to pull companies through such an extreme appreciation. Chairman Jiro Ushio of Ushio Ltd. advocates strict restraints on wages and jobs:

> Wages are where the biggest gap is between Japan and other countries. Leading companies in the US collect competitive resources from around the world. They employ talented people at high wages, conduct thorough studies to find sources of quality materials at low prices and use the weak dollar to make their products competitive. Industry is finally beginning to realize that there's no way Japan can compete by keeping wages the same and using the difference to provide more jobs. If we want to regain our competitiveness, we've got to hold down wages, cut our work force by about 10 per cent over the next 5 years and use the savings for bold research and development investments. Obviously, in clamping down on wages we are assuming that prices will continue to decline. Chairman Takeshi Nagano of the Japan Federation of Employers' Associations (*Nikkeiren*) estimates that if prices were to fall by 20 per cent over the next 5 years real wages would rise by an annual rate of 4 per cent, which would mean that nominal wages could be held at current levels. That's one of the goals we're going to have to focus on.

In doing that, sharp cost cuts would be needed, and while wages would be cut, companies would have to make bold increases in 'necessary' wage costs, while unrelentingly cutting 'unnecessary' wages.

When it comes to wages, Professor Haruo Shimada of Keio University advocates 'zero-base' management:

Japan doesn't distribute its wages just on the basis of performance and ability. We've always had this attitude that everybody's in this together, so let's raise everybody's wages together too. We don't have the sort of rigorous system in place where the conditions for dismissal and demotion are spelled out. That was fine when we could assume economic growth, but now that the pie is not growing, companies are going to have to become extremely selective about the people they employ or they are not going to function properly. That's why I think we need to go back to step one with our organizations, personnel systems and wage scales, and rethink them entirely. I call this 'zero-base' management.

The death knell for such hallmarks of Japanese-style management as lifetime employment and seniority-based wages? Certainly, if there are fewer jobs and more demanding performance evaluations to be met, Japan will be unable to look forward to the kind of easy job market it had in the past. Ushio thinks that the entire country will have to become involved in a programme to transfer jobs between industries.

It has already started in the US, and it has come time for Japan too to think seriously about transferring jobs from manufacturing into services and information. We have a different culture and language from people in Europe and North America, so I don't think our service sectors are going to earn us much foreign exchange. It'll take time to build these sectors up, and while we're doing that we'll have to look to lean, competitive manufacturers to bring in about 80 per cent of our foreign exchange earnings. Instead of trying to help Japanese society by maintaining employment levels over the short term, manufacturers would do better becoming leaders in their industries and even more internationally competitive than before.

After the war, Japan's companies developed and prospered with a speed that has never been equalled before or since. But as we have noted repeatedly throughout this book, the system that supported this development – Japanese-style management – is coming apart at the seams. As we face this historical transition, it is meaningless to keep singing about our past successes. Are we not a bit too drunk on the accomplishments of a time that is now over? We have achieved the overriding goal of the postwar years. We have caught up with the West. Now it is time for a new start. We must begin the search for true leadership and international competitiveness.

Notes

Chapter 1

1 My resumé (*Watakushi no rirekisho*), Group of Managers in Showa Era Series No. 4 (*Showa no keieisha gunzo shirizu No. 4*), Nihon Keizai Shimbunsha, Tokyo, 1992.
2 *The Source* (*Genryu*), 'In commemoration of the 40th anniversary of the founding of Sony'.
3 My resumé (*Watakushi no rirekisho*), Group of Managers in Showa Era Series No. 3 (*Showa no keieisha gunzo shirizu No. 3*), Nihon Keizai Shimbunsha, Tokyo, 1992.
4 Ono, Taiichi, *Toyota-Style Manufacturing* (*Toyota seisan hoshiki*), DIAMOND INC, Tokyo, 1978.
5 *Canon: Fifty Years of Technology and Products* (*Canon-shi – Gijutsu to seihin no 50 nen*), 1987.
6 Emmott, Bill, *The Sun Also Sets*, Simon & Schuster Ltd., Tokyo 1989.

Chapter 2

1 Ono, Taiichi, *Toyota-Style Manufacturing* (*Toyota seisan hoshiki*), DIAMOND INC, Tokyo, 1978.

Chapter 3

1 Roughly a million US dollars.

Chapter 4

1 *Seven-Eleven Japan: Endless Innovation 1973–1991* Seven-Eleven, Japan, Tokyo.
2 Computer-ordering terminals.

Chapter 6

1 English translation 1992, Capital Communications Corporation, Hong Kong.
2 English translation 1992, Capital Communications Corporation, Hong Kong, pp. 116–17.
3 English translation 1992, Capital Communications Corporation, Hong Kong, pp. 26–7.
4 English translation 1992, Capital Communications Corporation, Hong Kong, pp. 10–11.
5 English translation 1992, Capital Communications Corporation, Hong Kong, pp. 118–19.
6 English translation 1992, Capital Communications Corporation, Hong Kong, p. 23.
7 Wada, Kazuo, 1993, 'Yaohan's Kazuo Wada reports on business in China', *Keizaikai*, p. 113.
8 Wada, Kazuo, 1993 'Yaohan's Kazuo Wada reports on business in China', *Keizaikai*, p. 125.

Bibliography

Aoki, Masahiko, Koike, Kazuo and Nakatani Iwao, *Nihon kigyo no keizaigaku*, TBS Buritanika, Tokyo, 1986.

Canon, *Canon 50th anniversary*, Canon, Tokyo, 1987.

Drucker, Peter F., *The Practice of Management*, Harper & Brothers Publishers, New York, 1954.

Itami, Hiroyuki, *Zeminaru (seminar) keieigaku nyumon*, Nihon Keizai Shimbun-sha, Tokyo, 1989.

Itami, Hiroyuki, Itoh, Motoshige and Kagono, Taado, *Nihon no kigyo shisutemu (system) 1 ~ 4*, Yuhikaku, Tokyo, 1993.

Iwabuchi, Akio, *Seven-Eleven akinai no sinjigen he*, Oesus Huppan-sha, Tokyo, 1993.

Kakumoto, Ryohei, *Kokutetsukaikaku wo meguru masumedhia (Massmedia) no doko*, Kotsu Shimbun-sha, Tokyo, 1992.

Kanou, Yoshikazu, *Mineika ga nihon wo kaeru*, PHP Kenkyujo, Tokyo, 1991.

Katayama, Osamu, *JR yakushin no purosesu (process)*, Mainichi Shimbun-sha, Tokyo, 1989.

Katayama, Osamu, *Nihongata keiei no shinsenryaku*, PHP Kenkyujo, Tokyo, 1993.

Kojima, Takeshi, *Cho Riinkakumei*, Nihon Keizai Shimbun-sha, Tokyo, 1994.

Nakatani, Iwao, *Nihon kigyo fukkatsu no joken*, TOYO Shimpo-sha, Tokyo, 1993.

NHK joho nettowaku (network), *Johoka medhia (media)*, NHK joho nettowaku (network), Tokyo, 1992.

Nihon Keizai Shimbun-sha, *Zeminaru (seminar) nihonkeizainyumon*, Nihon Keizai Shimbun-sha, Tokyo, 1985.

Nihon Keizai Shimbun-sha, *Gendai keieigaku gaido (guide)*, Nihon Keizai Shimbun-sha, Tokyo, 1987.

Nihon Keizai Shimbun-sha, *Zeminaru (seminar) gendaikigyounyumon*, Nihon Keizai Shimbun-sha, Tokyo, 1990.

Nihon Keizai Shimbun-sha, *Watashi no rirekisho 6*, Nihon Keizai Shimbun-sha, Tokyo, 1992.

Nihon Keizai Shimbun-sha, *Watashi no rirekisho 8*, Nihon Keizai Shimbun-sha, Tokyo, 1992.

Nikkei ryutu shimbun, *Ryutsu gendaishi*, Nihon Keizai Shimbun-sha, Tokyo, 1993.

Nonaka, Ikujiro, *Kigyo shinkaron*, Nihon Keizai Shimbun-sha, Tokyo, 1985.

Nonaka, Ikujiro, *Chishiki sozo no keiei*, Nihon Keizai Shimbun-sha, Tokyo, 1990.

Ogata, Tomoyuki, *Seven-Eleven • ito yohkadoh no ryutsu joho kakumei*, TBS Buritanika, Tokyo, 1991.

Ono, Taiichi, *Toyota seisanhoshiki*, DIAMOND INC, Tokyo, 1978.

Okumura, Akihiro, *Kigyo inoveshon (innovation) heno chosen*, Nihon Keizai Shimbun-sha, Tokyo, 1986.

Sasaki, Naoto, *Keieikokusaika no ronri*, Nihon Keizai Shimbun-sha, Tokyo, 1983.

Seven-Eleven • Japan, *Seven-Eleven • Japan 1973–1991*, Seven-Eleven • Japan, Tokyo, 1991.

Sheff, David, *Game over*, KADOKAWA SHOTEN, Tokyo, 1993.

Sony, *Sony 40th anniversary*, Sony, Tokyo, 1986.

Sumita, Shoji, *Reru ni yume wo nosete*, TOYO KEIZAI INC, Tokyo, 1992.

Toyota, *Toyota 50th anniversary*, Toyota, Aichi, 1987.

Wada, Kazuo, *Yaohan's global strategy*, Capital Communications Corporation Ltd, Hong Kong, 1992.

Wada, Kazuo, *Chugoku bijinesu (business) hokoku*, Keizaikai, Tokyo, 1993.

Wada, Kazuo, Wada, Terumasa, Wada, Naomi, Wada, Mitumasa and Yamanishi, Yasuaki, *Yaohan runessansu (renaissance)*, Nihonkyobun-sha, Tokyo, 1994.

Yoshikawa, Hiroyuki, *Made in japan*, DIAMOND INC, Tokyo, 1994.

Index